Learning to be Professionals

Innovation and Change in Professional Education

VOLUME 4

SCOPE OF THE SERIES

The primary aim of this book series is to provide a platform for exchanging experiences and knowledge about educational innovation and change in professional education and post-secondary education (engineering, law, medicine, management, health sciences, etc.). The series provides an opportunity to publish reviews, issues of general significance to theory development and research in professional education, and critical analysis of professional practice to the enhancement of educational innovation in the professions.

The series promotes publications that deal with pedagogical issues that arise in the context of innovation and change of professional education. It publishes work from leading practitioners in the field, and cutting edge researchers. Each volume is dedicated to a specific theme in professional education, providing a convenient resource of publications dedicated to further development of professional education.

For further volumes:
http://www.springer.com/series/6087

Gloria Dall'Alba

Learning to be Professionals

 Springer

Dr. Gloria Dall'Alba
The University of Queensland
School of Education
Brisbane QLD 4072
Australia
g.dallalba@uq.edu.au

The quote from song lyrics to Leonard Cohen's *Anthem* in chapter 6 is used with permission.
The section of chapter 4 entitled 'Ambiguities in becoming professionals' draws upon the following journal article: Dall'Alba, G. (2009). Learning professional ways of being: Ambiguities of becoming. *Educational Philosophy and Theory*, *41*(1), 34-45.

ISBN 978-90-481-2607-1   e-ISBN 978-90-481-2608-8
DOI 10.1007/978-90-481-2608-8
Springer Dordrecht Heidelberg London New York

Library of Congress Control Number: 2009926829

Printed on acid-free paper

Springer is part of Springer Science+Business Media (www.springer.com)

To those with whom I have learned.

Acknowledgements

The generous participation of the medical students in the longitudinal research reported here is acknowledged with gratitude. The medical practitioners who supervised participating students in clinical contexts when the research was carried out readily provided access to the students and allowed me to observe their own interactions with them. I am grateful for the professional way in which they provided this access. Karolinksa Institute Research Fund and Karolinska Institute Research Foundation provided financial support for the interviews and observations in the longitudinal study reported here.

I warmly thank Robyn Barnacle, Michael Bonnett, Jules Kieser, Ravinder Sidhu, Carl-Magnus Stolt and Ann Webster-Wright for thoughtful comments on earlier versions of parts of this manuscript. John Bowden, Melanie Walker and the anonymous reviewers deserve particular thanks for generously commenting on the entire draft manuscript. They have each invested time and energy in engaging constructively with the ideas I sought to explore.

Oliver and Eliot have shown their interest in mum's writing project through their questions and amusing comments, which helped to keep me grounded in ways children do best. Their contribution is not to be underestimated and is acknowledged with love and gratitude.

Jörgen Sandberg has engaged in dialogue with me and provided constructive criticism throughout the longitudinal study reported here, as well as during the writing of this book. As well as commenting on most chapters, he carefully checked the accuracy of extracts from dialogue with students that I translated from Swedish into English, which appears in several chapters. His encouragement, support and genuine interest in my research over many years have contributed to bringing this book to fruition, as well as filling the process with warmth.

The editor of the series in which this book appears, Wim Gijselaers, and Astrid Noordermeer at Springer deserve special thanks for the positive and supportive way in which they have negotiated with me during this writing project.

This book has benefited from, or builds upon, the contributions of many others. Where possible, I have referenced these contributions in the text. As the book is a means of continuing scholarly discussion and debate about professional education, I have generally chosen not to use first person throughout the remainder of the text. The reason for this is not to create an illusion of "objectivity" or to avoid taking responsibility, but as an invitation to readers to engage collaboratively in exploring what it means to learn to become professionals. This book, then, is an invitation to dialogue.

Contents

Part I
Focus of the Inquiry

Chapter 1
A Deepening Crisis of Confidence in the Professions

> *The learning challenges that we all face in and through work . . . require of us not simply that we learn new techniques, or new ideas or new practices. They call upon us to change or at least to widen the very frameworks through which we interpret the world. They demand of us, in effect, that we become different kinds of human being.*
>
> (Barnett, 1999, p. 38)

The purpose of this monograph is to re-think current approaches to professional education programmes and the learning that occurs therein. Two arguments for re-thinking professional education are elaborated below. The first is that the contemporary context of professional practice has changed markedly; in particular, change is occurring at an intensified pace and there are increasing challenges to previously accepted frameworks for interpreting our world. The second argument is that a deepening crisis of confidence in the professions continues to spill over into professional education, signalling the inadequacy of current professional education programmes. Taken together, these arguments point to a pressing need to question the assumptions on which preparation for professional practice has conventionally been based. No longer is it sufficient to refine and adapt existing approaches. Re-visiting and critically scrutinising the assumptions implicit in current approaches is necessary for the renewal of professional education programmes. As John Furlong points out, "it is the crisis with conventional conceptions of professional knowledge that opens up the possibility of exploring alternatives" (2000, p. 21).

In the current context of change and uncertainty, the way in which aspiring professionals are prepared for the emerging demands and challenges of professional practice becomes a key issue for the development of society as a whole, as well as for professions and individual professionals. Given the similarities across many professional education programmes (see Chapter 3), critically examining preparation for professional practice is potentially of relevance to many forms of practice. This monograph seeks to make a timely contribution to, and stimulate dialogue on, innovation in professional education that directly targets the purpose of these programmes. While preparation for professional practice is of importance across the

G. Dall'Alba, *Learning to be Professionals*, Innovation and Change in Professional Education 4, DOI 10.1007/978-90-481-2608-8_1,
© Springer Science+Business Media B.V. 2009

globe, it is addressed in this book in the context of developed countries, although a number of the arguments apply more broadly.

This book systematically investigates professional education programmes and the assumptions on which they are based, as a means of exploring ways in which these programmes could more adequately enable aspiring professionals to meet the challenges of professional practice. It is not a book about learning to behave in a professional manner or to adopt a professional attitude in some generalised sense, regardless of the profession in question. More specifically, it draws upon the research literature to examine ways in which professional education programmes typically fall short in the preparation of professionals. Extending this literature, previously unreported empirical research is presented on what aspiring professionals learn about practising as professionals during preparation for professional practice. Implications for change and innovation within professional education programmes are also outlined.

A key tenet of this book is that the ways in which we currently prepare professionals for the world of work are generally limited in scope and inadequate for dealing with the change and uncertainty they encounter in contemporary professional practice. The book presents an alternative to existing approaches to learning to become professionals, as well as to researching this learning. The contribution it makes is both theoretical and methodological, with practical implications for professional education programmes. It provides an alternative model and way forward for those involved in designing and implementing professional education programmes, as well as those contributing to research about this important enterprise.

Contemporary Context of Professional Practice

Professionals in many countries around the globe are working in a context of continual change, including advances in biotechnology, computers and the internet, globalisation of the economy, expanding knowledge- and service-based industry, heightened threats to national and international security, and increased professionalisation of the workforce. The ensuing context of flux and uncertainty presents new and pressing challenges for professionals, while reliance upon their skilful participation in society is heightened. Professionals are being required to take new issues into account before those issues can be fully grasped, while continuing to make judgements, acting on the basis of those judgements, and facing the consequences of their actions. Ronald Barnett (1999; 2000; Barnett & Hallam, 1999) has described the context within which professionals currently work as one of not only complexity but, increasingly, of "supercomplexity":

> Supercomplexity is that state of affairs when one is faced with alternative frameworks of interpretation through which to make sense of one's world and to act purposively within it. . . . Situations such as these present their subjects with alternative and possibly incommensurable frameworks to understanding not just those situations but themselves. The dilemmas that supercomplexity presents us all with are dilemmas of understanding (the world), of action (in the world) and of identity and self-understanding (in that world).
>
> (Barnett & Hallam, 1999, p. 138)

In other words, supercomplexity "is that form of complexity in which frameworks for understanding the world are themselves challenged" (Barnett, 1999, p. 38).

In a similar vein, Zygmunt Bauman describes our contemporary social world as "liquid-modern":

> *All* modernity means incessant, obsessive modernization (there is no *state* of modernity; only a *process*; modernity would cease being modernity the moment that process ground to a halt); and *all* modernization consists in "disembedding", "disencumbering", "melting the solids", etc; in other words, in dismantling the received structures or at least weakening their grip. ... New is that the "disembedding" goes on unabated, while the prospects of "re-embedding" are nowhere in sight and unlikely to appear. (2004,p. 20)[1]

Bauman points to direct consequences of this fluidity and flux for learning:

> Routine, the habits it requires, and the learning that results in both, do not pay any longer. In a fluid setting, flexibility is the name of rationality. Skills do not retain usefulness for long, for what was yesterday a masterstroke may prove today inane or downright suicidal. Just as long-term commitments threaten to mortgage the future, habits too tightly embraced burden the present; learning may in the long run disempower as it empowers in the short. (p. 22)

It could be argued, however, that change has always been a feature of the social world, as it is integral to that world. We need to take care, then, not to overstate change as something new in the contemporary world, recognising it has always been part of life and of living. While the nature and impact of change in society might be debated (see, for example, Barnett, 1999; Bauman, 2004; Casey, 1999; Castells, 1996; McGuire, 1993), there seems to be general agreement, however, that the pace of change has intensified over recent years and that previously accepted interpretative frameworks have increasingly become subject to challenge. Influences of globalisation on many aspects of everyday economic and social life, re-thinking of knowledge boundaries through interdisciplinary endeavours, and emergence of newly developed information and communication technologies that have made space-time compression possible are examples of the flux and fluidity impacting on the practice of professionals. A heightened pace of flux and fluidity has, therefore, become an integral feature of living in our times. It is imperative that professional education programmes adequately prepare aspiring professionals to constructively deal with this contemporary context.

A Crisis of Confidence Re-Visited

In the context of flux and fluidity outlined above, the crisis of confidence in the professions that Donald Schön (1983) highlighted more than two decades ago can be seen to have deepened. The crisis of confidence takes several forms. First, as Schön pointed out, there is a discrepancy between the knowledge produced from traditional research and knowledge valued by practitioners. Second, although not explicitly noted by Schön, disagreement or internal conflict about central issues

---

[1]Emphasis in quotes throughout this book is from the original source.

is evident within professions. Third, there is increased questioning or mistrust of professional judgements, with an accompanying undermining of professional-client relationships.

As Schön (1983, 1987) convincingly argued, research on professional practice that is removed from the challenges and complexity of practice is of limited value to practitioners. Not only has such research lead to a crisis of confidence in professional knowledge, but also in professional education. Concerns about a theory-practice gap of the kind highlighted by Schön were subsequently echoed in research into a range of professions, including nursing (Benner, 1984), artificial intelligence (Dreyfus & Dreyfus, 1986; Winograd & Flores, 1986), psychology (Giorgi, 1990; Semin & Gergen, 1990), business administration (Flyvbjerg, 1992), and philosophy (Molander, 1993). A principal criticism has been that the knowledge generated by traditional research has distanced us from the human practices investigated, rather than deepening our understanding of them. Such research has failed to take into account the understanding and experience of practice it seeks to examine. While some aspects of Schön's work are open to criticism (see Chapter 2; see also Barnett, 1997; Dall'Alba & Sandberg, 1996; Rolf, Ekstedt, & Barnett, 1993; Usher, Bryant, & Johnston,1997; van Manen, 1999), an artificial theory-practice gap remains evident in professional education today, as Chapters 3 and 6 demonstrate.

The notion of an artificial theory-practice gap is not premised, however, on the assumption of a "functional fit" between professional education programmes and professional practice. The purpose of professional education programmes is broader than simply preparing aspiring professionals to perform specific tasks in the workplace. These programmes have a role to play, for instance, in promoting the development of a critical approach to current practice and the contribution this practice makes to the broader society. Moreover, those who graduate from a particular professional education programme typically proceed into a diverse range of workplaces and employment, where even the "same" profession is practised in a variety of ways. In addition, it has been argued that educational programmes and professional practice have a different logic and rationality (Kurtz, 2007), making a functional fit impossible to achieve. So, a precise functional fit would not be feasible even if it were desirable.

In contrast to the artificial separation of theory and practice that Schön called into question (see Chapter 2), in this book theory is seen as a form of systematised knowing or reflection about practice, which occurs at a general or abstract level. Theory presupposes practice (see also Ratcliffe, 2002) in the same way that knowing presupposes involvement in our world (see Chapter 2). Theory formation involves stepping back from everyday practices to allow scrutiny. It is a mode of practice that distances us from our ways of thinking, knowing and acting for the purpose of critical examination. Theory and practice are, then, necessarily interrelated. Theory is directed to making practice intelligible, as well as to questioning and enhancing practice (see, for example, Dall'Alba, 2005; McCuaig, 2007; Walker, 2001). In other words, theory formation involves research *about* the object of study that is simultaneously *for* the object of study (Kurtz, 2007, p. 285). Seen in this way, a theory-practice gap is artificially construed.

In addition to an artificial theory-practice gap, a crisis of confidence is also evident in lack of agreement about central issues within professions. Much of this lack of agreement relates to the increasingly supercomplex (Barnett, 1999, 2000; Barnett & Hallam, 1999) nature of practice in which competing, and often incompatible, frameworks are in evidence for understanding, acting, and being professionals. For instance, some economists argue developing countries would benefit economically from financial or trade liberalisation, while others caution such liberalisation would make these countries still more vulnerable to international markets. The role of journalism as a source of profit is in tension with the right of the public to be informed. A long-running debate within acting concerns whether actors should draw upon their personal emotional memory when portraying characters or develop their performance from careful analysis of the text itself.[2] Research scientists differ considerably in the way they regard the limits placed on experimentation by governments and the force of public opinion, for example, in gene manipulation of human foetuses. Health professionals debate the extent to which technology drives healthcare provision and its effects on quality of care. In early responses to the global financial crisis, proposed "rescue packages" by governments were applauded, as well as criticised on the grounds they undermined the notion of "free markets". Where these tensions and debates arise, deep-seated discrepancies are evident within professional communities about the nature of their practice.

Not only is there an artificial theory-practice gap and internal disagreement within professions, but also increasing criticism and questioning of professional expertise from within society at large. As Joanne Marshall (1993) points out, clients have expanding access to information that has meant more frequent challenges to professionals' control over decision making and more ready surveillance of professionals, with implications for professional-client relationships. Criticism and questioning of professionals can be seen within the popular media, through escalating insurance claims and legal action against professionals, in calls for greater accountability of professionals, and in increasing numbers of organisations whose purpose is to identify and uphold the rights of clients or consumers. A clear expression of a crisis of confidence, for instance, is the burgeoning forms of alternative medicine that have appeared in western countries in recent decades, due to dissatisfaction with treatments provided by conventional western medicine or its failure to provide treatment for some health conditions. At the same time, western medicine is making forays into eastern countries, at times displacing eastern medicine.

While it might be argued that questioning and criticism have come to characterise many societies in parallel with postmodern developments, the relevant point here is that professions and professionals are more often targets than was previously the case. As Michael Eraut notes, "cynics might argue that, whereas previously the State sought to protect its citizens from the unqualified practitioner, it now seeks to protect them from the qualified" (1994, p. 5). Scepticism or mistrust signifies

---

[2] Examples provided by James Laurenceson, Martin Hirst and Maryrose Casey relating to economics, journalism and acting, respectively, are acknowledged with gratitude.

an undermining of the professional-client relationship. In turn, professionals and aspiring professionals can develop misgivings about their chosen profession and its demands, at times leading to questioning of their career choice (see, for example, Arnman, 2004; Holmström, Sanner, & Rosenqvist, 2004) or even more desperate measures, such as seen in the higher than average suicide rates among medical practitioners (Juel, Mosbech, & Hansen, 1999; Schernhammer, 2005; Torre et al., 2005).

Not surprisingly, a deepening crisis of confidence in the professions continues to spill over into professional education. A decade after Schön called attention to this crisis, Donald McIntyre noted features that continue to be evident today:

> International and cross-professional comparisons of professional education provision seem to show a widespread sense of crisis but no coherence or consistency in the solutions being promoted. Thus the British government's current attempts to remove initial teacher education *from* the higher education sector contrast not only with the French government's radical moves in the opposite direction but also with the British government's own support for the movement of initial nurse education *into* higher education. (1994, pp. viii–ix)

A theory-practice gap, substantial disagreement or conflict within professions, and undermining of professional-client relationships present challenges in preparing aspiring professionals for contemporary professional practice. It is apparent that the crisis of confidence in the professions is unlikely to be resolved simply by increasing would-be professionals' knowledge and skills, at least not as these previously have been defined. It could be argued, however, that conventional professional education programmes, as well as much continuing professional development, typically focus precisely on such acquisition of knowledge and skills. Instead, re-thinking current approaches is needed to address these challenges.

An alternative approach to learning to be professionals will be proposed and elaborated in this book. This alternative approach is based upon the notion that the way in which we understand and embody professional practice is central to how we both perform and develop that practice. More specifically, learning to practise as professionals not only incorporates knowledge and skills, but also entails the development of professional ways of being (Dall'Alba, 2004, 2005). This alternative approach will be elaborated with reference to an empirical study of aspiring professionals as they proceed through a conventional professional education programme. In elaborating this alternative, some limitations of conventional professional education programmes will be identified.

In contrast to the focus of this book, it might be argued that much, or even most, of the learning involved in becoming professionals occurs not in professional education programmes but, subsequently, in the workplace. At the same time, professional education programmes provide some form of orientation to, and preparation for, professional practice that is a requirement within many societies in order to practise as professionals. Given this requirement, it is relevant to explore the learning that occurs as students proceed through these programmes. Professional education programmes may be regarded as an early phase in learning to be professionals; a phase in which much crucial learning occurs about the profession in question. Research that focuses on learning during these programmes can allow us to critically evaluate the appropriateness of the theories of learning and curriculum that are typically adopted, as well as the requirement for formal professional education itself. Research that explores the learning occurring on formal acceptance into a profession and among experienced professionals (for example, Billett, Fenwick, & Somerville, 2006; Boud & Garrick, 1999; Castleton, Gerber, & Pillay, 2006; Ellström, Ekholm, & Ellström, 2008; Sandberg & Dall'Alba, 2006; Webster-Wright, 2006, in press) is a necessary complement to the research reported here.

Structure of the Book

This book is in four Parts, I to IV. Part I identifies the focus of the book and consists of two chapters. Following from this first chapter that discusses a crisis of confidence in the professions, Chapter 2 explores the question of what professional practice entails, as a background to elaborating an alternative model for the education of aspiring professionals. This exploration includes the concept of a profession and the notion of practice portrayed in the research literature. Drawing upon this analysis, an alternative way of conceiving professional practice is proposed that places emphasis on developing and enacting professional ways of being in interaction with others.

Against this background, Part II examines the way in which we prepare aspiring professionals for the challenges of practice. In Chapter 3, the research literature is interrogated as a means of systematically examining the adequacy of preparation for professional practice in conventional programmes. The normative curriculum, with its emphasis on acquisition of knowledge and skills, is critically examined from a pedagogical point of view, as are curriculum innovations such as problem-based learning and newer forms of work-based learning. As part of this process of interrogating the design of curricula in professional education programmes, lived experience of students progressing through a medical programme at Karolinska Institute in Sweden is used to illuminate and elaborate the research literature. In Chapter 4, a re-conceptualisation of professional education programmes is proposed that is consistent with the theoretical framework described in Chapter 2. More specifically, a notion of learning and teaching is elaborated for supporting the process of becoming professionals.

The focus of Part III is professional ways of being that are learned for the purpose of engaging in professional practice. The practice of medicine in western societies is taken as an example through which to explore the formation of professional ways of being in interplay with traditions of practice in medicine. Chapter 5 provides the context for investigating this interplay through a brief history of western medicine, as well as examining the dominant contemporary biomedical model. Chapter 6 explores the interplay between emerging professional ways of being and the social context within which they are embedded. Some ways are explored in which the traditions of practice for medicine carry over to students at Karolinska Institute learning to be medical practitioners. Challenges and tensions are examined that relate to reproducing and renewing practice when learning to be professionals. These challenges and tensions are discussed in the light of related tensions within the profession and expectations in the broader society. Such challenges and tensions

that occur in learning to be professionals highlight the way in which this is not solely
a cognitive enterprise, but also entails the formation of professional ways of being in
interplay with prevailing traditions of practice. In Chapter 7, a closer investigation
is presented on what is learned about practising as professionals during preparation
for professional practice. More specifically, continuity and transformation in professional ways of being over time are explored, drawing substantially upon longitudinal
research of students studying medicine at Karolinska Institute.

Part IV addresses some implications of learning professional ways of being for
professional education. Chapter 8 discusses the significance of key ideas developed
in relation to the research literature and the empirical research reported in the book
for designing professional education programmes. In particular, a shift in focus from
acquisition of knowledge and skills to development of professional ways of being
that both sustain and renew professional practice can be seen to have far-reaching
implications.

Chapter 2
What Is Professional Practice?

> *Every inquiry is a seeking. . . . Inquiry, as a kind of seeking,*
> *must be guided beforehand by what is sought.*
>
> (Heidegger, 1962/1927, pp. 24–25, § 5–6)[1]

In investigating preparation for professional practice, it is relevant to address the question of what professional practice entails. As Martin Heidegger notes in the quote above, inquiry "must be guided beforehand by what is sought." Through its framing of practice, this chapter outlines a theoretical framework for the book. It seeks to make explicit the assumptions underlying this investigation of learning to be professionals.

We begin by considering the concept of a profession—which has a contested meaning—and then turn our attention to various ways in which practice is conceptualised in the research literature. The approaches to practice described below implicitly or explicitly deal with the relation between knowledge, persons and world, although they configure this relation in diverse ways. In conventional expertise research, individuals are regarded as separate from the world, while knowledge about the world is acquired and possessed by them, and applied to situations, as required. Donald Schön sought to overcome this separation of knowledge from the practice to which it relates, proposing the concept of knowing-in-action. The notion that knowledge is situated within participation in everyday activities extends this concept of knowing-in-action. The situatedness of knowledge is taken up by distributed cognition researchers, who argue that cognitions are not exclusively individual, but are distributed among people and their surroundings, including tools and artefacts. Activity theorists, too, explore the situated character of knowledge. Their focus is an activity system in which a shared activity serves to unify actors, tools, purposes and so on. Jean Lave and Etienne Wenger extended the notion of the inseparability of knowledge from practice by emphasising the embeddedness of knowledge within participation in communities of practice. These various approaches to

---

[1] Quotes from Heidegger's *Being and Time* are referred to using page numbers from both the translated and original German versions, respectively.

G. Dall'Alba, *Learning to be Professionals*, Innovation and Change in Professional
Education 4, DOI 10.1007/978-90-481-2608-8_2,
© Springer Science+Business Media B.V. 2009

practice typically consider practice in terms of either familiar routines or creative features.

Drawing on aspects of these various conceptualisations of practice, while calling into question other aspects, the chapter concludes with an outline of the notion of professional practice that underpins this book. Elaborating a lifeworld perspective on practice is put forward as a means of achieving an integrated framework for exploring and enhancing professional practice.

What Is a Profession?

A profession has conventionally been defined in terms of provision of a service that is based upon a systematic, scientific body of knowledge (for example, Parsons, 1968). Possession of this knowledge has afforded some degree of status and authority to professionals, as well as increased remuneration for service provision. This combination of status, authority and remuneration has vested certain power in the professions, although they vary considerably in the extent of this power. In return for the benefits of professional membership, professionals have been expected to exercise informed judgement, act ethically, and maintain confidentiality in providing a service to their clients. In other words, provision of a service by professionals has carried with it expectations of encounters based on knowledge and trust.

However, a range of scholars has challenged the accuracy of such an idealised view of the professions. For instance, Jeff Hearn (1982) acknowledges that membership of professions has traditionally been largely middle class and male. He argues, further, that professionalisation brought masculinisation of many areas of work, some of which had previously been predominantly female, such as healing, mediation of disputes, managing birthing and care of the dead. Capitalism reinforces and continues this masculinisation of work. Hearn notes that the so-called "established" professions, such as medicine and law, are those that traditionally came to be dominated by men and, it could be added, continue to be so in their management structures. As Hearn demonstrates, similar patterns of masculinisation could be seen as the "semi-professions" progressively moved toward professional status: "Within most of the semi-professions there is the strange contradiction of women occupying the majority of posts, as well as being diverted into the more specialist areas of work away from the centre of the profession" (p. 195). This is not to suggest women have simply been passive and entirely complicit in these developments; there are many instances of creative reinterpretation and resistance. For example, Hearn outlines historical changes in midwifery and the increasing influence of women in a number of professions.

Like Hearn, Thomas Popkewitz questions the accuracy of the ideals that have traditionally been espoused for the establishment of professions, taking the profession of teaching as an example:

> The Anglo-Saxon word "profession" is brought into the language of many countries to describe the social formations of work within the middle class, the increased importance of

expertise in the process of production/reproduction, and specifically, in teaching, the effort
toward upward mobility. (1994, p. 2)

In a similar vein, Mats Alvesson questions the claims to knowledge that are seen to
characterise professions, pointing out that such claims have several potential roles
and need to be problematised:

Knowledge, i.e. claims of knowledge in social contexts, play various roles, such as being:
(a) a means for creating community and social identity through offering organizational
members a shared language and a common way of relating to themselves and their world;
(b) a resource for persuasion in marketing and interactions with customers; (c) a means of
creating legitimacy and good faith with regard to actions and outcomes; and (d) obscuring
uncertainty and counteracting doubt and reflection. This last point indicates that "knowledge" and "knowledge work" may lead to the opposite of what they claim—to ignorance
and uncritical attitudes. (2001, p. 882)

Rather than accepting at face value espoused ideals of the professions as the basis
for their formation, Popkewitz points out the need to examine the formation of
professions within their cultural and historical context. He notes, further, that the
meaning of the term, profession, varies considerably across both cultural and historical contexts. It is difficult, then, to pin down what constitutes a profession when
"professions are not fixed and static but always in the process of being socially
constructed" (Slaughter & Leslie, 1997, p. 4).

While conventional definitions and professional ideals are open to challenge, a
trend toward professionalisation across a broad range of practice has called into
question and blurred customary boundaries. For instance, how specialised or scientific must their knowledge base be if a group of practitioners is to attain professional
status? When surgeons, teachers and nurses sought professional status, other professionals opposed each of these groups on the basis that their knowledge was not
sufficiently scientific. Surgeons, for example, were initially looked down upon as
practising manual skill, rather than basing their craft in scientific knowledge (see
Chapter 5). As noted in Chapter 1, the traditional authority and status afforded to
professionals is also being challenged and, in some respects, undermined by dis-
agreements within professions and questioning of professional expertise, as clients
and other stakeholders become more informed and aware of their rights.

Not only is the term ill-defined and the boundaries blurred relating to what constitutes a profession, but the notion of a systematic, scientific "body of knowledge"
has been extensively challenged. Rather than regarding knowledge as absolute and
foundational in this way, it has come to be seen as situated within particular settings
and in flux, changing across contexts and over time through a process of social
construction (for example, Lave, 1993; Säljö, 1991). Nonetheless, recent social
and economic developments, such as market globalisation and the emergence of
new technologies, have seen increased emphasis on knowledge-based professions,
although these developments occur alongside critique of conventional notions of
knowledge.

A parallel challenge to the notion of a scientific "body of knowledge" is renewed
attention to the body and the way in which we embody and enact our knowledge in
practice. As we interact with our world, the body is seen as central to this interaction,

as well as to the knowledge we develop and enact in practice. This way of conceiving knowledge challenges the idea that we "possess" knowledge or that it transcends the body. Rather than "bodies of knowledge", attention is being paid to "knowing bodies" (for example, Bresler, 2004; Peters, 2004).

Both the plural, dynamic character and embodiment of knowledge have become key features in epistemological debates (for example, see Bresler, 2004; Dall'Alba & Barnacle, 2005, 2007; Grosz, 1994; Mol, 2002; Williams & Bendelow, 1998), calling into question a systematic, scientific body of knowledge as a basis for professions. These features of knowledge have been highlighted across a range of fields, such as anthropology, cultural studies, education, philosophy, psychology and sociology, as well as from various theoretical perspectives including critical theory, ethnomethodology, feminism, phenomenology, structuralism and post-structuralism.

In addition to more fluid conceptions of knowledge or, more accurately, of knowing, there is renewed interest in questions of ontology within the humanities and social sciences. Questions relating to what is and who we are as human beings are, arguably, central to professional practice, although they have largely been neglected in research about such practice to date. As considerations of knowing and being are crucial to the approach to professional development put forward in this monograph, they are elaborated below and re-visited in the remaining chapters. In elaborating relevant features of knowing and being, we begin by exploring the notion of professional practice.

Exploring Professional Practice

In the research literature, practice is conceived in various ways that potentially have bearing upon preparing aspiring professionals for practice. Several of these ways of conceptualising practice can be seen as contributing to a practice turn in the human sciences (see, for example, Schatzki, Knorr Cetina, & von Savigny, 2001; van Manen, 1999). Some of these conceptualisations of practice are discussed below, as a means of elaborating a notion of practice and theoretical framework for the exploration of learning to be professionals in this book.

Decontextualised Knowledge and Skills

In the literature on expertise, efforts are made to identify the knowledge and skills that make up expert performance. This research highlights the importance of knowledge and skills to skilful performance. A common strategy in expertise research has been to contrast the performance of experts with that of novices in order to identify what the former group possesses that the latter lacks (for example, Boshuizen & Schmidt, 1992; Carter, Cushing, Sabers, Stein, & Berliner, 1988; Chi, Feltovich, & Glaser, 1981; Collier, 2004; Hung, 2003). For the most part, this research has been carried out in the form of experiments, away from everyday practices. One of the characteristic features of this research is that knowledge and skills are decontextu-alised from the settings and situations in which they form a part. Interestingly, recent novice/expert research (for example, Collier, 2004; Hung, 2003) acknowledges some limitations that can be attributed to this decontextualisation. For instance, Shin-Yuan Hung notes that the executive support systems used in an experimental study "may not be representative of real systems" and "other variables, such as organizational culture and climate, can be examined in the future research" (2003, p. 184).

Jean Lave describes such decontextualisation, as follows:

> To decontextualize knowledge is to form-alize it (to contain it, pour it into forms) at a more inclusive level.... It follows that abstraction from and generalization across "contexts" are mechanisms that are supposed to produce decontextualized (valuable, general) knowledge. (1993, p. 23)

Lave points out that this decontextualisation of knowledge assumes an understand-ing of context as a "container" that holds social interaction. She notes further that when knowledge is decontextualised in this manner, the head is typically regarded as a container for such knowledge, while language is a container for transmitting meaning (p. 22). She points to a key failure of such decontextualisation in that it offers an adequate account of neither thought nor action (p. 24).

This container metaphor supports the separation of knowledge acquisition (*into* the head) from its subsequent application (*in* practice), as well as an artificial sepa-ration of theory from practice, which Donald Schön (1983, 1987, 1995) challenged, as noted in Chapter 1 and elaborated below. Separating knowledge acquisition from application, and theory from practice, occurs, then, through decontextualising knowledge. So pervasive is such decontextualisation that it is evident throughout our language and is difficult to avoid or circumvent. For example, Martin Heidegger was at pains to point out he did not mean containment in the world when elaborating his notion of being-in-the-world (1962/1927, p. 79, § 54), a concept which is discussed below. Similarly, in writing this book, it has been a challenge to find language that allows expression of an alternative to this container view. For example, we speak of keeping *in* mind, *in* practice, and so on.

Knowing-in-Action

Schön proposed an alternative to a container metaphor when he sought to overcome a separation of knowledge from the practice to which it relates, in both research into the professions and professional education. He notes that such a move would require re-conceptualising professional knowledge, so it has relevance for our exploration of professional practice, as well as implications for professional education. Schön argues for a focus on "knowing-in-action", which refers to "the sorts of know-how we reveal in our intelligent action ... the knowing is *in* the action. We reveal it by our spontaneous, skilful execution of the performance" (Schön, 1987, p. 25; see Molander, 1993, for further elaboration). He points out that the concept of knowing-in-action does not imply scientific knowledge is dismissed or disregarded. This more formalised knowledge may be drawn upon during skilful performance along with other resources, such as prior experience and input from others.

Perhaps as compensation for the separation of knowing from doing and the higher status generally attributed to abstract knowledge than to practice, Schön often emphasises learning by doing. He points out that the purpose of the doing is knowing, for example, " to get the kind of experience that will help him [the design student] learn what designing means" (p. 93). However, on occasion, this point tends to be overshadowed by an emphasis on learning by doing. Schön's concept of knowing-in-action is more defensible in its integration of knowing with doing.

Based on investigations of professionals as diverse as architects and psychotherapists while they engaged in practice, Schön argues strongly against separating the acquisition and application of knowledge in professional education. He criticises the notion of applying theory and techniques in practice as inadequate and misleading, arguing that it artificially separates theory from practice. He regards such a separation as providing an inappropriate preparation for the complexities of professional practice.

Schön calls into question the notion of learning to intellectualise about practice as a separate activity from that practice, consistent with his notion of knowing-in-action. He notes, moreover, that in some professional education programmes, it is possible to see an implicit recognition of the inadequacy of separating theory from practice. He uses the example of aspiring medical practitioners working on hospital wards to illustrate his point:

> When interns and residents under the guidance of senior clinicians work with real patients on the wards, they learn more than application of medical science taught in the classroom. There is at least an implicit recognition that research-based models of diagnosis and treatment cannot be made to work until the students acquire an art that falls outside the models; and on this view, widely held by practicing physicians, the medical practicum is as much concerned with acquiring a quasi-autonomous art of clinical practice as with learning to apply research-based theory. (p. 16)

Although not a strong feature of his work—for which he has been criticised (for example, Usher et al., 1997, p. 139)—Schön notes that knowing is embedded within social structures shared by a community of practitioners:

> A professional's knowing-in-action is embedded in the socially and institutionally structured context shared by a community of practitioners. Knowing-in-*practice* is exercised in the institutional settings particular to the profession, organised in terms of its characteristic units of activity and its familiar types of practice situations, and constrained or facilitated by its common body of professional knowledge and its appreciative system. (1987, p. 33)

Situated Participation

Jean Lave and others (for example, Alvesson, 2001; Benner, 1984; Lave, 1993; Lave & Wenger, 1991; Säljö, 1991; Säljö & Wyndham, 1993; Seely Brown, Collins, & Duguid, 1989; Wenger, 1998) have highlighted this embeddedness of knowledge within social practice in their research. They argue, moreover, that knowledge and learning are situated within, and socially constituted through, participation in everyday activities. This claim is worthy of scrutiny as it potentially has importance for understanding professional practice and, in particular, for preparing aspiring professionals for practice.

Lave and Etienne Wenger (1991; Wenger, 1998) argue that learning occurs when we participate in communities of practice. They contrast learning about practice with learning through engagement in practice. They see school-based learning as typically concerned with learning about practice in a manner that is decontextualised from engagement in that practice. John Seely Brown and colleagues argue that when such decontextualisation occurs in school settings, school learning risks being "ersatz activity", rather than authentic learning (1989, p. 34). As Schön's work demonstrates, these arguments apply equally well to professional education programmes as to other areas of schooling (see also Dall'Alba & Barnacle, 2005, 2007; Vu & Dall'Alba, 2008).

According to Lave and Wenger, entry into practice communities occurs through a process of "legitimate peripheral participation". This process involves progressive movement from the periphery to full participation, through learning to participate in the activities of the community. Lave and Wenger provide examples of apprentices learning a craft or trade through progressively taking on increasingly complex tasks. For example, apprentice tailors learned first to sew by hand and iron clothes before moving to more complex tasks that were typically undertaken earlier in the process of tailoring, such as cutting out garments to be sewn. The apprentices learned from a range of people within a community of tailors, including masters and more experienced apprentices.

In learning to use the various tools and create relevant artefacts, for example, using a sewing machine to produce a finished garment, the apprentices not only learn the practice of tailoring, but also participate in a tradition through which the tools and artefacts are afforded meaning. While Lave locates participation in practice within historical traditions in this general way, historicity is not featured strongly in her analyses of empirical examples of such practice. For instance, ways in which traditions of practice—including potentially competing forms of practice—play out and become modified are not highlighted in her analyses. Her focus is largely appropriation of (a single form of) practice towards full participation. As Yrjö Engeström notes:

> For Lave, a setting is generated out of the person's activity and at the same time generates that activity. But this dialectical and constructive relation seems to stop short.... In other words, Lave has both the individual experience and the system, but they remain only externally, mechanically related to each other. (1993, p. 97)

Engeström and Reijo Miettinen (1999) also call into question the apparent unidirectional movement from novices at the periphery to experienced masters at the centre, when learning is understood as legitimate peripheral participation. They argue that movement outwards and in unexpected directions, as well as challenges to existing practice, are not adequately accounted for in Lave and Wenger's (1991) model. Alison Fuller and Lorna Unwin (2004) point out, too, that both newcomers and experienced practitioners report learning from each other.[2] In addition, Fuller and Unwin describe several forms of apprenticeship, some of which are not conducive to learning the practice in question beyond a narrow technicist mastery. It is possible to "learn" what to do, such as routines and procedures, with a limited or inappropriate understanding of what a broader practice entails, as Chapter 7 demonstrates. This is one of the potential risks associated with highlighting learning through practice at the expense of learning about practice; the two are not mutually exclusive (see Dall'Alba & Sandberg, 1996).

The apprenticeship model put forward by Lave and Wenger appears, then, somewhat romanticised. Nor do they identify implications of their model for learning in formal education or other settings (but see the epilogue in Wenger, 1998, which outlines some implications for learning). In later work, Wenger (1998) attempts to develop a social theory of learning (see below), which addresses some limitations of the earlier work. For example, he demonstrates ways in which practitioners resist or challenge existing practice, as well as simply complying or choosing not to resist in other ways. However, there remains an implication that novices learn from experienced practitioners, without clear acknowledgement that the reverse also occurs and that this learning may produce other than the desired outcomes.

In elaborating relationships and activities in communities of practice, more broadly, Lave points out there is no implication of "homogeneity of actors, goals, motives, and activity itself" (1993, p. 14). In addition:

> knowledge and learning will be found distributed throughout the complex structure of persons-acting-in-setting. They cannot be pinned down to the head of the individual or to assigned tasks or to external tools or to the environment, but lie instead in relations among them. (p. 9)

Distributed Cognition

The related notion of distributed cognition has recently received attention from researchers in educational psychology (for example, Karasavvidis, 2002; Resnick, Levine, & Behrend, 1991; Salomon, 1993a) and cognitive science (for example, Clark, 2001; Hutchins, 1995), although it has a longer history (see Cole & Engeström, 1993). Distributed cognition researchers draw attention to the impact of the surrounding world upon cognition, questioning a notion of cognition as exclusively internal and individual. Distributed cognitions are seen as mediated through others, as well as through features of the environment, tools or artefacts. For example, two students may collaborate in writing a report, using a computer. The students do not construct cognitions entirely independently, but their collaboration and use of tools, such as the computer, contribute to forming cognitions. These cognitions

---

[2] The mutual character of learning by participants of varying experience, not only by those "less knowledgeable", is also overlooked in Vygotsky's (1978) concept of the zone of proximal development or ZPD.

are seen as distributed among the students, computer, the language of the report they produce and any additional resources.

Some distributed cognition researchers hold to the notion that some cognitions are located within individuals, such that an individual's cognitions interact with cognitions distributed within the surroundings: an individual-surroundings interaction (for example, Perkins, 1993; Salomon, 1993b). This attempt to "have it both ways" appears to be a form of "mixed discourse" (Giorgi, 1994) with respect to both ontology and epistemology. For other distributed cognition researchers, cognition itself is considered generally distributed in character (for example, Clark, 2001; Cole & Engeström, 1993). These latter researchers argue for a change in the unit of analysis, from cognition as an individual possession to activities and practices within which cognition plays a central role and is distributed among actors, artefacts, tools and so on.

Activity System

In arguing for a shift away from a focus on individual cognition, Yrjö Engeström takes an activity system as his unit of analysis. The activity theory elaborated by Engeström and others (for example, see Engeström, 2005; Engeström, Miettinen, & Punamäki, 1999; Engeström & Kerosuo, 2007) is one of several approaches based upon the work of Soviet psychologists, such as Alexei Leont'ev (1978) and Lev Vygotsky (1978, 1987/1934), from the cultural-historical school. (For examples of other such approaches, see Chaiklin, 2001.) For Engeström:

> An activity integrates the subject, the object, and the instruments (material tools as well as signs and symbols) into a unified whole. An activity system incorporates both the object-oriented productive aspect and the person-oriented communicative aspect of the human conduct. ... Actually a human activity system always contains the subsystems of production, distribution, exchange, and consumption. (1993, p. 67)

In other words, an activity system is concerned with "object-oriented, collective, and culturally mediated human activity" (Engeström & Miettinen, 1999, p. 9). While "collective motive-driven activity" is distinguished from, but seen as related to, "individual goal-driven action" (ibid, p. 9), the extent to which the meaning or motive for an activity is common or shared appears to be glossed over. This is a crucial issue, given the importance placed on motive-driven activity that is collective in form. Etienne Wenger makes a related point when expressing his preference for practice, rather than activity, as a unit of analysis:

> By starting with practice as a context for the negotiation of meaning, I do not assume that activities carry their own meanings. This is one reason that I will not take discrete activities, or even systems of activities, as a unit of analysis. (1998, p. 286)

In elaborating an activity-theoretical approach, Engeström (1993) identifies three principles of such an approach: a collective activity system is the unit of analysis; the history of the system and its components are incorporated into the analysis; and disruptions, innovation and change for individuals and the system occur through inner contradictions. In line with these principles, Engeström points out that the unified whole which is an activity system is neither homogeneous nor unchanging:

> Besides accumulation and incremental change, there are crises, upheavals, and qualitative transformations. An activity system is not only a persistent formation; it is also a creative, novelty-producing formation.... [It] always contains sediments of earlier historical modes, as well as buds or shoots of its possible future. (1993, p. 68)

Engeström provides empirical analyses of the way in which historicity and cultural mediation are necessary components of an activity system. For instance, he examines the reorganization of medical work in a health centre in Finland (Engeström, 1993; Cole & Engeström, 1993). The reorganization, which addressed structural inefficiencies in work organization, was carried out with and by the staff of the health centre. In his analysis, Engeström demonstrates the way in which medical practice was mediated socially and through tool use, such as computerised patient records. In addition, he analyses ways in which "sediments of earlier historical modes" of medical practice, including potentially competing modes, played out in the health centre. For example, he describes medical work as directed to somatic diseases, as well as collaboration with patients on health issues. He also identifies what may be "buds or shoots" of a possible future for medical practice. In this way, Engeström's analysis involves a dialectic between particular and general, individual and collective, as his theory warrants. Through this dialectic, he seeks to relate the individual to social structure (see Engeström (2005) for additional empirical examples).

Communities of Practice

Etienne Wenger (1998), too, takes up the relation between the individual and social, but through analysis of practice. He puts forward a social theory of learning that focuses on "learning as social participation", where participation means:

> being active participants in the *practices* of social communities and constructing *identities* in relation to these communities. Participating... is both a kind of action and a form of belonging. Such participation shapes not only what we do, but also who we are and how we interpret what we do. (p. 4)

In this research, Wenger carries forward an emphasis on practice as social from his earlier work with Jean Lave:

> The concept of practice connotes doing... in a historical and social context that gives structure and meaning to what we do. In this sense, practice is always social practice.... Therefore, the concept of practice highlights the social and negotiated character of both the explicit and the tacit in our lives. (p. 47)

For Wenger, the process of negotiating practice involves both participation and reification, such as producing concepts and classification systems we use as part of our practice. Participating in practice means:

> Things have to be done, relationships worked out, processes invented, situations interpreted, artifacts produced, conflicts resolved. We may have different enterprises, which give our

practices different characters. Nevertheless, pursuing them always involves the same kind
of embodied, delicate, active, social, negotiated, complex process of participation. (p. 49)

Such participation provides coherence for a community through "mutual engagement, a joint enterprise, and a shared repertoire of ways of doing things" (p. 49).
Wenger illustrates such a community of practice through the everyday work of
claims processors who work together in a medical insurance company. His descriptions and theorising are based on observations he made while working among the
claims processors. He points out, though, that communities of practice are not
necessarily coincident with particular organisations and are informal; they emerge
through mutual engagement. For example, several researchers with a shared knowledge interest who interact over a period of time may form a community of practice.
In this way, Wenger highlights the meaning and significance of "communities of
practice", drawing upon and extending the earlier work.

Alessia Contu and Hugh Willmott (2003) argue, however, that Wenger's notion of
communities of practice is a conservative interpretation of the earlier notion developed with Lave, in that it assumes consensus and overlooks relations of power. They
acknowledge, though, that the importance of contradiction and power relations is
espoused in the earlier work, but not made evident in analyses of empirical material:

> Competing invocations of "community" illustrate how language may be deployed, more
> or less consciously or "politically," in ways that devalue or suppress social differences—
> including those of gender, ethnicity, and aspiration. In this respect, Lave and Wenger (1991)
> fail to align their use of the concept of contradiction to their emphasis on power relations
> and the historical embeddedness of learning in (social) practice. (Contu & Willmott, 2003,
> p. 288)

Contu and Willmott point to a risk that "in a conservative formulation of situated
learning ... 'communities of practice' become the self-referential founts of all relevant knowledge and learning" (p. 292). While this tendency is evident in Wenger's
(1998) work, he does not see practices as self-contained. Instead, boundaries that
develop in distinguishing a practice can shift as the practice changes. For instance,
nurses or ambulance paramedics may begin to provide a range of services that previously were only available from doctors. For Wenger, boundaries that distinguish
practices provide both discontinuities and interconnections with other practices and
the rest of the world. "Boundary objects", such as concepts or documents, can cross
boundaries, entering different practices in discontinuous or meaningful ways. For
example, a range of health professionals may consult and contribute to the medical
record of a hospitalised patient, often in different ways. In addition, "brokering"
involves creating connections by introducing elements of one practice to another.
The process of brokering requires an ability to participate while also being something of an outsider.

As noted above, Wenger's notion of participation in practice communities involves construction of identities relating to these communities. However, he points out
that he sees identities as neither exclusively individual nor social, but as relating the
two. He describes identity as "the social, the cultural, the historical with a human
face" (p. 145). Moreover, "membership in a community of practice translates into an

identity as a form of competence" (p. 153). His notion of identity embeds individuals within ongoing practice. Hence, identity has a temporal dimension in the form of a trajectory of becoming. Learning, then, is "an experience of identity" in terms of both a process and a place for participation (p. 215). It "belongs to the realm of experience and practice" (p. 225). This means that "learning—whatever form it takes—changes who we are by changing our ability to participate, to belong, to negotiate meaning" (p. 226).

Routine and Creativity

The developments outlined above relating to conceptualising knowing and learning as social, historical and cultural are associated with a practice turn noted earlier in this chapter. As part of this practice turn, some researchers highlight the routinised character of practice (for example, Bourdieu, 1977; Lave & Wenger, 1991; van Manen, 1999), while others emphasise creative, dynamic aspects (for example, Knorr Cetina, 2001; Schön, 1983). Karen Knorr Cetina (2001) argues that practices vary in terms of their reliance on routines or creativity. She argues, for example, that doing research is an example of a creative form of practice which can be distinguished in terms of its particular creativity: "Research work seems to be particular in that the definition of things, the consciousness of problems, etc., is deliberately looped through objects and the reaction granted by them" (p. 175). While highlighting creative, dynamic aspects of practice is a valuable complement to accounts emphasizing the routine and reproductive, Knorr Cetina appears to downplay the creative, responsive aspect of work other than research. For instance, using the example of cabinetmaking, Martin Heidegger points out that skilful practice requires that the cabinetmaker:

> answer and respond above all to the different kinds of wood and to the shapes slumbering within wood—to wood as it enters into man's dwelling with all the hidden riches of its nature. In fact, this relatedness to wood is what maintains the whole craft. Without that relatedness, the craft will never be anything but empty busywork. (1968, pp. 14–15)

Similarly, Donald Schön (1983) provides a detailed account of the way in which an architect responds to the situation at hand and to responses to actions from that situation, although he has been criticised for overstating the unique and underestimating the routinised aspects of practice (Rolf et al., 1993, p. 63). Seth Chaiklin and Jean Lave (1993) provide additional examples of enacting practice through responding to situations as they arise. In teaching, too, openness and responsiveness to the learners' unfolding understanding of the subject matter at hand can be seen as central (Bonnett, 2002; Dall'Alba, 2005; van Manen, 1991).

Typically, then, practice has both routinised and creative aspects. These two dimensions are not in opposition to one another, but are necessary dimensions of social practice. Even in the case of apparently routinised work, such as factory assembly lines, when breakdowns or deviations from expected outcomes occur, they require creative solutions. As new or modified assembly lines are designed and put in place, they also enable and demand new ways of working. At the very least, changes in the environment surrounding a practice demand some degree of dynamism, if not ensuring the capacity for creativity among its participants. Across social practice, then, routine and creativity are intertwined, with shifts from one to the other as practice proceeds.

A Lifeworld Perspective on Professional Practice

As noted in the introduction to this chapter, the approaches to practice described above configure the relation between knowledge, persons and world in varying ways. In conventional expertise research, individuals are regarded as separate from the world, while knowledge about the world is acquired and possessed by those individuals. This knowledge is then applied to situations in the world, as required. For some who advocate the situated and distributed nature of learning and cognition, some knowledge has similar status as for conventional expertise researchers, while other knowledge is distributed across individuals and their world. For other such researchers, knowledge is not a possession but a relation between persons and world, which is most clearly evident through engagement in collective activities or social practices. This latter research throws light on the significance for knowing of situatedness in activities and practices. In focusing on activities and practices, however, some of the latter approaches assume, but do not feature, the embodiment of knowledge, instead typically highlighting cognition and, sometimes, mind (for example, Cole and Engeström's "cultural theory of mind" (1993, p. 42)). While Andy Clark (1998) draws attention to the need to consider not only mind and world in cognitive science, but also body, he stops short of developing a convincing concept of embodiment for cognitive science.

The concept of the lifeworld provides a means of overcoming a separation into mind (or cognition), body and world as it is grounded in our entwinement with world. While the lifeworld is overlooked in conventional expertise literature, it is typically assumed—but its significance not explored—in situated cognition and distributed cognition approaches. Making explicit, and attending to, the lifeworld has the potential to deepen and enrich explorations of professional practice, through providing an integrated framework that highlights the significance of our entwinement with world for practice (see also Sandberg & Dall'Alba, in press).

The concept of the "lifeworld" in contemporary use is attributed to the philosopher, psychologist and mathematician, Edmund Husserl, the founder of modern phenomenology at the beginning of the 20th century. Husserl used this term to refer to the everyday world in which we are inevitably embedded and which we take for granted. This unitary concept describes, then, an inescapable relation between persons and their world, presenting a challenge to efforts that artificially separate them. As noted above, however, contemporary language sometimes obstructs the concepts we seek to develop, so that speaking in terms of person and world suggests independent entities and, so, is somewhat at odds with the relationality that the concept of the lifeworld seeks to highlight.

The lifeworld is simultaneously my world and a world shared with others and things. It incorporates the social, historical, cultural, material and biological, as well as their interrelations. Given this understanding of the lifeworld, Theodore Schatzki's (2001, p. 3) claim that practice approaches are at odds with lifeworld accounts is untenable. Rather, practice approaches assume the lifeworld. In some cases (for example, Wenger, 1998), this assumption is made explicit. According to Husserl, the lifeworld provides the point of departure for all our endeavours, including scientific investigation and philosophical reflection. It is, therefore, pre-scientific and pre-reflective. In calling attention to our pre-scientific and pre-reflective world, the concept of the lifeworld is consistent with a defining maxim of phenomenology: To the things themselves! This maxim should not be misinterpreted as a call to a kind of naturalism or investigation of "things as they really are". On the contrary, through this maxim, phenomenology urges a close and attentive account of our world as we engage with and experience it, both individually and collectively. In other words, phenomenology argues for recognition of, and attentiveness to, the lifeworld as the basis for our theorising and reflection. The concept of the lifeworld provides a point of departure, then, for investigations of professional practice.

The concept of the lifeworld is central to Husserl's epistemological project, although it is not entirely consistent with his later transcendental phenomenology, where he sought to achieve a foundation for all knowledge that was to transcend human experience. Phenomenologists who came after Husserl, such as Martin Heidegger and Maurice Merleau-Ponty, drew upon his work in various ways, but rejected his transcendental turn. The concept of the lifeworld is one of the common concepts within the various branches of phenomenology that have developed since Husserl. Herbert Spiegelberg (1982) describes some of these various developments in *The Phenomenological Movement*. Through the relational concept of the lifeworld, then, phenomenology provides an approach to knowing, including its social character (for example, see Berger & Luckmann, 1966), which was a radical departure from earlier accounts that treated subject and world as independent entities. The substantial impact of the concept of the lifeworld extends across the humanities and social sciences, well beyond its origins in philosophy and, more specifically, in phenomenology.

Being-in-the-World

As Husserl's philosophical project focused on epistemology, his concept of the lifeworld also has such a focus. While issues relating to how we develop knowledge are central to professional practice, a limitation of such a focus is that it stops short of considerations about ontology, such as who we become as professionals and how this process of becoming occurs. Conventional expertise and distributed cognition research, as well as most situated cognition research, also overlooks ontology. Heidegger recognised this limitation of Husserl's phenomenology. He extended Husserl's concept of the lifeworld through the concept of "being-in-the-world", giving it a heightened ontological character. Like Husserl, Heidegger emphasised that we are always already embedded in, and entwined with, our world. But he also sought to renew interest in exploring "the question of the meaning of being" (1962/1927, p. 21, § 2). This question is the focus of Heidegger's magnum opus, *Being and Time*, as well as many of his later works.

Heidegger is critical of lack of attention to the question of being in philosophy after Plato and Aristotle. He challenges what he saw as myth-like beliefs about being that had encouraged such neglect, namely, that the concept of being is universal, indefinable, and self-evident (pp. 22–23, § 3–4). Instead, Heidegger identifies a paradox: "that we already live in an understanding of Being and that the meaning of Being is still veiled in darkness" (p. 23, § 4). For example, our everyday lives are premised on an understanding of what it means to be human, although we are far from clear about what being human entails. Heidegger points out that it is a particular being—with a certain understanding of being—who asks the question about what is being. He called this being, Dasein (literally, Being-there (p. 81, § 55)), referring to both human being and being human (Dreyfus, 1991, pp. 13–14; Inwood, 1997, p. 137).

Heidegger regards modes of knowing, such as architecture, biology, history and so on, as ways of being-in-the-world (1962/1927, p. 408, § 357). He considered it necessary to clarify being-in-the-world if we are more fully to understand knowing. He turned to clarifying the being of Dasein in order to understand these various ways of being, since he saw Dasein as the "site of the understanding of being" (1996/1927, p. 7, §8).[3] This means that if we are fully to understand knowing within various forms of professional practice, we must understand the being of those who know.

Grounded in his concept of being-in-the-world, Heidegger explores characteristic features of being human, which have relevance for professional practice. These features include existence (or possible ways of being) and "mineness" (or always "belonging" to someone):

> *The essence of Dasein lies in its existence* [or] possible ways for it to be.... Dasein is mine to be in one way or another.... In each case Dasein *is* its possibility, and it "has" this possibility, but not just as a property. (p. 68, § 42)

These possible ways of being and "mineness" mean human beings have agency. As we engage with the world, we do not merely follow a pre-determined path or course of action, but contribute to creating our lives. As we enact particular ways of being, we incorporate aspects of our past as well as anticipating a future we contribute to producing. For Heidegger, temporality—or historicity—is a central feature of being human. Given our possible ways of being and temporality, we are in a process of becoming throughout our lives: "Because Dasein ... is temporal, it realizes its possibilities of understanding only through becoming" (Huntington, 2001, p. 23). Becoming professionals, then, is open-ended and always incomplete.

---

[3] While the remaining quotes from *Being and Time* in this book are taken from a translation by John Macquarrie and Edward Robinson, this quote is from a note written in the margin by Heidegger, which is included in a later translation (Heidegger, 1996/1927) by Joan Stambaugh.

We typically do not attend to this process of becoming or to understanding our own being, more generally, according to Heidegger. This is because we are absorbed in a range of activities and projects, generally carrying them out in a mode of "average everydayness". That is, we are usually absorbed in, but take for granted, the routine and everyday. Operating in a mode of average everydayness is not a deficient mode of being; it allows us to complete the tasks we have before us. Although we typically do not bring the routine and everyday under scrutiny, we nonetheless actualise particular ways of being as we go about our activities and projects. While we are open to possibilities, our ways of being are constrained by the specific situations we inhabit and their history, as well as by our own past that we carry forward with us.

When we are absorbed in our various activities and projects, we use tools or equipment—sometimes with unexpected consequences (see, for example, Arnold, 2003)—and we produce artefacts. These equipment and artefacts are not simply objects that occur within our world, but Heidegger describes them as "ready-to-hand" for us. For instance, if I am ill and visit a doctor, a stethoscope or thermometer may be used in diagnosing my ailment, which is recorded in my medical record. These instruments and artefacts are integral to the practice that is medicine. Their usage within this practice is typically taken for granted by both doctor and patient. Only when instruments or artefacts are broken or missing from where we expect to find them, do we become aware of them as entities or things. Equipment and artefacts are, then, integral to engagement with, and shaping of, our world.

Not only are equipment and artefacts integral to being-in-the-world, but so, too, is "being-with" others, including those who are only implicated, such as the author of a resource we read about our diagnosed ailment. Throughout our lives, being with others is a feature of being-in-the-world. Through being with others, we learn to think and act as (the collective and general) "they" do. For instance, we learn how "one" acts during a visit to the doctor. Learning and knowing are possible, then, through being with others, where language has a key role.

Heidegger concludes, then, that "knowing has the phenomenal character of a Being which is in and towards the world" (1962/1927, p. 87, § 60), again emphasising the inseparable relation of epistemology with ontology. In contrast, decontextualisation from everyday practices in conventional research on expertise (see above) not only undermines the situatedness of the knower in relation to those practices, but also overlooks being-in and being-towards the world. If we ignore these features of being-in-the-world in research on professional practice, we neglect key features of this practice. In other words, the ontology-epistemology nexus is central to this research.

In later work, Heidegger (1993/1954) highlights questions of ontology as they relate to the use of technology. He expresses disquiet about the way in which our increasingly technologised world frames human being and nature. In particular, he argues that our unquestioning production and use of technologies encourages an instrumental way of treating both nature and human beings as resources to be used or exploited. Iain Thomson explains Heidegger's concern, as follows:

As technology colonizes the lifeworld, everything "sucked up" into its purview, including the modern subject, is reduced to the ontological status of a resource to be optimised. . . . For Heidegger, the "greatest danger" of our spreading technological understanding of being is the possibility that we will lose the capacity to understand ourselves in any other way. (Thomson, 2000, pp. 206–207)

Bronwyn Davies (2003) and Paul Gibbs (2004) provide thought-provoking analyses of the trend to treat human beings as exploitable resources in the university context (see also Dall'Alba, 2005; Dall'Alba & Barnacle, 2005). While Heidegger acknowledges technology can be used thoughtfully, he argues that, for the most part, it is being used in a way that fails to take account of the consequences of its use. It is possible to take a somewhat less pessimistic view of the use of technologies, as they can have both positive and negative consequences (Dall'Alba & Barnacle, 2005; Ihde, 2002). For instance, technologies can provide more ready access to educational opportunities or healthcare for people who are geographically isolated or those with some disabilities.

A key insight from Heidegger's ontological investigations of technology is that they are not neutral instruments, but afford particular human-technology relations and, thereby, specific ways of framing human being and our entwinement with world. This insight has relevance for professional practice, especially in a context where such practice increasingly incorporates technologies. For the most part, there is little debate about the ontological significance of the production and use of technologies in professional practice, underscoring the concern expressed by Heidegger.

Related to Heidegger's concerns about technology is his concept of "care", which differs from the English meaning of this term in its ontological emphasis. For Heidegger, being human is to care (Heidegger, 1962/1927, p. 84, § 57), in other words, to concern ourselves with people and things that matter to us. As noted above, we concern ourselves with, or become absorbed in, the projects, activities and things that make up our world. Care also takes the form of being with others, which has particular relevance to professional practice. At one extreme, being with another can "take away 'care' from the Other . . . it can *leap in* for him [so that] the Other can become one who is dominated and dependent, even if this domination is a tacit one and remains hidden from him" (p. 158, § 122). Heidegger's concerns about the way in which use of technologies can frame being human can be seen in the context of a potential risk of domination through these technologies. For example, some health professionals argue that employing extraordinary measures to extend the life of terminally ill patients can remove from them the possibility of a dignified death. Conversely, being with others may not involve domination, but "collaboration which enables personal freedom to be grasped" (Gibbs, 2004, p. 77). Heidegger describes this form of care as:

a kind of solicitude [care for the Other] which does not so much leap in for the Other as *leap ahead* of him . . . not in order to take away his "care" but rather to give it back to him authentically as such for the first time. This kind of solicitude pertains essentially to authentic care—that is, to the existence [or possible ways of being] of the Other, not to a "what" with which he is concerned; it helps the Other to become transparent to himself *in* his care to become *free for* it. (1962/1927, pp. 158–159, § 122)

For the most part, being with others takes various forms between these two extremes of "that which leaps in and dominates, and that which leaps forth and liberates" (p. 159, § 122). A trend towards patient-centred healthcare in many countries can be seen as an attempt to care without domination (see, for example, Coulter, 2002), although there may be gaps between rhetoric and practice. Patricia Huntington argues that "Heidegger supplies a rich vocabulary for reconceptualizing human nature as care—custodian for what appears—rather than as the rational animal who lords over the earth" (2001, p. 27). She points out, however, that "in *Being and Time* Heidegger still made all systems of meaning take their point of reference from Dasein, even as he sought to decenter 'man' as the source of knowledge and meaning" (p. 30), but that the notion of "letting be" he develops in later works seeks to address this limitation.

Through highlighting ontology, then, Heidegger's concept of being-in-the-world extends and enriches the notion of the lifeworld. A significant contribution is that, through the concept of being-in-the-world, Heidegger places emphasis on being human through entwinement with others and things, rather than on mind or cognition, in contrast to many other approaches. Those approaches that emphasise cognition have overtones of René Descartes' *cogito sum*: "I think, therefore I am". Heidegger pointed out Descartes' oversight: "Not until the nature of this Being has been determined can we grasp the kind of Being which belongs to *cogitationes*" (p. 72, § 46). In other words, only when we have clarified what it means to be human (that is, the "I am") is it possible to comprehend thinking as a mode of being human. Heidegger makes a similar argument that knowing presupposes being.

Heidegger has contributed to awakening a renewed interest in questions of ontology, both within and beyond philosophy (see, for example, Barnacle, 2005; Barnett, 1997, 2004; Dall'Alba, 2005; Dall'Alba & Barnacle, 2005, 2007; Grosz, 2004; Merleau-Ponty, 1962/1945; Mol, 2002; Ratcliffe, 2002; Thomson, 2001; Walker, 2006). By highlighting questions of ontology, he has extended our understanding of what it means to be human and to engage with our world as human beings, with implications for professional practice and research about this practice.

Lived Body

While enriching our understanding of what it means to be human, one of the limitations of Heidegger's ontological investigations is that they assume, but do not explore, embodiment (See Huntington, 2001, for discussion about how embodiment is assumed in Heidegger's work). Maurice Merleau-Ponty has sought to address this limitation. He draws upon both Husserl's concept of the lifeworld and Heidegger's being-in-the-world, extending these concepts through highlighting embodiment. Below we explore several aspects of Merleau-Ponty's notion of embodiment through his concept of "lived body". These aspects include adopting a perspective due to our situatedness, commitment to projects, ambiguity in relating to the world, body extension and overlapping of individual with social. We then consider some limitations of Merleau-Ponty's concept of the lived body before drawing the chapter to a close by pointing to features of the lifeworld that can enrich explorations of professional practice and learning to be professionals.

While Heidegger emphasises entwinement with others and things in our world, Merleau-Ponty highlights the body as the medium for embeddedness in, and engagement with, the world:

> The body is the vehicle of being in the world, and having a body is, for a living creature, to be intervolved in a definite environment, to identify oneself with certain projects and be continually committed to them. . . . I am conscious of my body *via* the world . . . [and] I am conscious of the world through the medium of my body. (1962/1945, p. 82)

Merleau-Ponty's notion of embodiment incorporates, then, situatedness and commitment to specific projects and activities. Due to our situatedness, we always adopt a particular perspective in encounters with our world, so that our perceptions and understandings are necessarily incomplete, as Heidegger also acknowledged. Rather than something to be overcome, this incompleteness is a feature of our embodiment. Adopting a perspective and commitment to projects are, then, aspects of being in, and oriented towards, the world. In contrast to the concept of situated cognition outlined above, through highlighting embodiment Merleau-Ponty overcomes the problem of how cognition and world meet: "The body is our general medium for having a world" (p. 146). He goes on to clarify that "consciousness projects itself into a physical world and has a body, as it projects itself into a cultural world and has its habits. . . . Consciousness is in the first place not a matter of 'I think that' but of 'I can'" (p. 137). In this way, Merleau-Ponty made a radical and fruitful break with a Cartesian mind/body and subject/object duality (see also Dall'Alba & Barnacle, 2005).

Merleau-Ponty points out that our body differs from other objects in the world in that it is always with us: "I have no need to look for it, it is already with me" (p. 94). More specifically, I am my body (p. 150). The body to which Merleau-Ponty refers here is not limited to the physical body as a set of interconnected organs, but is the body as *lived*. Through our body, we are directed towards and engage with things and others in our world, giving concrete form to possible ways of being. This lived body is both subject and object simultaneously: "I apprehend my body as a subject-object, as capable of 'seeing' and 'suffering'" (p. 95). Merleau-Ponty highlights the complexity of being human and of our relation to our world through identification of ambiguities, such as the body as subject-object: "In other words, ambiguity is of the essence of human existence, and everything we live or think has always several meanings" (p. 169). He resists a tendency to isolate and categorise, demonstrating that our categories and entities often spill over into one another. For example:

> When I press my two hands together, it is not a matter of two sensations felt together as one perceives two objects placed side by side, but of an ambiguous set-up in which both hands can alternate the roles of "touching" and "being touched." (p. 93)

A further blurring of boundaries that Merleau-Ponty features is the way in which objects outside our body can become an extension of the body, such as a blind person's cane, a car we drive, or a computer we use to "reach" a text in a library and to compose our own text (see Dall'Alba & Barnacle, 2005; Ihde, 2002). He describes such body extension in terms of being in the world:

> To get used to a hat, a car or a stick [for example, a blind person's cane] is to be transplanted into them, or conversely, to incorporate them into the bulk of our own body. Habit expresses our power of dilating our being-in-the-world, or changing our existence by appropriating fresh instruments. (p. 143)

The extension of the body in this way may appear to have some similarities to the concept of distributed cognition. However, Merleau-Ponty's way of considering body extension is not limited to cognition, but concerns embodiment and being in the world. His notion of embodiment is itself a rejection of a tendency to separate cognition from the physical body, a legacy in western thought from Plato and Descartes (Dall'Alba & Barnacle, 2005; Peters, 2004). As Wayne Bowman notes:

> The habit of treating body as the disavowed condition of knowledge (the subordinated counterpart of mind) is an extraordinarily difficult one to shake. Deeply built into our inherited languages are the remains of conceptual structures in which mind is separate from and superordinate to things bodily, and teaching old words new tricks is extraordinarily challenging. (2004, p. 30)

Similar to Heidegger, Merleau-Ponty rejects a notion of containment in a world: "We must therefore avoid saying that our body is *in* space, or *in* time. It *inhabits* space and time" (p. 139). There is, moreover, reciprocity between space and time, and my body: "I am not in space and time, nor do I conceive space and time; I belong to them, my body combines with them and includes them" (p. 140). For Merleau-Ponty, embodiment is not bounded by, nor contained within, my own body. Rather, my body allows access to and extends into other bodies and entities that make up the world. In a similar way, the lived body is both individual and social. As Minette Mans expresses it, "the body individual is a reflection and confirmation of the body social" (2004, p. 83). Pierre Bourdieu's concept of "social field" (1977), which has been influenced by Merleau-Ponty's philosophy (Dreyfus, 1991, p. 9), is an elaboration of this overlapping of individual with social, as is his concept of "habitus".

For Merleau-Ponty, the body, as social and temporal, merges with and flows into collective history:

> As my living present opens upon a past which I nevertheless am no longer living through, and on a future which I do not yet live, and perhaps never shall, it can also open on to temporalities outside my living experience and acquire a social horizon, with the result that my world is expanded to the dimensions of that collective history which my private existence takes up and carries forward. (1962/1945, p. 433)

Traditions of practice that constitute a profession are examples of the collective history we take up and carry forward through the lived body. Embodiment, then, is a condition for knowing. The lived body makes knowing possible. Knowing occurs through, and by means of, the lived body.

While knowing relies upon embodiment, Merleau-Ponty's concept of the lived body makes clear that embodiment cannot be reduced to "doing", especially mindless doing. As Pirkko Markula points out, "the engagement in bodily practices or promotion of bodily practices does not alone guarantee the construction of an embodied subjectivity" (2004, p. 74). At the same time, Mans points out that "bodies in performance always enfold and reveal diverse histories of gender, social status, kinship, ethnicity and power as well as the bodily experience" (2004, p. 79). These aspects of embodiment that Mans identifies are not explored in Merleau-Ponty's account, however, which can be seen as a limitation. For example, Elizabeth Grosz (1994) explores ways in which Merleau-Ponty's notion of the body overlooks gender and power.

While Merleau-Ponty's account of the lived body features some aspects, but not others, feminist scholars have drawn upon this concept to advance feminist and queer theory (for example, Grosz, 1994; Moi, 2001; Young, 1990, 2003). Iris Marion Young (2003) refers to the work of Toril Moi (2001) in arguing that the concept of the lived body can be elaborated to disclose additional aspects of embodiment:

> The idea of the lived body...can bring the physical facts of different bodies into theory without the reductionist and dichotomous implications of the category of "sex". The idea of the lived body, moreover, refuses the distinction between nature and culture that grounds a distinction between sex and gender....The diverse phenomena that have come under the rubric of "gender" in feminist theory can be redescribed in the idea of lived body as some among many forms of bodily habitus and interactions with others that we enact and experience....The idea of the lived body thus does the work the category "gender" has done, but better and more. It does this work better because the category of lived body allows description of the habits and interactions of men with women, women with women, and men with men in ways that can attend to the plural possibilities of comportment, without necessary reduction to the normative heterosexual binary of "masculine" and "feminine". It does more because it helps avoid a problem generated by use of ascriptive general categories such as "gender", "race", "nationality", "sexual orientation", to describe the constructed identities of individuals, namely the additive character that identities appear to have under this description. (Young, 2003, pp. 99–100)

Young argues, however, that in addition to issues of experience, identity and subjectivity, there is a need to address the way in which social structures constrain opportunities for some, while opening them to others. She sees the concept of the lived body as providing a means of connecting analysis of social structures with experience and subjectivity:

> Another reason that turning to a concept of lived body may be productive for feminist and queer theory is precisely that it can offer a way of articulating how persons live out their positioning in social structures along with the opportunities and constraints they produce. (p. 109)

In a similar vein, Grosz (1994) draws upon, as well as extending, Merleau-Ponty's concept of lived body. As Young also does, Grosz demonstrates that relations of power are largely overlooked in Merleau-Ponty's analyses. Grosz discusses the way in which, in contrast, Michel Foucault highlights the relation between materiality and power:

> In Foucault, the body is the object, target, and instrument of power, the field of greatest investment for power's operations, a stake in the struggle for power's control over a materiality that is dangerous to it, precisely because it is unpredictable and able to be used in

potentially infinite ways, according to infinitely variable cultural dictates.... The body is
that materiality, almost a medium, on which power operates and through which it functions.
(1994, p. 146)

Grosz points out, too, that not only is the body an object and instrument of power,
it is also "constrained by its biological limits" but that "while there must be some
kinds of biological limit or constraint, these constraints are perpetually capable of
being superseded, overcome" (p. 187). This tension or interplay between biological
limits and overcoming those limits (that is, limits that are not entirely limits) is a
further example of the blurring of boundaries or ambiguity of which Merleau-Ponty
speaks in his notion of the lived body. Some implications of ambiguity for learning
professional ways of being are explored in Chapter 4.

The concept of the lived body brings embodiment into the notion of the lifeworld.
The lived body provides a means of exploring ways in which the social, historical,
cultural, material and biological are interwoven in constituting the lifeworld. These
various aspects of being-in-the-world are relevant to professional practice. Hence,
an extended concept of the lifeworld offers an integrated framework for exploring
professional practice, including both epistemological and ontological dimensions
(see Sandberg & Dall'Alba, in press, for elaboration). The challenge is to take
account of the lifeworld in efforts to investigate and enrich professional practice
in ways that acknowledge our entwinement with world but do not privilege human
being at the expense of other beings.

Professional Practice Presupposes the Lifeworld

From the preceding inquiry into professional practice, we see that professional practice presupposes the lifeworld. Consistent with an extended concept of the lifeworld,
we see that individuals and collectives enact and embody professional practice.
Such practice is spatially and temporally located in specific contexts, so we adopt
particular perspectives on practice and our understanding of practice is thereby
always incomplete. Our understanding of practice includes both epistemological
and ontological dimensions. Not only is our knowing enacted and embodied in and
through practice, but also who we are as professionals. Given we are always already
embedded in and entwined with our world, we embody social structures that frame
traditions of practice, although we continue to have agency in relation to how these
structures play out in our practice. For instance, if we teach in ways that teachers
do, engage in medical practice in ways that medical practitioners do and so on, we
may also resist, bend or renew some of these accepted practices and structures to
the extent this is possible in particular places and times. While social structures and
traditions of practice frame what we do and who we are as professionals, they also
provide openings for a range of ways of being professionals in our contemporary
world. As we engage with these structures and practice traditions in the present, we
carry forward the past in anticipating possible ways of being.

Professional practice evolves and becomes renewed over time through its temporal character. It incorporates continuity and transformation, for both individuals and

collectives, in and through their entwinement with world. Practice is dynamic and complex, routinised as well as creative. This means that practice is not singular, but that the "same" practice is enacted and embodied in multiple ways (see, for example, Billett, 2001; Dall'Alba, 2002; Lamiani et al., 2008; Mol, 2002), as "everything we live or think has always several meanings" (Merleau-Ponty, 1962/1945, p. 169). Some of these ways of enacting practice may not be entirely consistent with each other. For example, there are inconsistencies between patient-centred healthcare and medical practice that primarily seeks to manage disease (for example, Stålsby Lundborg, Wahlstrom, & Dall'Alba, 1999; see also Chapter 5). Those who engage with a practice community encounter not one practice, but various enactments and embodiments of the practice in question, albeit with shared dimensions that allow us to recognise it as a particular practice.

The perspective on professional practice adopted here is consistent with a practice turn evident in some approaches to the humanities and social sciences. This practice turn incorporates the pluralisation and embodiment of knowing and of practice outlined above. Less often, attention is drawn to ontological dimensions of being in, and being oriented towards, the world. However, it is through, and in terms of, our being towards the world that practice is meaningful at all. Professional practice presupposes being towards the world. Both epistemological and ontological dimensions are considered central to professional practice in the account put forward here. Hence, professional practice incorporates not only our knowing and how we act, but also who we are as professionals. Given knowing, acting and being are integral to professional practice, emphasis in this book is placed on learning professional ways of being through entwinement with our world.

Learning to become professionals involves, then, what we know, how we act, and who we are becoming (Dall'Alba, 2005; Dall'Alba & Barnacle, 2007), as these relate to our interaction with others and things in our world. Professional education programmes must address these various aspects if they are to enhance the process of learning to be professionals. A conventional focus on acquisition of knowledge and skills in such programmes is, therefore, inadequate. A key task of these programmes is to promote integration of knowing, acting and being in our world as they relate to particular professional practice, including opening new possibilities for being the professionals in question. In the remainder of this book, we explore what such a process of becoming entails.

Part II
Professional Education as Preparation

Chapter 3
Investigating Preparation for Professional Practice

Learning cannot be designed: it can only be designed
for—that is, facilitated or frustrated.

(Wenger, 1998, p. 229)

Against the background of the current context of flux and fluidity outlined in Chapter 1 and the framing of professional practice developed in Chapter 2, this part of the book critically examines preparation for professional practice in conventional educational programmes. Two arguments from previous chapters also contribute to forming the background as we begin this investigation, namely, that appropriate preparation for professional practice does not imply a functional fit between preparation and practice (see Chapter 1), and there may be various rationales for the formation of particular professions (see Chapter 2). Notwithstanding these two arguments, those aspiring to enter the professions must be adequately prepared for providing specific services, especially given the important role these services can have for society and the lives of clients. This chapter begins an examination of the adequacy of preparation for professional practice in broad terms from a pedagogical point of view.

In critically examining conventional professional education programmes, the chapter draws on relevant research literature as well as reflections from students as they completed a medical programme at Karolinska Institute in Stockholm, Sweden. The students' reflections were made between 1997 and 2000, during longitudinal research in which 13 medical students were observed in consultations with patients and interviewed during the clinical part of their programme. This longitudinal research is reported more fully in Chapters 6 and 7, and was conducted as part of research on a whole medical student cohort (Dall'Alba, 1998, 2004). While changes to the Karolinska medical programme have occurred since the longitudinal research was carried out, many issues identified in the research remain relevant to professional education programmes, as we see in the chapters that follow. Students' reflections are used here to illustrate and elaborate some of the issues identified in the research literature about professional education.

A key argument in the present chapter is that conventional preparation for the increasingly complex world of professional practice is generally limited in scope and inadequate for continued professional development. While this argument is not new, when we scrutinise the curriculum design and implementation of many

G. Dall'Alba, *Learning to be Professionals*, Innovation and Change in Professional
Education 4, DOI 10.1007/978-90-481-2608-8_3,
© Springer Science+Business Media B.V. 2009

professional education programmes we see that, despite some innovations, many of these programmes largely continue in a similar vein as their precursors.

Critically examining the curriculum in this chapter is not intended to suggest, however, that curriculum design can resolve all challenges for learning in professional education programmes. Nor does it suggest that curriculum design can "cause" students to achieve desired learning outcomes, even in cases where efforts have been made to clarify what those outcomes might be. Rather, the quote that introduces this chapter identifies a central principle of learning: *"Learning cannot be designed*: it can only be designed *for*—that is, facilitated or frustrated" (Wenger, 1998, p. 229). Moreover, any form of curriculum design has strengths and limitations in promoting learning. Curriculum design is, nonetheless, one of the major means we have for contributing to learning among students in professional education programmes. It is important, therefore, that we thoughtfully use the opportunity for promoting learning that it affords:

> Whatever effects a curriculum has—whether intended or unintended—effects there are. What is apparent is that the range of possible effects on students is increasing and is open for decision. Unless, at the strategic level, we become reflective practitioners, our curricular decisions may be influenced by unrecognized forces at work, or may lead to effects on students with uncertain value, or both. (Barnett, 1992, p. 14)

Adopting a critical, reflective approach to curriculum includes continually interrogating and monitoring its effects to ensure that planned curricula and students' experiences of those curricula contribute to learning.

A major reason for critically examining the curriculum design of professional education programmes in this chapter is that our understanding of learning, and of the promotion of learning, is expressed and enacted in the way we design curricula. Adopting a critical stance on the design of the curriculum provides us with a means of interrogating our understanding of learning and of how to enhance learning.

Technical Rationality and the Normative Curriculum

Although two decades have passed since Donald Schön (1987) critiqued the normative curriculum in professional education programmes, his description still has currency today:

> The professional schools of the modern research university are premised on technical rationality. Their normative curriculum, first adopted in the early decades of the twentieth century as the professions sought to gain prestige by establishing their schools in universities, still embodies the idea that practical competence becomes professional when its instrumental problem solving is grounded in systematic, preferably scientific knowledge.... As professional schools have sought to attain higher levels of academic rigor and status, they have oriented themselves toward an ideal most vividly represented by a particular view of medical education: physicians are thought to be trained as biotechnical problem solvers by immersion, first in medical science and then in supervised clinical practice where they learn to apply research-based techniques.... The greater one's proximity to basic science, as a rule, the higher one's academic status.... And the relative status of the various professions is largely correlated with the extent to which they are able to present themselves as rigorous

practitioners of a science-based professional knowledge and embody in their schools a version of the normative professional curriculum. (pp. 8–9)

Robin Usher and colleagues (1997) elaborate the epistemology that Schön called technical rationality, as follows:

> The technical-rationality model assumes that theoretical knowledge must be the foundation of practice because it is research-generated, systematic and "scientific" knowledge.... Furthermore, the "worthwhileness" of theoretical knowledge is reinforced because of the apparent power of this kind of knowledge to make predictions about events in the world and hence to be able to control these events.... The condition of practice is the learning of a body of theoretical knowledge, and practice therefore becomes the application of this body of knowledge in repeated and predictable ways to achieve predefined ends. A certain kind of rationality, an essentially technical and instrumental rationality, is presupposed here. It is hardly surprising then, that practice comes to be seen as mere technique, the efficient matching of means to ends in predictable and routine ways. The practitioner is consequently reduced to the role of "technician", the applier of techniques. (1997, pp. 125–126)

This technicist view of practice suggests a functional fit between professional education and practice is both feasible and desirable. However, Schön challenges an epistemology of technical rationality for professional education when he demonstrates it is at odds with the way in which experienced professionals engage in practice and aspiring professionals learn to do so (Schön, 1983, 1987). Despite this discrepancy, as the education of lawyers, engineers, architects, teachers, accountants, nurses, social workers and so on moved into universities, the normative curriculum was generally introduced across these programmes for the reasons Schön outlined above. Over time, some innovations have been introduced, such as through the use of new information and communication technologies, and earlier contact with clients or patients. However, these innovations have usually been introduced without substantial change to the organisation of the curriculum or the pedagogies employed (see, for example, Alexander & Boud, 2001; Dall'Alba & Barnacle, 2005). While there are exceptions to the pervasive normative curriculum, including problem-based learning, work-based learning and curricula emphasising process over content, these alternatives remain less prevalent. In addition, where alternative curriculum designs are in place, residues of conventional designs often remain. For instance, student achievement may be assessed in the form of knowledge retention and/or acquisition of specific skills, such as communication techniques.

As noted in Chapter 2, Schön is critical of the separation between acquisition and application of knowledge and skills that was cemented through the normative curriculum. This form of curriculum organisation assumes knowledge and skills are first acquired and then applied in practice, as the need arises. John Bowden and Ference Marton, too, question such a separation:

> Sorting situations into two categories—learning situations on the one hand and situations of application on the other—seems hard to defend. Every "learning situation" includes the potential for application (of something previously learned) and every "situation of application" implies the potential for learning (something new). (1998, p. 41)

Separating acquisition from application is based on a questionable notion that knowledge and skills can meaningfully be learned as decontextualised entities (see Chapter 2; see also Dall'Alba & Barnacle, 2005, 2007; Lave, 1993). It also begs the question of how knowledge and skills become integrated into professional practice. More specifically, it ignores the situational awareness required about when, how and why particular knowledge and skills are appropriate, and in what circumstances. As Usher and colleagues point out:

> Every context of practice has its own distinctive features which provide possibilities and impose constraints on what can be done.... [Theoretical knowledge] cannot tell practitioners what is the right action in relation to a concrete problem in a specific context; it is simply impossible to translate it into rules and techniques which can be applied by practitioners in concrete situations. For them, what is always at stake is the very relevance of theoretical generalisations. The problem is compounded because theoretical knowledge is not monolithic. Thus, there could be many generalisations which might be relevant in any practice situation, and some of them might be in conflict with others. (1997, pp. 126–127)

Like Schön, several students in the Karolinska medical programme questioned the effectiveness of the normative curriculum design. Their medical curriculum largely followed the technical rationalist model described by Schön, with two preclinical years followed by three-and-a-half years of clinical studies, although there were innovative elements in some courses.[1] All 13 of the students who were observed and interviewed acknowledged the importance of the knowledge they had obtained from the medical programme, but many questioned the way the curriculum was organised. In her third year, Ingrid[2] made the following reflections on the two preclinical years in which the focus had been knowledge acquisition:

> *I thought the preclinical was quite boring.... In the middle of the first semester, you wondered whether you'd ever get to be a doctor. Couldn't sort of relate it really....Back then you sat and pounded in answers to what you were reading. Now you wish in some way, now you have another picture of the whole thing...you could relate it in a different way. Not, not like, not just read about diabetes without maybe seeing a diabetes patient and seeing the complications there can be and see, like, the damaged foot. Then you don't just read about, like, if they have changes in blood vessels and things like that, but you have more a picture of, like, what it really can look like and what they get, like, see what an insulin injection looks like, for example....Get an idea...when you've been able to see it and maybe talked with people with diabetes and heard their view of the disease and things like that. And not just read about a disease you have to learn about: these are the symptoms and you do this and this. Because then you have to also, like, match it later with a patient who comes. But that's what I think is really difficult....Yeah, I think*

---

[1] In this book, 'course' is used to designate discrete units of study, such as anatomy or paediatrics, that together make up an educational programme, such as medical education.

[2] Names of students have been changed for anonymity and quotes from students translated from Swedish.

it's easier to go from the other direction [having contact with patients from the beginning]. (2nd semester of 3rd year, pp. 41–44)

Several other medical students in the study also pointed to the difficulty of relating knowledge gained from books and lectures to patient problems. For example, Lotta said:

It's really difficult to learn about an individual patient's problem from books and lectures. You can learn very quickly when you're on a ward, it takes a day or so. You have a bit better insight then. But linking it to knowledge in books is really difficult. (2nd semester of 3rd year, p. 74)

In her final semester of the medical programme, reflecting back on the preclinical years, Lotta observed: "For the first two years I didn't know anything about how everything works and what it's like to be a doctor" (p. 69). Erik was openly critical of the separation between knowledge acquisition and its subsequent application:

I think it's a scandal, as someone who's already been out and worked, I think the whole medical programme is laid out in the wrong way. Two and a half years locked up inside Karolinska Institute!...It's quite an odd system if you're going to be a doctor....Medical education is a practical kind of work so that, but Karolinska is very research-focused, so that would be why. (2nd semester of 4th year, pp. 25–26)

In Schön's critique of the normative curriculum, he calls into question learning to intellectualise about practice as a separate activity from that practice. Through this separation, the relation between theory and practice is not interrogated or problematised. Such separation is not, of course, limited to the normative curriculum. It continues to be evident in some of the curriculum innovations that incorporate early practicum or clinical experience when it is not well-integrated with the remainder of the programme, in disconnections between learning in university and practice contexts, and even in some uses of reflective practicum components that may serve to separate reflection from practice, rather than making it an integral, ongoing part of practice. Current trends in the evidence-based practice movement also carry the risk of continuing to reinforce a bifurcation of theory and practice, as well as failing to problematise the relationship between the two (see also Davies, 2003; Nutley, Isabel Walter, & Davies, 2003).

Given the normative curriculum is based on technical rationality, the acquisition and application of science-based knowledge is prioritised over learning professional practice. Such an emphasis is evident, for instance, in medical programmes in which a large component of clinical placements is located in hospitals, while placements with general practitioners may be featured only marginally:

The population of patients which is referred to hospital is a subset of that which attends general practitioners, a subset in which serious disease is overrepresented and people's other needs underrepresented. As a result, medical students whose clinical experience is confined to hospital, often in highly specialized units, have a distorted view of the prevalence of

disease in the community and people's real needs. This brings in its wake errors in diagnosis
and the inappropriate use of investigations. (McCormick, 1992, p. 161)

A lack of focus on learning central aspects of professional practice also occurred
in several courses in the Karolinska programme when medical practitioners in the
hospitals selected medical conditions for students to observe: "Sometimes there's
the attitude that what's unusual is more exciting and that's what we should look at.
But, for us, it's best to see what's most common" (Max, 1st semester of 5th year,
p. 21).

An inappropriate epistemology of technical rationality and associated failure to
focus on learning professional practice mean the normative curriculum is untenable
for adequately preparing aspiring professionals for professional practice. In addition, the rapidly expanding knowledge in many fields, increasingly interdisciplinary
nature of professional practice, complexities of the work professionals do, and the
open, fluid character of many situations in which professionals carry out their work
present challenges to this form of curriculum organisation. But still the normative
curriculum persists, so that questioning it can be construed as lowering standards.

Sally Cavanaugh identifies some of the reasons the status quo is maintained
despite the inappropriateness of the normative curriculum, with some similarities
to points raised above by Erik:

> The organization of academic departments by discipline, coupled with institutional adher-
> ence to a narrow definition of scholarship, influences faculty roles and priorities, which
> in turn influence the teaching and learning process in professional education programs. In
> sum, higher education's organization by academic discipline serves to facilitate research
> productivity, but it does not lend itself well to the development of flexible integrated learn-
> ing that students need to function effectively in complex and dynamic professional practice
> environments. (Cavanaugh, 1993, p. 114)

A discipline-based funding model for teaching of courses remains common in universities, which serves to reinforce and maintain discipline-based curricula. Reward
systems that generally prioritise research over teaching or entrench the status quo in
other ways provide no incentive for re-thinking the organisation of these curricula
or for developing as teachers (see Laurillard, 2002, for related arguments).

Curriculum organisation based on separate disciplines in line with an epistemology of technical rationality leads to fragmentation into parts that typically do not
become integrated in the study experience of students. For instance, students are
left with the challenge of bringing together the large range of topics and courses
they study, as well as the knowledge and skills they learn within the university and
in practice contexts. It is not difficult to appreciate the enormity of such a task, especially for novices. In the final semester of the medical programme, Ingrid provided
an example of this challenge during consultations with patients. She realised that
some diseases or symptoms are related to events occurring in patients' lives, but that
while the relationship between the social and somatic is important, she considered
it difficult to bring the two together:

> *[In the medical programme] there have been too many pieces to take hold
> of all at once when you haven't even had a sense of the whole. . . . So, as a*

student, it's often very easy to either focus on the disease and its symptoms as they are, or to focus on the underlying social factors. It's hard to bring, tie the two together. You don't have either the time or opportunity or ability to do that, and at the same time you can't do it in case a supervisor comes in afterwards and says exactly the opposite. Then you've got in the way more than helped. (final semester, pp. 59–60)

Kristina, too, described difficulties for learning from a fragmented curriculum:

There are two sides to everything. I've found things very disjointed and bitsy for our part. We've been pulled out of one hospital department on Friday afternoon and then to a new one on Monday morning. And then there've been a heap of seminars you have to run to and things like that, and then move on again next Friday and things. It's been small, short visits. But it also, then you get breadth. It's hard to get it all to work out. (final semester, p. 21)

Fragmented curriculum organisation is so prevalent that it tends to be taken for granted, even by those who strive to improve the student learning experience. For example, in arguing for the need to "put *education* back into medical training", Robin Downie and Bruce Charlton make the following statement: "Generally speaking, we feel that if the parts are properly educational the whole will take care of itself" (1992, p. 5). They appear to be referring to learning the "parts" that make a good doctor. A common focus on an array of parts occurs at the expense of integrating those parts and understanding the importance of the parts for the whole, that is, of enhancing understanding and performance of professional practice. Achieving integration of this kind is arguably one of the most challenging aspects of learning to be professionals. Efforts to achieve such integration are evident in some professional education programmes. For example, research on teacher education shows:

teacher education programs that have coherent visions of teaching and learning, and that integrate related strategies across courses and field placements, have a greater impact on the initial conceptions and practices of prospective teachers than those that remain a collection of relatively disconnected courses. In a set of studies of seven exemplary teacher education programs—programs in which graduates and their employers find they are significantly better prepared than most other beginning teachers—one of the most striking characteristics is that the programs are particularly well integrated and coherent: they have integrated clinical work with coursework so that it reinforces and reflects key ideas and both aspects of the program build toward a deeper understanding of teaching and learning. These programs are founded on a set of big ideas that are continuously revisited and hence more deeply understood. (Darling-Hammond, Hammerness, Grossman, Rust, & Shulman, 2005, p. 392)

In other words, integrated curricula enhance the learning of professional practice in ways that might be expected but, nonetheless, are not common in curriculum design:

Learning ideas within the context of an overarching conceptual framework not only helps students understand the "big picture" but also enables them to begin to recognize how all the individual ideas and theories fit together and relate to one another. Having this structure explicitly described and explained is helpful to candidates' later learning. (Darling-Hammond, Hammerness, et al., 2005, p. 397).

Moreover, "helping candidates understand the bigger picture allows them to locate what they are learning" (p. 398). This view of curriculum contrasts starkly with a set of courses that appear disconnected to students and in which content must be "covered" by the teacher, often using an approach described as "once over lightly" (Darling-Hammond, Pacheco, et al., 2005, p. 443). In curricula of the latter kind, what students learn is clearly not in focus.

Deborah Ball and David Cohen point to what is required in professional education if students are to understand the "big picture" for their profession:

> First, professional education must be education for professional practice if it is to be either professionally responsible or usable. Thus a conception of the practice itself, and what it takes to practice well, should lie at the foundation of professional education. Second, any defensible education requires a sense of its purposes, a map of the relevant terrains in which to work, and a conception of what is involved in learning to operate in that terrain. . . . Third, since such schemes do not apply themselves, ideas are needed about the kinds of knowledge, skill, and other qualities crucial to teaching in these ways. To satisfy these three basic requirements would be to realize key elements of professional education for . . . practice. (1999, p. 12)

It seems likely that neglect of systematic integration within the curriculum and lack of focus on learning professional practice is contributing to a situation where comprehensive understandings of practice are uncommon among both aspiring and experienced professionals. This situation is evident in a number of empirical studies across a range of professions (for example, Benner, 1984; Benner, Tanner, & Chesla, 1996; Dall'Alba, 2004; Kieser, Dall'Alba, & Livingstone, in press; Sandberg, 2000; Stålsby Lundborg et al., 1999). The criticism being directed at professionals and professional education (see Chapter 1) may partly be due to incomplete understanding that is encountered among professionals.

When we critically examine the limitations of conventional professional education programmes in this way, we see they are inappropriate for preparing aspiring professionals for practice in the current context of fluidity and flux. The inadequacy of these programmes demands we question the assumptions on which preparation for professional practice has conventionally been based. To this end, we now turn to considering two forms of curriculum organisation, problem-based learning and recent forms of work-based learning, which have sought to overcome a separation of acquisition of knowledge and skills from their application. These curriculum designs are discussed here as two among many possible options for curriculum organisation that provide alternatives to the normative curriculum in professional education. These alternatives demonstrate that other forms of curriculum organisation are not only possible, but also feasible, for professional education programmes in contemporary universities.

Problem-Based Learning

While Donald Schön was arguing for a re-structure of the curriculum in education for the professions, an innovative departure from the normative curriculum had been

taking shape in the form of problem-based learning (PBL). This approach origin-
ated in the mid-1960s in medical education at McMaster University in Canada (see
Barrows & Tamblyn, 1980). It was a radical curriculum move at the time, especially
given the dominance of the normative curriculum in professional education. While
PBL attracted some enthusiasts in its early days, Brian Jolly relates a conversation
he had after a visit to McMaster in 1974 that captures some of the sceptical response
it also received:

> I remember having a conversation with a Professor of Anatomy at London University who
> simply refused to see any merit in a group of students, who "knew nothing", sitting around
> discussing what might be wrong with a patient in order to improve their understanding of
> science. They would, of course, have been much better off cutting up some cadavers to
> isolate the anatomical structures that were causing the patient's discomfort and probable
> death. (2006, p. 494)

It is unsurprising PBL met some strong resistance, given its challenge to the prevailing epistemology of technical rationality and the normative curriculum. Shifting
control of the learning process from teachers to students was also a controversial
feature, especially when proponents of PBL considered such a shift was necessary
and desirable. As Howard Barrows and Robyn Tamblyn point out when arguing for
this shift, "It is more important to consider how much the student learns than how
much the teacher teaches" (1980, p. 16). However, as noted above, when reward
systems prioritise research over teaching and entrench the status quo, there is little
incentive for developing as teachers or questioning established forms of curriculum design. As Barrows and Tamblyn note, this situation presents a paradox for
programmes whose purpose is to prepare aspiring professionals for practice:

> Each member of a medical faculty has spent many arduous years gaining the knowledge and
> skills necessary to successfully carry out tasks in research and patient care. Few have taken
> the time to gain any specific or formal preparation to aid them in carrying out their respon-
> sibilities in medical education. While this is considered acceptable, medical schools would
> not tolerate such an amateur status in those responsible for research or patient care.... The
> reasons for this paradoxical situation are a matter of history and reflect the reward system
> used in medical schools, where faculty development in education is not encouraged. There
> are few schools who would put the education of students as their highest priority, or who
> would allow faculty promotion and remuneration to reflect educational knowledge and skills
> equal to or above research and patient-care productivity. (pp. 2–3)

The impetus for PBL curriculum design came from dissatisfaction with conventional medical curricula. Reflecting on the early days of PBL, Barrows (1996) draws
upon the account of a colleague at McMaster in outlining the motivation for curriculum innovation there at the time:

> The McMaster group noted that students were disenchanted and bored with their medi-
> cal education because they were saturated by the vast amounts of information they had to
> absorb, much of which was perceived to have little relevance to medical practice. They also
> noted that, by contrast, during residency, students were excited by working with patients
> and solving problems. (Spaulding, 1991, p. 28 cited in Barrows 1996, p. 4)

These comments mirror those above by Ingrid and other medical students who considered their preclinical years to be boring due to the lack of relation to medical

practice and large quantities of information to be remembered. The students reported that the separation of theoretical knowledge from practice created difficulties for relating what had been learned previously to patients who presented for treatment. In the Karolinska medical programme during the longitudinal study, one course that ran for a full semester adopted a PBL format, while other courses were hybrids in which some features of PBL were included alongside more conventional teaching methods. Near the end of the fourth year PBL semester, Max commented, as follows:

> [With PBL] you don't really have control over what you're studying and that.... You don't read as systematically as you maybe do in other kinds of study. But at the same time I think you've learned a lot without it being difficult.... You're active. You pose questions before you sit down and read. And that's quite good compared with sitting and reading from page one. It isn't so effective to do that, in fact. Even if you feel very satisfied when you're got to the last page, there's no guarantee so much of it has stuck. (2nd semester of 4th year, pp. 22–23)

Barrows explains the need for the curriculum to focus not on knowledge acquisition, but on the problem solving that is central to clinical practice:

> Studies of the clinical reasoning of students and resident physicians in neurology suggested that the conventional methods of teaching probably inhibit, if not destroy, any clinical reasoning ability (Barrows and Bennett, 1972) [and] that students had forgotten their freshman neuroanatomy by the time of their clinical neurology course as juniors. (Barrows 1996, p. 4)

Moreover, Barrows and Tamblyn identify in PBL the importance of the need to continue to learn as professionals, which requires that students learn how to learn:

> Almost all of the learning a physician will need to accomplish in his forty or more years of professional work, after his formal medical education, will be his own responsibility. [A logical task, therefore,] is to continuously evaluate his own abilities, determine when new skills and knowledge are needed, and effectively use available resources to meet these identified needs. (1980, p. 5)

Barrows identifies the characteristic features of the McMaster PBL, as follows: (a) learning is student-centred in the sense that students are active and take responsibility for their own learning; (b) students work in small groups (typically of about 5–9 in the early days at McMaster) and then are re-grouped at the end of each unit of study; (c) under the guidance of a tutor, students in the group learn to pose questions to each other that will enable them to address the problem at hand; (d) realistic problems from professional practice form the focus and stimulus for learning; (e) practice-based problems are a vehicle for development of problem solving and are presented in the way they would be in practice; and (f) students work together to gain new knowledge through self-directed learning (1996, pp. 5–6).

A defining feature of PBL is that students are not first presented with the necessary knowledge and then given a problem to solve—as commonly occurs in the normative curriculum—but, conversely, they "analyze and resolve the problem as far as possible before acquiring any information needed for better understanding" (pp. 6–7). Moreover, "essential to the method is that students' prior knowledge of the problem is, in itself, insufficient for them to understand it in depth" (Norman & Schmidt, 1992, p. 557). In this way, practice-based problems are the organising framework and stimulus for student learning:

> The curricular linchpin in PBL—the thing that holds it together and keeps it on track—is the collection of problems in any given course or curriculum with each problem designed to stimulate student learning in areas relevant to the curriculum. (Barrows, 1996, p. 8)

This form of curriculum organisation is consistent with Schön's argument that "the question of the relationship between practice competence and professional knowledge needs to be turned upside down" in the normative curriculum (1987, p. 13). Where there is deviation from starting with realistic, practice-based problems that students work through in small groups under the guidance of a tutor and monitor their own learning in addressing these problems, it is doubtful that curricula can claim to have adopted PBL.

More specifically, in problem-based learning:

> the problem is not offered as an example of the relevance of prior learning or as an exercise for applying information already learned. . . . Finding an answer to a question is not problem-based learning. The use of a known principle or solution to explain an observation or phenomenon is not problem-based learning. (Barrows & Tamblyn, 1980, p. 18)

Instead, it is "the learning that results from the process of working toward the understanding or resolution of a problem. The problem is encountered *first* in the learning process!" (p. 1). Barrows warns against "the damage that apparently easy or trivial compromises in curricular design can do" to achieving the potential of PBL (1996, p. 7). Contrary to misconceptions about PBL, tutors can respond to students' questions in guiding them as they analyse the problem being investigated. Moreover, PBL does not preclude the use of lectures that are relevant to the problem students are working through, although lectures are not the main method of teaching and learning.

During the period since its inception, PBL has spread across a range of medical education programmes internationally and also to other professional programmes, such as in dentistry, nursing, pharmacy, veterinary medicine, law, engineering, business, teacher education and to various areas within the natural sciences, as well as to early childhood, primary and secondary school curricula. Adoption of PBL is continuing to occur into the present. In some instances, whole new medical programmes were designed around PBL principles based on the McMaster model, such as at Maastricht in the Netherlands, Newcastle in Australia and Linköping in Sweden. In other cases, specific courses or parts of courses within professional and other educational programmes have adopted PBL principles.

As PBL spread widely from its origins in Canada, modifications to its implementation occurred in response to local conditions, efforts to refine aspects of its implementation, misunderstanding of its intent, resistance from sceptical administrators and teaching staff, or failure to adequately prepare teaching staff to work with students in the unfamiliar ways that PBL demanded. Although there are exceptions, there frequently appears to have been a preoccupation with "doing PBL" at the expense of paying careful attention to its pedagogical principles. The result often has been a focus on the routine of going through steps in solving a problem, rather than adopting a reflective approach to learning to solve problems based in practice. The latter approach includes reflecting on the effectiveness of both the process used in solving a problem and the learning that takes place about the problem or topic.

PBL has been adopted, then, in a broad variety of ways, accompanied by debates in the literature about its usefulness and effectiveness. As Jolly notes, "The debate has widened from "it works!"—"no it doesn't" to a dispute about the know-ability of whether, how and why it works; and if it does what effect size would it be, and is it big enough?" (2006, p. 494). The merits or limitations of PBL will not be debated here, although it can be noted that the appropriateness of some of the measures used to evaluate PBL have been questioned (for example, Breton, 1999; Major & Palmer, 2001). When attempts to evaluate the effectiveness of PBL used conventional notions of epistemology based on students' knowledge acquisition, results were inconclusive and any differences found were small (see, for example, Dochy, Segers, Van den Bossche, & Gijbels, 2003; Norman & Schmidt, 1992; Vernon & Blake, 1993). These results suggested students from conventional programmes may demonstrate better knowledge of basic sciences, while those in PBL programmes may show better clinical knowledge. When assessments considered critical thinking (for example, Tiwari, Lai, So, & Yuen, 2006) or knowledge retention over time (Dochy et al., 2003; Norman & Schmidt, 1992), students from PBL programmes typically performed better than those in conventional curricula. Graduates from PBL programmes were more positive towards the programme they had experienced and felt better prepared for professional practice than those from conventional programmes (Antepohl, Domeij, Forsberg, & Ludvigsson, 2003; Norman & Schmidt, 1992; Prince, van Eijs, Boshuizen, van der Vleuten, & Scherpbier, 2005; Schmidt, Vermeulen, & van der Molen, 2006).

Comparisons between performance of students and graduates of PBL with conventional programmes are difficult because, over time, "there has been considerable drift and accommodation of curriculum models so the differences are less clear cut" (Jolly, 2006, p. 494). It should be noted that, like PBL, conventional curricula continue to be implemented in a range of ways, although the epistemology and rationale that Schön identified in the normative curriculum remains prevalent. PBL exemplifies an alternative form of curriculum organisation in preparation for professional practice. A further point that implementations of PBL demonstrates is that curriculum innovations become modified across sites and contexts, with variation in the extent to which they are based on sound pedagogical principles. The ways in which innovations such as PBL are implemented can be expected to impact upon the learning that occurs and, therefore, upon the extent to which students are adequately prepared for professional practice.

Work-Based Learning

A more recent, but no less radical, curriculum innovation has emerged in the newer forms of work-based learning (see Boud & Solomon, 2001c, for examples). Although not originating specifically as a form of preparation for professional practice, work-based learning is outlined here as it provides another form of curriculum organisation that addresses some of the criticisms of the normative curriculum. Incorporation of work-based components into professional education programmes is not new. These components have been included in higher education programmes for many years, including in professional education. The forms they take include practicum placements, fieldwork and sandwich courses, in which students spend initial and final years in the university, with an extended, intervening period located in workplaces. Newer forms of work-based learning have a relatively recent history, with developments largely beginning during the later part of the 1980s and into the 1990s. David Boud and colleagues (2001) provide an historical outline of developments contributing to current forms of work-based learning, while Norman Evans (2001) gives an historical account of the context in which work-based learning has been used in a range of programmes in the UK.

Unlike earlier work-based components, in newer forms of work-based learning, work and the workplace take precedence over disciplinary knowledge or university programmes. In other words, "work is the curriculum" (Boud, Solomon, & Symes, 2001, p. 5). These programmes are intended to be of mutual benefit for the learner and the workplace: "Learning is designed not just to extend the knowledge and skills of the individual, but to make a difference to the organization. . . . Organizational and individual capabilities are thus linked. This grounds learning and gives a focus to it" (p. 6).

Boud and colleagues identify characteristics of work-based learning, as follows: (a) a partnership that includes ongoing formal agreements is established between an educational institution and a public, private or community organisation, with the purpose of fostering learning; (b) learners are employees of, or in a contractual relationship with, the external organisation and they negotiate learning plans with both the organisation and educational institution; (c) the programme followed is based on the needs of the workplace and the learner; (d) the starting point and educational level is determined once the learner's desired learning and current competencies, rather than educational qualifications or past achievements, have been identified; (e) learning projects that make a contribution to the organisation are undertaken in the workplace, while external resources may be drawn upon, including courses or training; and (f) the educational institution assesses learning outcomes against a transdisciplinary framework of standards and levels, leading to an educational qualification (2001, pp. 4–7). Similar to PBL and other curriculum innovations, there are hybrids of work-based learning and conventional programmes (for example, Brown, Harte, & Warnes, 2007; Nicholls & Walsh, 2007) that vary in the extent to which they incorporate these characteristics. Work-based learning, too, has attracted some enthusiastic proponents, as well as meeting resistance to its challenges to re-structuring the conventional higher education curriculum.

Work-based learning, like PBL, has turned on its head not only the relationship between practice competence and professional knowledge, which Schön advocated (1987, p. 13), but also the relationship between the university and the workplace: "In work-based learning the structural arrangements, as well as the sequence of learning episodes, begin with the learners and their workplaces, and end with the university" (Boud & Solomon, 2001b, p. 21). As the various parties come together to negotiate learning that is valued by them all, it is not surprising tensions arise that need to be addressed if the collaboration demanded by work-based learning is to eventuate (see, for example, Garrick & Kirkpatrick, 1998; Rhodes & Shiel, 2007; Sobiechowska & Maisch, 2007).

Boud and Solomon identify three broad challenges that work-based learning presents for universities: the challenge of *equivalence* between conventional academic standards and work-based learning outcomes; challenges to teaching and learning *practices*; and challenges to the *identity* of the university, academic and learner (2001b, pp. 26–30; see also Garrick & Kirkpatrick, 1998). As well as challenges for universities, there are challenges for learners: "In work-based learning learners have to deal with the complexities of being both a worker and learner and of having an increased responsibility in the learning process" (Boud & Solomon, 2001b, p. 31; see, for example, Rhodes & Shiel, 2007; Sobiechowska & Maisch, 2007). While some research has investigated the ways in which the challenges for universities and learners are being addressed in work-based learning, these challenges are, as yet, not adequately researched.

There is also a need for thoughtful research that interrogates and problematises the notion of work-based learning itself. Such research would benefit from taking into account the policy framework within which work-based learning has developed, "including the pressures on universities to adopt more vocational approaches to higher education, accompanied by the development of a new corporate mentality and the insertion of the 'market form' into higher education" (Garrick & Kirkpatrick, 1998, p. 174). In debates about the vocationalisation and marketisation of higher education (see, for example, Barnett, 1994; Bowden & Marton, 1998; Garrick & Kirkpatrick, 1998; Heidegger, 1998/1967; Sidhu, 2006; Slaughter & Leslie, 1997; Thomson, 2001; Walker, 2006) it has been argued that the role and purpose of higher education is broader than preparation for work, boosting national economies or international competitiveness, although the contribution of higher education to these pragmatic imperatives has also been acknowledged.

As higher education and society form closer ties in a range of ways, including through work-based learning, Ronald Barnett identifies an ideological shift in higher education "from knowing as contemplation to knowing as operation" (1994, p. 15). More specifically, an academic view "built around a sense of the student's mastery within a discipline" is being displaced by an operational/instrumental view, "essentially reproducing wider societal interest in performance, especially performance likely to enhance the economic performance" of the nation (p. 159). Barnett argues that the academic and operational views of knowing are both flawed, relying upon a questionable separation of thought and action: "Doing at any level of complexity involves thinking, and thinking conducted with any seriousness is a form of action" (p. 160). While work-based learning can be seen as part of a shift from contemplation and disciplinary knowledge to operation and performance, the various forms it takes vary in the extent to which they embody such a shift.

Whatever its merits and challenges, it remains to be seen whether work-based learning will be incorporated into greater numbers of educational programmes and higher education institutions. While interest in this form of curriculum organisation continues, it is not apparent that, on any large scale in the foreseeable future, work-based learning will replace conventional programmes that provide preparation for professional practice. However, work-based learning has called into question some of the assumptions underlying many higher education programmes:

> Work-based learning as a pedagogical site challenges most of our conventional assumptions about teaching, learning, knowledge and curriculum. . . . Indeed, work-based learning in higher education institutions disturbs most of the conventional binaries that have framed our academic work, including: organizational learning and university learning; performance outcomes and learning outcomes; organizational discourses and academic discourses; theory and practice; and disciplinary knowledge and workplace knowledge. (Boud & Solomon, 2001a, p. 225)

It is not apparent, however, that work-based learning offers benefits over conventional programmes relating to the development of a critical approach to practice or its role in society. Nonetheless, the development of work-based learning raises important questions for professional education. These include questions relating to the forms of knowing that are relevant for professional practice and for professional education programmes, the contributions that professional education can make to preparing aspiring professionals for the challenges of practice, and ways in which higher education institutions can work more collaboratively with external organisations in promoting learning to be professionals. For these reasons alone, it is a development worth noting and monitoring.

Curriculum Design for Professional Preparation

Scrutiny of the normative curriculum, particularly in the light of other forms of curriculum organisation, such as problem-based learning and work-based learning, reveals limitations in the ways in which we conventionally prepare professionals for the complexities of professional practice. Despite its limitations, however, the normative curriculum highlights the need for professionals to be knowledgeable about the practice in which they are engaged. The need for knowledge about professional practice, and capacity for skilfully engaging in that practice, is not in dispute. The forms such knowledge and skilfulness should take and ways in which it can be developed are contentious issues, however. These issues are debated across a range of approaches to professional education, as noted above.

Schön's critique of the normative curriculum, as well as problem-based learning and work-based learning, point to the need to develop knowledge in ways that does not artificially separate it from embeddedness in practice. As we noted in Chapter 2, Martin Heidegger emphasises the way in which we are always already embedded in, and entwined with, particular situations and projects; we cannot step outside this embeddedness in our world. Highlighting the importance of such embeddedness in practice contexts can be achieved through various means, including inquiry directed to practice-relevant problems or issues arising at work, as problem-based learning and work-based learning demonstrate. It does not imply all parts of professional education programmes must be located geographically in those practice settings, for example, in schools, law courts, architecture studios or building sites, hospital wards or health clinics. Nor does it imply a functional fit between preparation and practice. Instead, as Deborah Ball and David Cohen argue, professional education can "use practice as a site for inquiry" (1999, p. 19). This means focusing on key questions and issues relating to practice, including adopting a critical approach to the significance, and current ways of dealing with, those questions and issues. Approaches to curriculum that emphasise inquiry directed to practice also underscore the importance of such inquiry for attaining an integrated curriculum. Curriculum integration must be made visible to, and be experienced by, students if it is to contribute to learning. In addition, problem-based learning and work-based learning highlight the importance of developing ways of learning and of knowing that continue to be relevant beyond professional education and into professional practice.

Despite some efforts in curriculum innovation, the continued prevalence of the normative curriculum demonstrates a persistent understanding of learning as knowledge acquisition for subsequent application. Even where innovations have been introduced into the curriculum, this understanding often remains evident. The persistence of this understanding of learning and knowledge limits substantial curriculum innovation in many settings. This is because our efforts to promote learning among students occur in the context of our own understanding of learning, as it develops over time. In other words, our understanding of learning affords opportunities for improving the curriculum, as well as constraining those efforts. As this understanding develops, the design of the curriculum can change shape and focus. Problem-based learning and work-based learning demonstrate such change through their attempts to address limitations for learning of the normative curriculum.

Chapter 4
Professional Education as a Process of Becoming

> *To make real changes in education . . . we have to set aside the deadly notion that the . . . first priority should be intellectual development.*
>
> (Noddings, 1992, p. 12)

In the previous chapter it was argued that enhancing learning as students progress through professional education programmes requires a clear focus on preparation for practice. This is because these programmes are not ends in themselves; their key purpose is preparation for professional practice. As shown in Chapter 3, one of the ways in which the normative curriculum is inadequate for students in professional programmes is that the primary purpose of these programmes is not consistent with the focus of the curriculum. Rather, emphasis on the acquisition and application of knowledge occurs at the expense of a clear focus on preparation for practice. Moreover, research demonstrates that professional development does not simply involve acquiring and applying knowledge, but learning to deal with the situations encountered in practice in qualitatively different and more complex ways (for example, Benner, 1984; Benner et al., 1996; Borko, Davinroy, Bliem, & Cumbo, 2000; Borko, Mayfield, Marion, Flexer, & Cumbo, 1997; Schön, 1983, 1987).

What, then, does a focus on preparation for professional practice entail? The way in which this question is approached will depend, among other things, upon the epistemological and ontological assumptions being made. The lifeworld perspective adopted in this book, drawing particularly upon Martin Heidegger and Maurice Merleau-Ponty (see Chapter 2), throws new light on the question of preparing for professional practice. Merleau-Ponty's work can contribute to our inquiry in several ways, particularly through his emphasis on ambiguity in our relation to our world, embodiment and knowing through the lived body. Heidegger, on the other hand, has written specifically on the question of higher education and on a range of educationally significant issues.

Consistent with Heidegger's broader efforts toward re-thinking ontology (see Chapter 2), he engages in ontological inquiry into higher education. Iain Thomson (2004) argues that this enduring theme for Heidegger is largely unacknowledged in the research literature about Heidegger's work. He notes that "a radical re-thinking of education—in a word, an ontologization of education—forms one of the deep thematic undercurrents of Heidegger's work, early as well as late" (p. 439). For Thomson, this theme permeates *Being and Time* with a "quiet presence" that will be detected by those already familiar with Heidegger's philosophy of education (p. 440). Michael Bonnett (2002), too, identifies powerful ideas for education in Heidegger's early and later work. He points out that Heidegger addresses questions such as thinking, understanding and learning that have direct educational significance, as well as questions relating to language and human being that have profound importance for education. An example is Heidegger's notion of care without domination (see Chapter 2), which has strong ethical implications for the pedagogical relation. Bonnett illustrates how Heideggerian notions of teaching and learning have contemporary resonance, while calling into question an instrumental view of education. Similar arguments have been made specifically in relation to higher education (Dall'Alba, 2005; Dall'Alba & Barnacle, 2005, 2007; Gibbs, 2004).

While the research literature on professional education programmes pays close attention to the development of knowledge and skills, or an epistemological dimension, there is scant attention to an ontological dimension of the learning that occurs. While there is passing reference to a need for "transformation" in a small proportion of this literature, the form this transformation would take is rarely clarified and its importance is downplayed through a clearer focus on knowledge and skills development. Little has changed in this respect since early in the 20th century when Heidegger began arguing for close attention to the ontological dimension of human being (for example, Heidegger, 1962/1927; 1998/1967). A focus on epistemology— or what students know and can do—occurs at the expense of this ontological dimension or who students are becoming. A similar lack of attention to an ontological dimension in research on professional practice was noted in Chapter 2. For example, aspects of professional practice or qualities of being a professional that have a clearly ontological dimension, such as "moral character" (Tirri, Husu, & Kansanen, 1999; see also Self & Olivarez, 1996), are typically presented only in terms of skills and competencies to be acquired. As professional practice incorporates not only our knowing and how we act, but also who we are as professionals, all of these aspects must be developed in relation to one another in professional education programmes. Moreover, they can only be developed in relation to the social practice in question; they are not simply individual attributes. Developing knowing, acting and being can also be seen to be relevant, in some sense, to all educational endeavour.

When preparation for professional practice is approached in this way, professional education is reconfigured as a process of becoming. The key purpose of these programmes is then seen as developing professional ways of being that relate to particular professions, rather than simply in terms of developing knowledge and skills. While knowledge and skills are important, they are insufficient for embodying and enacting skilful professional practice, as well as for the process of becoming that learning such practice entails. Knowledge and skills are gained in order to contribute to this process of becoming; epistemology is in the service of ontology (Dall'Alba, 2005; Dall'Alba & Barnacle, 2007). This chapter brings to bear the theoretical framework outlined in Chapter 2 in exploring this process of becoming in which aspiring professionals learn to be professionals. Learning and teaching that supports this process of becoming is also outlined.

Becoming Professionals

While processes of becoming often go unacknowledged or are given only passing reference in theorising and practice relating to professional education, these processes are typically assumed in such programmes. For instance, we expect transformation from students to engineers, lawyers, nurses, teachers and so on. While this is an implicit expectation of such programmes, nonetheless, they typically do not make this transformation their focus. More recently, theorising about higher education programmes has begun to take this ontological dimension more seriously (for example, Barnacle, 2005; Barnett, 1997, 2004, 2005; Dall'Alba, 2005; 2009; Dall'Alba & Barnacle, 2005, 2007; Thomson, 2001; Vu & Dall'Alba, 2008; Walker, 2006). Higher education programmes promote—directly or indirectly—particular ways of knowing, acting and being. For example, medical programmes develop knowledge about medical practice, such as knowledge about diseases and symptoms; they encourage ways of acting, including how to examine patients for signs of disease without inflicting harm or injury; and, in doing so, they foster ways of being medical practitioners that impact upon patients' personal integrity. These ways of knowing, acting and being are interdependent. They are formed and shaped through processes of becoming that involve an unfolding and transformation of the self over time. As Ronald Barnett points out: "A higher education is necessarily a process of becoming. The question is, what kind of becoming?" (1994, p. 190).

As we noted in Chapter 2, having possibilities, or possible ways to be, is a central feature of being human for Heidegger (1962/1927, p. 40, § 42). We also understand ourselves in terms of possibilities (p. 185, § 145), so we are continually in a process of becoming that is open-ended, never complete. Not only do we negotiate possibilities, but we are already (oriented to) what we are "not yet" (Heidegger, 1962/1927, pp. 185–186, § 145). For instance, while medical students are not yet medical practitioners, they engage in various activities and projects that orient and commit them to being medical practitioners. What they seek to know, how they act and who they are becoming is oriented to, and directed by, this commitment. One of the Karolinska medical students, Gunnar, pointed to a paradox in this early commitment to a profession: "It's strange that you can be so sure you want to become something you actually know so little about" (final semester, p. 23). While some of the students in the longitudinal study occasionally questioned their choice of profession, especially early in the medical programme, for the most part they progressively confirmed their commitment over time.

The students' engagement in various activities and courses within the programme was an expression and demonstration of this commitment. In taking up some possibilities and not others within the options available to them, they contributed to shaping and actualising their becoming. For example, they chose to go to some classes, but not others; they studied particular elective courses, while forgoing others; they sought opportunities to discuss questions of interest with some professionals or fellow students rather than others. In describing this process of contributing to our own becoming, Thomson points to a distinction made by Heidegger (1962/1927, pp. 185–186 § 145) between "being-possible" and "ability-to-be":

> As Blattner nicely puts it, "there are two functions here: opening up the range of possibilities, and pressing ahead into one of them." We become what we are "not yet," then, by pressing ahead into (or projecting ourselves upon) our projects. (Thomson, 2004, p. 450)

Forming and shaping our own present and future in this way carries with it both anticipation and anxiety, which is clearly evident as students approach the end of a professional education programme:

> *You really want to try taking more responsibility, because you know you're getting close to the end. So you also want to test, to try out your wings a little, to see how far they hold. You have to be bolder. And that's, that's like what comes with time.... It'll go in waves. Then when you start you'll, when you start working for real you'll also feel again that you can't manage this.... No, it's going to be really demanding, for sure. You feel really inadequate and that. Because anyway there's quite a lot you haven't got involved in so much, or you can't do.* (Elisabet, 2nd semester of 5th year, pp. 131–132)

Paul Gibbs considers that facing the uncertainty of our becoming is "both courageous and unsettling, for it challenges us in what we are and what we intend ourselves to be, rather than accepting a spectatorial account of ourselves" that simply reflects the expectations of others (2004, p. 122). Facing this uncertainty and attempting to deal with it is one of the ways in which we can shape our own becoming. In contrast, "being perceived as 'bright', getting ahead, not to delve into oneself, but rather to understand how to meet outer expectations is to master the art of inauthenticity" (Giugliano, 1988, p. 152, cited in Gibbs, 2004, p. 120). This is to risk being carried along unthinkingly with what the generalised "they" do. Professional education programmes play a part in promoting ways of addressing, or avoiding facing up to, the uncertainty of becoming (see also Vu & Dall'Alba, 2008).

In becoming professionals, knowing, acting and being are integrated into professional ways of being that unfold over time. Various development trajectories open as possibilities, while we press ahead into shaping and forming our development within, or sometimes despite, existing constraints, as Chapter 7 illustrates. This view challenges a common assumption that professional development proceeds in a stepwise manner through a fixed sequence of stages (for example, Benner, 1984; Benner et al., 1996; Dreyfus & Dreyfus, 1986; Fook, Ryan, & Hawkins, 2000). Viewing professional development in terms of stages does not feature the agency we demonstrate in shaping our development trajectory, including when we make decisions in the present or about the future, as well as when we avoid making such decisions. Developmental stages also veil more central aspects of professional development, such as knowing, acting and being the professionals in question (Dall'Alba & Sandberg, 2006).

While we have a range of possible ways to be, it matters to us who we are and who we are becoming. We are "a being who takes a stand on its being and is defined by that stand" (Thomson, 2004, p. 453). The stands we take are significant for us in that "the very way reality shows up for us is filtered through and circumscribed by the stands we take on ourselves, the embodied life-projects which organize our practical activities and so shape the intelligibility of our worlds" (p. 444). As it matters to us who we are becoming, we do not simply take up opportunities available to us in a straightforward manner. Rather, as our activities and projects shape our becoming, we are likely to take up those opportunities that are consistent with or advance our sense of self, while resisting those that undermine our sense of who we are.

Our becoming is not solely an individual matter, however. Heidegger points out that we are also entwined in traditions that tend to cover over what is being passed on down the generations (1962/1927, pp. 42–43 § 21). For example, history students learn routines and procedures that are part of the practice of history and of being historians. The traditions of which we are a part tend to be taken for granted and are generally not transparent to us, especially when they become familiar to us. Through examining practice traditions, the interdependence of individual professionals and the profession of which they are a part is made clear; one cannot exist without the other. These practice traditions constrain opportunities for some, while opening them to others. For example, as we noted in Chapter 2, Jeff Hearn (1982) argues that the formation of professions has typically been accompanied by marginalisation of women, especially from positions of influence. However, where there is some openness to re-thinking assumptions and relinquishing established power differentials, new ways of acting and of being can come into play, bringing about a renewal of practice at both individual and collective levels. As Gibbs points out:

> If we are not satisfied with what is we can imagine a state not yet present that can or ought to be brought into being by the choice of actions we make. How we come to understand and enact these possibilities is often only through the act of engagement with others, thus grounding our potentiality within a social temporal condition. (2004, p. 118)

Professional education has a key part to play in forming and shaping the stands students take on both themselves and the professional practice to which they aspire: what they come to know, how they act and who they are as professionals. In this way, the stands they take are entwined with their knowing and acting. In other words, epistemology and ontology are inseparable. As Thomson explains:

> Our very "being-in-the-world" is shaped by the knowledge we pursue, uncover, and embody. [There is] a troubling sense in which it seems that we cannot help practicing what we know, since we are "always already" implicitly shaped by our guiding metaphysical presuppositions. (2001, p. 250)

As we noted in Chapter 2, Maurice Merleau-Ponty (1962/1945) points out that embodying and enacting what we know is made possible through the lived body. The lived body allows access to, and engagement with, our world. Through the lived body we come to know, act upon and inhabit our world, so it unites epistemology and ontology. Our knowing and what we can do are not simply something we possess, but who we are. Formalised knowledge, too, presupposes embodied knowing and being-in-the-world in the same way that theory presupposes practice (see Chapters 1 and 2). In other words, formal knowledge is only possible through the embodied way in which we engage with our world.

The inseparability of epistemology and ontology is no excuse, however, for overlooking ontology in professional education programmes. If we focus only on epistemology, we risk stopping short of accomplishing the transformations expected through such programmes. The interrelation of epistemology and ontology is to be nurtured if professional education programmes are to enhance processes of becoming.

Ambiguities in Becoming Professionals

While professional education has a central role to play in enhancing processes of becoming, our ambiguous relation to our world (see Chapter 2) opens a range of possible ways to know, to act and to be professionals. For example, during the Karolinska medical programme, Ingrid came to recognise that the problems patients needed help with were not always those they initially identified as the reason for the visit to the doctor. This realisation and the reflexive approach she adopted, opened new possibilities for her way of being a medical practitioner:

> *You've got a slightly different view of people, in some way, than what you had before. Maybe that's positive. I think it's probably one of the most important things [I've learned from the medical programme].*
>
> Interviewer: *So what's your view now? Can you describe it?*
>
> *That you don't always think and see things in the way you say. Or if I can express it this way, that you've learnt you're not the only one who often puts up a facade outwards, but everyone else does it, too. And you've learnt that. And maybe in some way you start to deal with that a bit.*
>
> Interviewer: *Mm. How do you think it's important for you, as someone who's becoming a doctor, to realise this?*
>
> *I think it's really important. And it's something that you, that you, when you know it, maybe you can work around it in some way. Because it's actually what's behind that you're after. At the same time, maybe you yourself can let someone else in, too, if I can put it that way. So you don't only put on a white coat and stay in there, but you invite others in a bit. You have to do that, maybe that's something. But it's also something you wish for [that you could achieve]. [Pauses, then laughs] (2nd semester of 3rd year, pp. 46–47)*

Questioning her prior assumptions in this way enabled Ingrid to re-consider what it means both to practise medicine and to be a skilful, committed medical practitioner.

While we may sometimes be open to extending or challenging our familiar ways of understanding ourselves or some aspect of our world, we continue to be constrained by the possibilities available in the particular situations we inhabit, as well as by our past and what we anticipate for the future. For instance, the extent to which Ingrid is able to "invite others in", or open herself to others, is likely to be influenced by the responses she receives when she does so, as well as by her previous experiences of interacting with others. In this way, our becoming incorporates both continuity and transformation, as Chapter 7 demonstrates.

Exploring implications of our ambiguous relation to our world for professional education can enable us to better grasp what it means to learn to be professionals. Several features of learning to be professionals are outlined below as we explore the ambiguity that is integral to professional practice. These features are principally explored in relation to the period of transition from aspiring to practising professionals, although they also have relevance for continuing to learn as professionals. The features include: *continuity* over time *with change* in ways of being professionals; *possibilities* in the ways we can be *with constraints* on those possibilities; *openness* in taking up possibilities *with resistance* to doing so; and *individuals* who are becoming professionals *with others* involved in this process. Attending to, and dwelling with, these ambiguities—while recognising them as ambiguities, not simply conflicts to be resolved—can open possibilities for enriching professional education programmes. In so doing, these programmes can become more meaningful for those who are learning ways of being that relate to particular professions.

Continuity with Change

Both continuity and change occur through the passage of time as part of our everyday life. Our world today is both the world it was yesterday and a changed world. In some sense, we are the persons we were yesterday and will be tomorrow, but also not the same. For Heidegger and Merleau-Ponty, temporality—or historicity—is not only inevitable but also central to being human. Both these scholars resist the everyday conception that we are contained in time as it flows around us, perhaps carrying us along (see Chapter 2).

According to Heidegger, we are our past. The past not only "pushes along 'behind' ", but is also our way of being in the present, which anticipates and creates the future (1962/1927, p. 17 § 20). The past does not determine the present or future, but it opens possible ways of being. The past, present and future do not form a linear trajectory, then, but the past opens a range of possibilities that can be taken up in the present, while directing us away from other possibilities. At the same time, the past becomes a resource in the present and for the future. Elizabeth Grosz considers temporality in a way that is reminiscent of Heidegger when she points out the past is never fixed nor determines the present and future, but inheres in them:

> Life is a becoming beyond what it is because the past, not fixed in itself, never fixes or
> determines the present and future but underlies them, inheres in them, makes them rich in
> resources, and forces them to differ from themselves. (Grosz, 2004, p. 255)

This folding of past into present, into future ensures continuity with change in our lives, while opening up a range of possible development trajectories. Even aspiring professionals who may have no prior experience of being an archaeologist, economist or dentist bring with them some notion of what these professions entail that, initially at least, underpins their becoming. However, when these aspiring professionals gain entry to their chosen profession, they have undergone substantial change, not least in their ways of being professionals. This process of change with continuity continues throughout our professional lives; it is integral to both being professionals and continuing to learn as professionals (Webster-Wright, 2006), as well as integral to being human and continuing to learn, more generally. There is ambiguity, then, in who we are (becoming) as professionals through this enfolding of continuity with change.

For instance, aspiring accountants embarking on their studies in accounting continue to be the persons they are in some respects, within the context of a world that continues to operate largely as before. At the same time, these trainee accountants undergo change in their capacity to engage in accounting practices and in their understanding of what accounting involves. As they learn to become accountants, both epistemology and ontology are involved. The aspiring accountants continue to be who they are and to be recognisable to those who know them, while also being transformed.

Grosz, who draws upon Merleau-Ponty's concept of the lived body in some of her work (for example, Grosz, 1994), describes this temporal ambiguity as doubling; allowing past, present and future to form a continuity:

> The present not only acts, it also consolidates, the past; it doubles itself as both present
> and past, actual and virtual. And it is only this doubling that enables it to resonate with the
> resources, the virtual, that the past endows to it and to the future. (Grosz, 2004, p. 251)

Inherent in this continuity are the conditions for change in the future: "The present acts, is active, makes. But what it makes is never self-identical, stable, given as such to the next moment. What it acts or makes is the condition of the transformative effects of the future" (p. 251). For example, as aspiring medical practitioners learn to practise medicine, their own positive and negative experiences of seeking medical advice can serve as a resource. Threads carried forward from the past can serve as resources in the present, as well as providing openings for change that continues into the future. These threads may afford opportunities for interrogating and transforming understanding of medical practice when it does not lead to the desired outcomes or patients do not respond as expected. Temporality ensures, then, some degree of sameness or continuity, while opening up for other ways of being: "inherence of the past in the present, for the capacity to become other" (Grosz, 2004, p. 252).

Possibilities with Constraints

The interweaving of continuity with change ensures some routines and regularities—including those permeated by domination or, conversely, by mutual respect—while at the same time there are openings for other possibilities; things could be otherwise. These possibilities are not limitless, however. Our possible ways of acting and of being are constrained by the specific situations we inhabit with their history and traditions. Familiar routines and ready-made solutions cover over the range of possibilities open to us in any situation as we go about our activities in a mode of average everydayness, which tends to be the path of least resistance. Our own past that we carry forward also places limits on the possibilities open to us. Heidegger points out that we "grow into" a familiar way of interpreting ourselves that is reflected from our world. He argues that we understand ourselves in terms of this interpretation, which opens possibilities for being as well as constraining those possibilities (1962/1927, pp. 17–18 § 20).

For example, some teacher trainees may strive to engage their students in learning that is challenging and transformative. The efforts they make to achieve this are afforded opportunities, as well as constrained, by their understanding of themselves as teachers in interrelation with traditions of practice relating to teaching. Certain practices, such as involving students in assessing the work of their peers, may be considered acceptable by students and colleagues, while other practices, such as allowing students to determine their own course of study, may be regarded as inappropriate or negligent by some, while exciting or innovative by others. So, traditions of practice for teaching simultaneously open possibilities and constrain. These traditions interrelate with other changes in society, so that teacher trainees and/or experienced teachers may begin to challenge and transform the notion of what it means to teach through their practice.

Opening of possibilities and associated constraints also play out through the aspirations of those who seek to become professionals, although these aspirations may change over time. Doret de Ruyter and Jim Conroy (2002) point to the importance of "ideal identity", or aspirations about what the person in question wants to be, for formation of a sense of self. They argue that these aspirations contribute to the formation of a sense of self through:

(a) clarifying what kind of person the individual wishes to be; and
(b) an interrogation of how she sets about achieving her ideal identity, intimating what kind of person she is at a particular moment by virtue of the way in which she strives to achieve her ideal. (p. 509)

Studies of workplace learning (for example, Webster-Wright, 2006) demonstrate that failure to achieve an unrealistic ideal (perpetuated by organisations, professional associations and/or professionals themselves) can result in feelings of impostership; of never being good enough or as accomplished as others.

The ambiguity associated with possibilities and constraints does not operate in a neutral manner. Practice traditions and social structures constrain opportunities for some, while opening them to others, as noted above. Bronwyn Davies (2003, 2005) describes constraints on contemporary university teachers arising from a neoliberal agenda, which she argues curtails creative or intellectual work. In short, power relations permeate professional practice and efforts to become professionals.

Openness with Resistance

In a context of opportunities and constraints, we demonstrate openness to possibilities that are presented to us, as well as resistance. While aspiring professionals often demonstrate some openness to learning new ways of knowing and acting, sustaining such changes so they become incorporated into customary ways of being can be challenging. Heidegger points out that such "a movement of passage" (1998/1967, p. 166), or transformation, takes time to become a stable way of dwelling or being in the world. One of the reasons for this is that it changes the way we relate to others and things in our world, so considerable adjustment may be called for. We may resort to familiar ways of acting when challenges are met (see, for example, Virta, 2002). Another reason such transformation takes time is that it may be resisted. Transforming our ways of being professionals is likely to be confronting, as it may be experienced as undermining the self or familiar ways of being. Drawing on Heidegger, Glenn Gray notes "there is always a struggle to advance a new way of seeing things because customary ways and preconceptions about it stand in the way" (1968, p. xxi). In a similar vein, Charlie Leadbeater points out that "what holds people back from taking risks is often as not . . . their knowledge, not their ignorance" (2000, p. 4, cited in McWilliam, 2005, p. 4). At the same time, the openness to possibilities we demonstrate occurs in relation to, and sometimes by means of, our customary ways and preconceptions. This struggle or interplay between openness and resistance can apply to any aspect of our relation to our world; it relates to individuals and professions as a whole.

Interplay between openness and resistance not only challenges our knowing or actions, but also who we are and understand ourselves to be. For instance, innovative ideas brought by aspiring architects sometimes challenge preconceptions about architecture among experienced architects, or vice versa. Challenges of this kind can occur for individuals, as well as flowing over to the profession as a whole. Addressing such tensions requires questioning assumptions, not only about what architecture involves and its role in society, but also about what it means to be an architect. Once again, not only epistemology but also ontology is at stake.

Interplay of openness with resistance is linked to the ways in which continuity in routines is interrupted or displaced by efforts toward renewal. Established routines and associated professional ways of being may exert themselves to such an extent that renewal of practice is obstructed. This can present difficulties for aspiring and recently graduated professionals, as well as for experienced professionals, who see the potential for improved practices but experience resistance or disapproval from others. Power differentials often play a key role in influencing the outcome of challenges to established routines and practices. However, where there is some openness to re-thinking assumptions and mutual respect among practitioners, a renewal of practice is possible at both individual and collective levels.

Individuals with Others

It is evident from each of the preceding features of learning to be professionals that engaging with others is integral to professional practice, with language playing a key role. As noted in Chapter 2, being with others includes those who are only implicated, such as members of our profession who developed a tool we use but whom we may never meet. While being with others enables us to learn to think and act as "they" do, we also take a stand on those thoughts and actions, as well as on who we are becoming, even if this means we simply fall into line with how "one" should think, act and be. For instance, aspiring journalists learn various ways in which one acts as a member of the journalism profession, while taking a stand on the ways and extent to which they will follow what one is expected to do. At the same time, being with others—including those within and outside the profession—extends possibilities for being, potentially enriching the process of becoming. Trainee and experienced journalists, for example, are likely to learn from their encounters with members of the public, as well as from colleagues.

The process of becoming professionals occurs, then, through continual interaction with other professionals, as well as those outside the professions. It is misleading to attempt to separate the individual from engagement with others in this process of becoming. Quite simply, an individual does not become a professional in isolation; conversely, a profession cannot exist without individual professionals. The two are interdependent and spill over into one another, as well as being entangled in the broader social world.

Avoidance of Addressing Ontology in Professional Education

In contrast to features of becoming professionals discussed above, in the introduction to this chapter it was argued that professional education programmes typically pay scant attention to an ontological dimension of learning to be professionals. It was argued, further, that professional education programmes must address not only epistemology, but also ontology. What would it mean to nurture an ontological dimension in professional education programmes, that is, to focus on forming and transforming persons as professionals? First we consider what it does *not* mean, before exploring what such a focus entails. As Heidegger makes clear with reference to Plato, such a focus does not involve "merely pouring knowledge into the unprepared soul as if it were some container held out empty and waiting" (Heidegger, 1998/1967, p. 167; see also Freire's 1970 critique of a "banking model" of education). Nor does such a focus simply mean coming to know through doing (see Chapter 2).

An ontological focus of the kind Heidegger proposes is also at odds with treating human beings instrumentally, as resources to be exploited, which he considers is encouraged in our increasingly technologised world, as noted in Chapter 2. Iain Thomson argues, with reference to Heidegger, that through the pervasiveness of framing human being in this way, we come to treat ourselves as "one more resource to be optimized, ordered, and enhanced with maximal efficiency—whether cosmetically, psychopharmacologically, or educationally" (2001, p. 250; see also Foucault, 1980). Heidegger (1993/1954; 1998/1967) challenges such a way of framing human being and education, expressing concern that we "increasingly instrumentalize, professionalize, vocationalize, corporatize, and ultimately *technologize* education" (Thomson, 2001, p. 244).

We see evidence of such an instrumental view of human being and of education in discourses and policy documents that emphasise the contribution of higher education to income earned by graduates, the skill level of workforces and national economies. Unease with this prevalent view is evident in arguments that education is more than preparation for work or an economic resource, as noted previously. Gibbs argues that a "crisis of higher education" in the sense of finance, access and external quality assurance has been artificially created in furthering this instrumental agenda:

> The use of managerial discourse to create the crisis of higher education which ostensibly can only be solved through the use of techniques borrowed from industry and commerce is meant more to shape the form of higher education under the market than to help it sustain itself as a forward-looking critic of the way we are. (2004, pp. 22–23)

Michael Bonnett, too, points to "the market and managerial models of education that increasingly set the tone for so much that has come to be regarded as educational reform" (2002, p. 236). An instrumental agenda is also evident in the fragmentation of the curriculum and the university into separate disciplines that no longer have a shared goal (see also Thomson, 2001). Valerie Wilson and Anne Pirrie argue that "learners' active engagement with their educational experiences, which provides the key to transforming both the experience and themselves (in our case into competent doctors) is discouraged by a system which atomises those experiences" (1999, p. 212). Even innovative curriculum design, such as problem-based learning and work-based learning, generally appears to take for granted that the purpose of higher education is primarily the development of knowledge and skills.

Nel Noddings points out that when we value our students only for what they achieve, "they become resources" in an instrumental sense (1992, p. 13; see also Bonnett, 2002). Drawing on Heidegger's concept of care as an essential feature of being human (see Chapter 2), she argues, instead, for an approach to education that begins with, and promotes, care for the other. She notes that such an approach is not anti-intellectual (p. 19), pointing out that "if we decide that the capacity to care is as much a mark of personhood as reason or rationality, then we will want to find ways to increase this capacity" (p. 24). Approaching education through the concept of care illustrates an alternative to an instrumental view, highlighting the ontological dimension of education and its role in contributing to who students are becoming.

Noddings points out that confirming the other in his or her becoming has a central place in education that develops the capacity to care: "When we confirm someone, we spot a better self and encourage its development. We can do this only if we know the other well enough to see what he or she is trying to become" (p. 25).

Nigel Blake and colleagues (Blake, Smeyers, Smith, & Standish, 2000), too, argue against an instrumental view of education. They point out that reducing the practice of medicine, social work or engineering to "skills" or "competencies" over-looks the engagement, commitment and risk involved: "what are commonly called skills are not activities to which we give anything of *ourselves*" (p. 26). For instance, in order to skilfully engage in professional practice, health of patients must matter to medical practitioners, social workers must be concerned about the well-being of their clients and it must matter to engineers that a bridge they build will support the weight of vehicles travelling over it. Gibbs argues that "scholarly activities can be more than just exercises in gaining accreditation of prescribed skill; they can offer a way towards practical wisdom" (2004, p. 25). A focus on narrowly defined skills or competencies overlooks and undervalues the ontological dimension of professional practice and of learning to be professionals. It thereby undermines the relationships among what we know, how we act and who we are (see also van Manen, 1977).

Pursuing Ontological Education for the Professions

If we reject the form of social engineering that an instrumental view of education represents, developing professional ways of being in the sense intended here cannot simply mean replacing one form of social engineering with another; one desired "product" with another. It cannot mean narrow pre-specification of "approved" subjectivity or becoming. This would be a process that "leaps in and dominates," taking away possibilities to be from the other (Heidegger, 1962/1927, p. 159, § 122; see Chapter 2). A process of education for becoming professionals would promote openness to possibilities for being and becoming, within the constraints that are relevant for the profession in question at particular historical points. In other words, rather than indoctrinating aspiring professionals into particular ways of being, professional education must open and interrogate possibilities for being the professionals in question. This is not to deny that some ways of being profes-sionals may be found wanting, for example, acting unethically or unresponsively in a way that fails to respect and show due care for clients. All ways of practising as professionals will not be acceptable and professional education should not shy away from addressing challenging issues of this kind. Careful, thoughtful work is needed in contributing towards developing professionals who are responsive to, and attuned with, the professional practice they seek to learn, as discussed below.

If professional education is to accomplish its purpose of promoting the integra-tion of knowing, acting and being professionals, this must be done in a way that engages. It cannot be a process that shirks responsibility for learning or fails to touch the being of those being educated. On the other hand, they must continue to have the freedom to shape their life courses and form their development trajectories, while becoming increasingly aware of what it means to practise as professionals within their chosen profession. The purpose of professional education programmes, then, is to promote this form of becoming.

Conceiving professional education programmes as a process of becoming gives rise to challenging ontological and ethical questions. For instance, in what ways and to what extent is it appropriate to shape another's becoming? Whose knowing, acting and being serve as "golden standards"? Questions such as these underpin all professional education programmes, as these programmes assume we can educate others for the professions, contributing to transforming them into professionals in the process. Engaging with deep questions about the purposes of professional education and how those purposes can be realised is necessary to thoughtfully and responsively enhancing the process of becoming professionals. Heidegger expresses concern about the danger in avoiding thinking deeply and simply falling into line with an instrumental approach, so we eventually cannot think or act in any other way (1993/1954). In other words, his concern relates to "the danger of being overcome by the claim of the common 'reality' to be the only reality" (1998/1967, p. 171). He provocatively remarks that, in this deeper sense, "we are still not thinking" (1968, p. 14).

How, then, can we think more deeply in reconfiguring professional education programmes as a process of becoming? As Erik observed towards the end of the Karolinska medical programme: "You can't read in a book what you should do [in a particular situation] or how you should be" (2nd semester of 5th year, p. 37). On the contrary, Heidegger draws on Plato to argue that what is called for is education as formation: "turning around the whole human being. It means removing human beings from the region where they first encounter things and transferring and accustoming them to another realm where beings appear" (1998/1967, p. 167). He explains that "the turning around has to do with one's being and thus takes place in the very ground of one's essence" (p. 166). Here Heidegger is not referring to essence as something fixed and unchanging, but to our way of being. This "turning around" involves "a disruption of customary behavior and of current opinion" (p. 165). In other words, for Heidegger, education involves troubling our taken-for-granted assumptions, including about what is and who we are. Thomson points out the purpose of this turning around: "to bring us full circle back to ourselves, first by turning us away from the world in which we are most immediately immersed, then by turning us back to this world in a more reflexive way" (2001, p. 254).

Ronald Barnett (2005) discusses higher education in a way that resonates with Heidegger's notion of troubling taken-for-granted assumptions. He argues for "curricula that present awkward spaces to and for students," which bring them into contact with the multiple perspectives and frameworks that are a feature of our uncertain and unpredictable contemporary world (p. 795; see also Chapter 1). Encountering multiple perspectives and frameworks in this way can promote tolerance for this multiplicity. Not only are students to learn to tolerate strangeness in an uncertain world, but also to produce it, "for, ultimately, the only way, amid strangeness, to become fully human, to achieve agency and authenticity, is to have the capacity to go on producing strangeness by and for oneself" (p. 794).

Ambiguity, or alternative meanings, cannot be eliminated or resolved once and for all. As ambiguity is a feature of our relation to our world, students will encounter some of these multiple meanings as they learn to practise as professionals and in their subsequent professional practice. For example, the Karolinska students noted differences in procedure across medical practice settings, as well as different ways of enacting medical practice among experienced practitioners (see Chapters 6 and 7 for examples; see also Mol, 2002; Stålsby Lundborg et al., 1999). Calling attention to this ambiguity is necessary for enabling students to address it when they encounter a range of ways of enacting professional practice. More particularly, this ambiguity can also be used in presenting the familiar in unfamiliar ways, for troubling taken-for-granted assumptions. When we experience the familiar or everyday in new ways, this opens new possibilities, or other ways of being. Through calling into question and re-shaping assumptions about what it means to practise medicine, to design computer software or to apply the rule of law, other ways of being are opened up. This can contribute to the process of "turning around" aspiring professionals in a way that is directed to, and attuned with, the professional practice in which they are learning to engage.

As this turning around "takes place in the very ground of one's essence" or way of being, it brings about formation and transformation of the self, so that we become accustomed "to another realm where beings appear". In other words, through education we can become attuned to the situations in which we find ourselves and be responsive to those situations: a responsive, attuned dwelling with others and things. Heidegger illustrates this attunement and responsiveness using the example of a cabinetmaker's apprentice who is learning the craft:

> His learning is not mere practice, to gain facility in the use of tools. Nor does he merely gather knowledge about the customary forms of the things he is to build. If he is to become a true cabinetmaker, he makes himself answer and respond above all to the different kinds of wood and to the shapes slumbering within wood—to wood as it enters into man's dwelling with all the hidden riches of its nature. In fact, this relatedness to wood is what maintains the whole craft. Without that relatedness, the craft will never be anything but empty busywork. (1968, pp. 14–15)

An approach that emphasises attunement and responsiveness is arguably highly suited to education for the professions, given the need for professionals to be attuned to, and responsive in, providing services to the community. For Ingrid, providing a service to those who sought medical help was central to her task as a doctor:

To help and be available. Either helping by listening, that's a type of help. Or helping by relieving pain. Or helping by operating. Or helping by comforting. . . . I see my work as a service to someone else. And I'm available to someone else and offer them something.

Interviewer: *And what do you offer, then?*

Mm, the knowledge you have, both in the area, the pure medical knowledge. Perhaps also knowledge about how to listen. And knowledge that you don't

*become afraid when someone begins to cry or you comfort them, if you know
what I mean. That's what I have to offer.* (final semester, pp. 53–54)

Later in the interview Ingrid summed up by describing a good doctor as follows:
" I think it's someone who wants to help, on the patient's terms" (p. 64); and, similarly, "someone who's available and who helps in the way that's needed, depending
on the situation and circumstances" (p. 65). A view of education as enabling attunement and responsiveness is also consistent with the broader call of phenomenology
for us to be attentive to the lifeworld (see Chapter 2). Through enabling us to learn
such attentiveness and responsiveness in specific situations, education contributes
to forming and transforming us. Indeed, this is its purpose.

Encouragement to be open to becoming professionals in this reflexive sense
can be a liberating and empowering process for aspiring professionals. Developing attunement and responsiveness gives a clearer sense of their own agency and a
focus for their efforts towards becoming skilful professionals. In the earlier example, Ingrid's recognition that patients may be protecting their sense of self when
they come to medical consultations demonstrates attunement and her responsiveness to this realisation allowed her to work more closely with patients in addressing
the reason for their visit. Her attunement and responsiveness gave her direction in
enhancing her practice as an aspiring medical practitioner.

Letting Learn

Heidegger clarifies what learning means when education involves formation or
becoming: "To learn means to make everything we do answer to whatever essentials
address themselves to us at a given time" (1968, p. 14). This is the attunement and
responsiveness to which we referred above. This way of being contrasts starkly with
"mastering the art of inauthenticity" in order to meet others' expectations, noted
above. Instead, through developing a capacity for attuned responsiveness, education
"consists in making the human being free and strong for the clarity and constancy
of insight" into being human (p. 176). However, this form of learning cannot be
explicitly "taught" in the conventional sense. This is one of the reasons that Heidegger considers teaching to be challenging:

> Teaching is even more difficult than learning. We know that; but we rarely think about
> it. And why is teaching more difficult than learning? Not because the teacher must have a
> larger store of information, and have it always ready. Teaching is more difficult than learning
> because what teaching calls for is this: to let learn. The real teacher, in fact, lets nothing else
> be learned than—learning. His conduct, therefore, often produces the impression that we
> properly learn nothing from him, if by "learning" we now suddenly understand merely the
> procurement of useful information. The teacher is ahead of his apprentices in this alone,
> that he has still far more to learn than they—he has to learn to let them learn. (1968, p. 15)

Letting learn requires that we create space and opportunities for learning. It
demands a curriculum that is not overloaded or closed to inquiry, but allows
and encourages students to pursue the questions they bring, including about the

profession to which they aspire and who they are becoming. This includes providing space and encouragement for students to take a stand on what they are learning, as well as who they are becoming. It involves granting some degree of autonomy to learners:

> We grant autonomy to teachers or doctors when we accept that they know what they are doing, even if we don't understand it; the same autonomy ought to be granted the pupil or the patient, because they know things about learning or being sick which the person teaching or treating them might not fathom. (Sennett, 2003, p. 122)

An objection may be raised that students are not sufficiently knowledgeable or responsible to be granted any form of autonomy. However, this runs counter to experience in higher education programmes (for example, Gonzalez, 2001, as well as problem-based learning and work-based learning). On the other hand, we can be assured we do not promote responsibility or commitment among our students if they are not granted some degree of autonomy. Nor do we enhance their knowing, as such commitment is necessary for learning. Through letting students learn to be professionals in this way, we are able to promote integration of knowing, acting and being, so that learning professional ways of being is foregrounded.

Letting learn can be seen as a form of caring relation of the kind that Nel Noddings describes: "Caring is a way of being in relation, not a set of specific behaviors . . . or an individual attribute" (1992, p. 17). This form of caring does not dominate, nor leap in to "take over the learner's problems and hand them back sorted out, for this would simply be to displace the learner from his unique engagement, to leave him free-wheeling—disengaged and dependent" (Bonnett, p. 240). Creating space and opportunities for learning demands that we acknowledge and bring into play the openness, commitment, passion and wonder that are integral to learning, while also addressing the misconceptions, prejudices, resistance and anxieties that limit learning. Letting learn means we challenge and support the other in interrogating, forming and transforming ways of being professionals. It frees the other, in and for becoming.

In contrast to "letting learn", a common theme among the Karolinska medical students was they often felt in the way during clinical placements: "a category without function" (Max, 1st semester of 4th year, p. 7). Their displacement created difficulties for learning and also for dealing with the challenging situations the students encountered in clinical practice. As they often had no role or function in a context where those around them were busy, they were reluctant to promote their own learning in a way that required assistance or interaction with experienced professionals. When space is not created for learning, "going through the motions" is likely to be adopted as a default position. For instance, Lotta related such an incident involving a group of students:

> *It was very embarrassing when I was on the cardiac ward. We were supposed to go in and listen to a patient who'd had a heart attack and then the senior doctor said: "What are you listening for?" And we couldn't answer* [laughing]. *Yeaahh, mm, what are we listening for? No idea!* [laughing] (2nd semester of 3rd year, p. 74)

Ingrid pointed out another consequence of lack of space and opportunities for learning: "You're very often left out as a medical student. And that means you have to take initiative and that. And that's a bit silly, because often it can mean there's competition between us students, too" (2nd semester of 3rd year, p. 35).

These examples point to the need for mutual commitment to learning for professional practice, by teachers and learners alike. Simply completing required tasks in a way that does not engage the students will not assist in forming and transforming professional ways of being. Letting learn applies not only to the pedagogical relation in which teachers provide guidance and support for their students, but also highlights the need for reflexive space for teachers themselves. Such reflexive space is necessary if teachers are to enhance their understanding of how to promote student learning, as well as the self-understanding that contributes to their own becoming.

There are clearly challenges for staff who are to both care for patients and assist students to learn, which the Karolinska students acknowledged. However, questions arise about the appropriateness of the lack of space and opportunities for learning in the organisation of the clinical curriculum, or, perhaps frequently, in its lack of organisation. The difficulty for students in creating opportunities for learning also highlights an inadequate focus on preparation for professional practice in the curriculum. Not only did the limited opportunities and space for learning impede students' preparation for professional practice, but it meant they did not receive the support they needed, although the students identified some exceptions. The result was that students were sometimes left feeling alienated, as Ingrid pointed out above. This was particularly the case when they encountered difficult situations, such as the sudden death of a patient. Kristina observed that the approach that seemed to be required of students in the medical programme was "a 'pull yourself up by the socks' idea. Forced in head first all the time, you're to learn from that, in some way" (final semester, p. 17). This approach seems consistent with an expectation that students will either sink or swim, rather than taking seriously the responsibility and commitment to challenge and support them in their learning. It shows a lack of attunement and responsiveness to students' learning, which would be necessary to enhancing the formation and transformation of professional ways of being in a manner that prepares them for professional practice.

A theme throughout this book is that professional education programmes are not ends in themselves, but their purpose is preparation for professional practice. These programmes can stimulate a process of learning throughout professional life in which learning from colleagues and others, as well as through experience of everyday practice, are key components (Ball & Cohen, 1999; Billett et al., 2006; Boud, Cressey, & Docherty, 2006; Boud & Garrick, 1999; Cavanaugh, 1993; Sandberg & Dall'Alba, 2006; Webster-Wright, 2006, in press). Professional education programmes have a key role to play, then, in enabling aspiring professionals to learn for life. This will only occur if the learning that is required in forming and transforming professional ways of being is taken seriously and given space in the curriculum.

Part III
Professional Ways of Being

Chapter 5
Contextualising Professional Ways of Being

> *The historical life of a tradition depends on being constantly*
> *assimilated and interpreted. An interpretation that was correct*
> *in itself would be a foolish ideal that mistook the nature of*
> *tradition. Every interpretation has to adapt itself to the*
> *hermeneutical situation to which it belongs.*
> (Gadamer, 1994/1960, p. 397)

A recurring theme in the preceding chapters is that learning to practise as professionals not only includes knowledge and skills, but also entails the development of professional ways of being in interplay with prevailing traditions of practice. This part of the book, consisting of three chapters, focuses on professional ways of being that are under formation, especially in their early phases. This chapter and the next explore the interplay between emerging professional ways of being and the social, cultural, historical, material world in which they are embedded. The context in which these professional ways of being are formed consists of various interdependent spheres that include: the educational programme that is to prepare aspiring professionals for skilful practice; traditions of practice for the profession with which the programme is associated; and the broader society to which the profession provides a service. Through exploring the interplay between the social, cultural, historical, material context and professional ways of being, the way in which aspiring professionals learn to become professionals can be further elaborated.

This part of the book takes the practice of medicine as an example through which to explore the formation of professional ways of being. The use of the "established" profession of medicine as an empirical example of professional practice is not intended to suggest it is more worthy or relevant of study than other professions. There are several reasons, however, that medicine and medical education are appropriate for research on learning to be professionals. The first of these is that, like other professions, medicine is in need of continuing critical scrutiny, as is medical education, which has had impact on other professional education programmes at various points in time (see Chapter 3). Second, while medicine is an established profession with a relatively long history, it also has similarities to some of the newer

G. Dall'Alba, *Learning to be Professionals*, Innovation and Change in Professional
Education 4, DOI 10.1007/978-90-481-2608-8_5,
© Springer Science+Business Media B.V. 2009

professions that are knowledge-intensive and undergoing rapid development. Third, contemporary medicine provides clear examples of an instrumental approach to human being, which was critiqued in Chapter 4 and is at risk of becoming still more prevalent in professional practice in our increasingly marketised and technologised age. Fourth, although alternative curriculum models are evident, such as problem-based learning, educating medical practitioners is still commonly carried out with overtones of the normative curriculum, emphasising acquisition and application of knowledge and skills, as discussed in Chapter 3. In this respect, too, medical education is similar to other professional education programmes. Fifth, when medicine and medical education were largely male domains, men wrote most of the related, published literature. As more women move into the professions, it is important that women also continue to scrutinise established professions such as medicine and the programmes that provide preparation for the professions. Finally, medicine is of interest in this book as an example of the professions because it clearly brings together scientific knowledge and human encounters. This somewhat uneasy marriage throws light on central relationships that have relevance for the professions and for learning to be professionals. While medicine is taken as an empirical example, then, the issues that are discussed through exploring the interplay between practice traditions and professional ways of being have broader relevance for the professions, more generally.

The chapter begins with a brief historical account of the changing traditions of practice that have formed medicine as an interpretative practice. The ambiguity—or other possible meanings—of any "one" professional practice is illustrated through exploring these changes over time, as well as through a critique of the dominant, biomedical approach to contemporary medicine. The accounts drawn upon in this chapter include those of experienced medical practitioners, patients, social scientists and humanities scholars, with some overlap in these categories. Against this background, the next chapter shifts focus to investigate learning to be medical practitioners in the context of traditions of practice for medicine. The present chapter and the next one provide the context for Chapter 7, where we look more closely at the longitudinal study of students progressing through a medical programme at Karolinska Institute.

A Brief History of Western Medicine

2000 BC—Here, eat this root.
1000 AD—That root is heathen. Here, say this prayer.
1850 AD—That prayer is superstition. Here, drink this potion.
1940 AD—That potion is snake oil. Here, swallow this pill.
1985 AD—That pill is ineffective. Here, take this antibiotic.
2000 AD—That antibiotic doesn't work anymore. Here eat this root....
(Anonymous statement circulating on the internet since the late 1990s)

Through historical accounts of professions over extended periods of time, we see that professions are social, cultural, embodied practices that are constituted intersubjectively (see also Chapter 2). This is particularly evident in the case of professions with longer periods of professionalisation, where the ways in which they are understood and enacted has changed noticeably over time and across cultural contexts. Medicine is one such profession with a comparatively long history, including an extended period prior to recognition as a profession. The history of medicine shows distinct changes over time and across contexts in the way medicine has been understood by insiders and viewed by outsiders. Briefly reviewing the history of medicine here provides a context for explorations of learning to be medical practitioners in the next two chapters.

As the quote above suggests, the changes that have occurred in the history of medicine may not always represent progress. Moreover, as Lois Magner (1992) and David Wootton (2006) show, when challenges to long-standing dogmas have been mounted throughout the history of medicine, strong opposition from medical practitioners and others has often substantially delayed acceptance of new insights. Medicine is similar to other fields of inquiry in this respect (see Kuhn, 1962). The history of medicine highlights, then, the way in which the practice of medicine is entwined with the societies of which it forms a part, as Roy Porter points out:

> The war between disease and doctors fought out on the battleground of the flesh has a beginning and a middle but no end. The history of medicine, in other words, is far from a simple tale of triumphant progress. As is hinted by the story of Pandora's box or the Christian Fall, plagues and pestilences are more than inevitable natural hazards which can, we hope, be overcome: they are largely of mankind's own making. Epidemics arose with society, and sickness has been, and will remain, a social product no less than the medicine which opposes it. Civilization brings not just discontents but diseases. (2003, p. 1)

Human activities such as agriculture, domestication of animals, travel, trade, invasion and war have all contributed to the spread of disease, sometimes in epidemic proportions. Levels of hygiene and poverty have affected the spread of disease, with diseases associated with affluence becoming common in the western world more recently.

In addition to their own efforts to protect themselves and their families from disease, people have sought help from various kinds of healers. The brief historical account of these healers and their practices that follows draws largely upon more detailed studies by Magner (1992) and Porter (2003; see also Porter, 1997, for a more elaborated account). The account provided here primarily focuses on western medicine. A risk in such a focus is that it can tend to overlook or downplay the contribution to health and health care by other groups, such as families, friends, nurses, allied health practitioners and those providing alternative forms of health care. A focus on western medicine can also neglect the significance of influences beyond the west. For histories of medicine that are broader than western influences, readers are directed to accounts by Nancy Duin and Jenny Sutcliffe (1992) and Magner (1992). While the account presented here has limitations, it sketches the historical context in which aspiring medical practitioners are educated in Sweden. It should be acknowledged at the outset, however, that sketching a brief history of western medicine is an almost impossible task, given the broad range of social, material and cultural contexts that have had a bearing on its development. The detail of specific developments is not in focus in this account, given the necessity of skimming over much of the detail in the interests of brevity. Rather, a broad brush sketch provides an historical context for what follows.

Early Healers and the Emergence of Western Secular Medicine

Early healers were often diviners and witch doctors, who offered remedies and ritual dances for appeasing the gods. Then came herbalists, birth-attendants, bone-setters and healer-priests. Among indigenous healers, the shaman was believed to have spiritual powers that allowed the use of magic and rituals for healing, combating sorcery and ensuring fertility. As the size of settled populations grew, religious rites and empirical treatments combined, and began to be recorded in written form. In ancient Mesopotamia and Egypt, healers included experts in divination, priests and practitioners of medicine, who could be women or men. In ancient Greece, health and disease were linked with gods and heroes.

In the fifth century BC, secular medicine began to appear in Greece with the Hippocratic medical practitioners, who rejected links with the supernatural and root-gatherers, although a range of other healers continued with these crafts. In Hippocratic medicine, disease was seen to be a natural process, not a result of supernatural forces. Hippocrates, considered the founder of western medicine, is thought to have been born on the Greek island of Cos, although there is some doubt he was a real person. According to legend, Hippocrates was knowledgeable in medicine and lived an honourable life. His legacy includes the still revered Hippocratic oath, which sets out ethical principles for the conduct of medical practitioners. These principles included helping the sick and doing no harm. As the principles within this oath show, tensions between medicine as a means of helping the sick and as merely a business transaction were already in evidence. Hippocratic medicine focused on providing assistance to individual patients, although often with an audience of interested relatives or bystanders.

During the height of Hippocratic medicine, health and disease were associated with the four humours, or bodily fluids. These were blood, gastric juices, phlegm and black bile. The humours had their equivalents in the four elements identified in Greek science, which were air, fire, water and earth. It was considered essential for good health that the humours were kept in balance, so the task of the medical practitioner was to work in harmony with the healing processes of the body. The idea of the need for balance within the body for good health is also found in ancient Chinese and Indian medicine (Magner, 1992). The humours accounted for temperature, colour and skin texture. Their relative balance in the body was also seen to influence body shape and physique, as well as later being associated with temperament. Imbalance in the humours could be corrected through lifestyle changes, such as diet or exercise, as well as through medical or surgical treatments. For example, excess or unhealthy blood could be corrected by bloodletting, a procedure that was still being used into the 20th century, but has now largely been abandoned as it is deemed ineffective. In contrast to the supernatural beliefs of their predecessors, the Hippocratic medical practitioners' tools of trade were reason and careful observation—but not physical examination—informed by the system of the humours and experience they had gained. When medicine failed to provide help for the sick, however, people turned to the gods for help, often at the suggestion of medical practitioners.

Medicine Begins to Claim Status as a Science

Following Hippocrates, the influence of Greek medicine spread increasingly to the Roman empire. The renowned medical practitioner, Galen, was born around 129 AD in Pergamum (now part of Turkey) in what was then part of the Roman empire. Galen studied Hippocratic medicine and held it in high regard, including the need for balance among the humours. He considered himself not only a clinician, but also a man of science. Through experimenting on animals and dissecting animal corpses—but not human, as this was not considered acceptable—he drew conclusions about human anatomy. Not surprisingly, these conclusions were not always correct, but they contributed to understanding anatomy. Some 400 years earlier in Hellenistic Alexandria, however, human cadavers had been dissected, reportedly in public, but this practice did not spread as there was public opposition in other places. As the Roman empire became Christian, medicine and religion overlapped and sometimes clashed. Echoing earlier Greek times, saints and martyrs became associated with healing and health. Hospitals, which had previously been used by slaves and soldiers, began to provide refuge and care for the sick or the poor in both Christian and Islamic countries. They were usually not sites of specialised medicine and were generally controlled by religious orders or patrons.

After Galenic medicine, in the "Dark Ages" monks, nuns and priests played a key role in continuing the work of healing and learning in Europe. In the Islamic world, however, the work of Galen was being carefully studied and extended. When universities were established in Europe during the 12th century, western medicine experienced renewed development, beginning in Salerno, Italy. Translations of Islamic medical texts provided some continuity with Galenic medicine. While both women and men were educated as medical practitioners at Salerno, as universities gained in prestige and spread throughout Europe, some universities excluded women from university studies. In parallel with being excluded from medical studies, women healers began to be associated with witchcraft (Hearn, 1982). Universities offered education for medical practitioners in the form of formal studies in science and philosophy, although most medical practitioners in the mediaeval period continued to learn as apprentices to experienced practitioners. Physically examining the body was still not part of the practice of medicine, with the exception of checking the pulse. Instead, medical practitioners relied on accounts from patients and their physical appearance.

From the early 1300s, demonstrations of human dissections were carried out in Bologna as part of medical studies and spread throughout Italy, as well as being carried out by artists such as Leonardo da Vinci. When the Church granted permission for human dissections, this was premised upon an agreement that the body would be the realm of interest for scientific investigation, while the mind or soul was the province of the Church. This splitting of mind from body became a characteristic feature of the development of a scientific medicine. Anatomy became an essential part of medical studies in Italy, although there was continued resistance to human dissection in other countries. The closer observation of human flesh and organs that human dissection allowed lead to the challenging of earlier Galenic theories, with resultant developments in physiology and neurology. These developments brought with them a reductionist tendency to regard the body as a form of machine (see Osherson & AmaraSingham, 1981). This view and further work in anatomy brought the notion that disease left its mark in specific locations within the body in a way that could be identified through post-mortem analysis. As Roy Porter describes it: "Here was the medicine of the all-powerful gaze, one which saw—almost with X-ray eyes—through the patient to the underlying disease" (2003, p. 74; see also Foucault, 1973/1963). While it contributed to understanding disease, this diagnosis was of no benefit to the patient as it occurred post-mortem.

Medicine Becomes Institutionalised

As urban populations grew and medical practitioners increased in number, beginning in Italy they began to organise themselves into guilds that took responsibility for apprenticeships, examinations for aspiring medical practitioners, overseeing of pharmacists and drugs, and eventually regulation of medical practice. The medical guilds and colleges that were established came to be criticised for protecting the privileged at the expense of patients and other medical practitioners. Surgeons largely dealt with injuries and other ailments through hands-on measures such as bone-setting and amputation, and they often also worked as barbers. They were generally looked down upon as practising manual skill, rather than having a base in scientific knowledge. From the mid-1700s, the heightened status of anatomy and a break with barbers began to change the way surgeons were viewed, so that surgery is now one of the highest status, most powerful and well-remunerated medical specialisations.

Despite increasing understanding of the physical body, there was little improvement in dealing with disease. In a context where disease was an accepted part of life, medical practitioners were able to do little more than provide comfort and advice, although they sometimes provided treatments that had little effect on ailments. As Porter points out:

> In this situation, the old-style doctor had a choice between conservative Hippocratic options (waiting and watching, bed-rest, tonics, care, soothing words, calm and hope) or "heroic" possibilities, including violent purges, drastic blood-letting (Galen's preference), or some pet nostrum of his own. (2003, pp. 38–39)

Wealthy patients often influenced the decision on treatment they would receive. While medical treatments and advice were initially available only to the wealthy, they were later also made available to poorer patients.

Medicine Turns to Diagnosis of Disease and Clinical Trials

Although developments in medicine had been relatively slow, a number of advances in related fields lead to more rapid changes from the mid-1800s (Duin & Sutcliffe, 1992; Porter, 2003; Wootton, 2006). Perhaps most significant about these changes is that they began to impact upon diagnosis of disease in living patients, rather than simply at autopsy. The invention of instruments such as thermometers and stethoscopes brought with it growing interest in physical examination of patients, while diagnostic laboratories later allowed the analysis of body fluids. There was some initial opposition to the use of instruments for examining patients among medical practitioners, however, as these instruments were seen as requiring a form of manual labour more suited to surgeons. There is a certain irony to this resistance, given the stethoscope came almost to symbolise medicine and to be as necessary to a medical practitioner's attire as the white coat. The "scientific medicine" associated with the use of progressively more sophisticated technologies spread most rapidly in the United States, where there was least resistance. Later developments have seen medicine become increasingly technologised, while Lois Magner points out that research has shown over-reliance on new technologies has contributed to major errors in diagnosis of disease (1992, p. 341).

The use of instruments and laboratories in medical assessments impressed some medical practitioners and patients, while making others wary of the consequences of their intrusion into the caring relationship between the two. Moreover, improved diagnosis did not necessarily lead to better treatments for disease. The synthesis of strong drugs such as morphine and heroin meant they could be used as painkillers, although addiction might be the price unexpectedly paid for easing of pain. Also from the mid-1800s, female medical practitioners once again became qualified through university studies, first in the United States and then in Britain. In some universities, however, women continued to be excluded from studying medicine until the 20th century.

In Paris, the French Revolution brought about the centralisation of patients in large public hospitals, providing a ready source of material for the development of medical science. This centralisation of patients in what were typically squalid conditions, however, was associated with the regular occurrence of infections obtained during hospitalisation. A shift in focus from symptoms reported by patients to observable signs of disease identified during physical examinations was made possible through the use of instruments and by regarding the body in what was seen to be an objective, scientific manner. As Porter observes, "endlessly exposed to the dying poor, the Paris doctors rated diagnostics above therapeutics" (2003, p. 77). The scale of patient material in public hospitals lent itself to early versions of what would come to be known as clinical trials, with attention shifting from individual patients to statistical probabilities. During this period, disease came to be seen as an identifiable entity, with a distinction made between normal and pathological bodies. However, there was some resistance to this distinction in the form of a view that the pathological and normal were not fundamentally different but lay on a continuum, such that disease occurred when bodily functions did not proceed as usual.

As emphasis came to be placed on clinical trials and diagnosis, hospitals became key sites for medical education across Europe and North America. They also gradually became sites of specialised medical diagnosis and treatment, with associated personnel hierarchies and progressively more sophisticated technologies. In western countries, hospitals have typically become the most costly component of health care provision. Alongside hospitals, the laboratory took on an important function in controlled experimentation, including the study and production of drugs and other remedies in the treatment of disease. Some of these remedies have been shown to be effective, while the ineffectiveness of others has become apparent over time. In some cases, the associated side effects have been shown to be substantially more harmful than the initial disease or ailment. The drug, thalidomide, is a clear example. It was prescribed as an aid in sleep and a tranquilliser for pregnant women, resulting in severe deformities and death in their children. Similarly, the frequent use of antibiotics against bacterial infection has lead to more resistant strands of harmful bacteria.

Laboratory experimentation was particularly developed in Germany, where the experimental science of physiology enjoyed high status. Through emphasis on experimentation and physiology, the body came to be regarded as a set of interrelated chemical systems. Improvements in the microscope made possible the study of cells and their role in biological functions, such as growth and reproduction, as well as in pathology, where abnormal changes to cells were seen to multiply, leading to cancer. Diseases were linked to cells, although there was disagreement about whether the cause of disease was internal or external to the cell. Bodies of higher level organisms, however, were seen to have physiological functions that maintained a form of equilibrium—later known as homeostasis—in vital features such as oxygen concentration and body temperature.

The question of what causes disease continued to be debated, but not resolved. There were many theories, including that disease comes from the atmosphere and soil, that it is transmitted from one person to another, or that it is passed on by microscopic organisms. These debates were brought to a head as epidemics spread throughout Europe, against which medicine was powerless. A breakthrough occurred when the French chemist, Louis Pasteur, demonstrated a link between specific microbes and specific diseases in animals and, later, in humans, providing support for a germ theory of disease. Demonstration of this theory lead to the development of a vaccine used in counteracting the spread of smallpox. Advances relating to the germ theory allowed developments in tropical medicine, which were used in the spread of western power through colonisation. However, attention to the germ theory coupled with the increasing threat of infectious diseases diverted attention from disease of other kinds. As early as the 1700s, for instance, links had been made between nutrition and disease through the treatment of scurvy with fresh citrus. Enhanced hygiene, standards of living and immunity have lead to substantial improvements in public health, prior to the associated medical developments to which these health improvements are often attributed (Magner, 1992; McKeown & Lowe, 1966; Mishler, 1981b; Wootton, 2006).

During the 20th century, new medical discoveries and technological advances strengthened the status of a range of medical specialties, while also giving rise to new specialties. Developments in areas such as microbiology, genetics, molecular biology, immunology, anaesthesia, obstetrics and transplantation surgery created a veritable industry of biomedical research, while hospitals in western countries have continued to consume increasing proportions of health budgets. Porter estimates that an astonishing "nine out of ten of those employed in the modern medical enterprise never directly treat the sick," in stark contrast to 200 years ago (2003, p. 155). Despite this unprecedented investment in medicine, unfulfilled expectations of "miracle" cures for a range of diseases, such as acquired immune deficiency syndrome (AIDS), provide a cautionary tale. Ironically, medicine has had a key role in promoting this expectation of miracle cures that often fail to eventuate.

As medicine has become more technologised, institutionalised and bureaucratised, there has been heightened concern about perceived lack of care for the person who is the patient among some medical practitioners, other health professionals and the general public. Jack Coulehan argues, as follows:

> Over the past several decades, medicine in the United States has evolved into a vast, increasingly expensive technological profit center, in which self-interest is all too easily conflated with altruism.... As technology advanced, patients developed higher expectations of cure, but at the same time they became progressively less satisfied with the personal aspects of medical care.... The costs of the system skyrocketed but it nonetheless remained inequitable and inaccessible to significant segments of the population.... Yet our lingering cultural belief in equitable and relationship-based medicine haunts us and casts a pall over today's machine-based medical practice. (2005, p. 893)

Moreover, growing dissatisfaction with treatment of some diseases and ailments, particularly chronic disease, has seen increasing numbers of people seeking help from alternative medicine, such as acupuncture and homeopathy. The interest in various forms of alternative medicine among a steadily growing number of practitioners of conventional medicine has seen its inclusion in a number of medical education programmes. In addition, research has demonstrated the efficacy of a number of practices and remedies used in alternative medicine, long derided by the medical profession.

Shifts in the Medical Practitioner-Patient Relationship

Research on the relationship between medical practitioners and patients supports the historical trends sketched above. Yrjö Engeström (1993) draws on the work of previous scholars in identifying several historical layers of medical practice impacting upon this practitioner-patient relationship that are consistent with the account above. The first of these is a successive move from bedside medicine then hospital medicine to laboratory medicine. This move has meant a changing focus from the patient with a psychosomatic ailment to a disease located within the body and, later, to cell clusters and their associated processes. The prevalent use of laboratory tests as part of medical diagnosis is evidence of this change in focus. A second change over time has been from a private, fee-based service to corporatised, rationalised medical practice. Engeström describes the focus in the latter form of medical practice as "an input-output unit that fulfills the requirements of accounting (a visit, a procedure, a hospital day)" (p. 90). He points out the need to distinguish "the privately owned corporatized medicine operating for profit, and the publicly owned bureaucratic and rationalized medicine striving for cost efficiency" (p. 90). A third broad change over time has been towards what is referred to as holistic or humanistic medicine, based either on psychoanalysis or social psychology and communication, with emphasis on understanding and empathy.

As Engeström points out—and Heideggerian philosophy highlights (see Chapter 2)—these diverse strands in the history of medicine are carried forward in various ways into contemporary medical practice. They are, however, not entirely consistent with each other, so they can introduce tensions into, and contestation about, the way in which medicine is practised.

Medicalisation of Life

As its status and budgets have increased, medicine is no longer primarily directed to care for the sick, but has moved into virtually every facet of life: a "medicalization of life" (Illich, 1977; see also Mishler, 1981a; Rose, 1994). As standards of living have risen in the western world, medicine has moved into lifestyle, behaviour, nutrition, physical appearance, fertility and sexual performance. Widespread use of anti-depressants, a range of medication for behavioural problems, nutrition supplements, cosmetic surgery, in vitro fertilisation (IVF) and drugs for enhancing sexual performance demonstrate a shift away from a primary focus on care of the sick. With increasing costs associated with hospitalisation and sophisticated technologies in contemporary medicine, this broader range of services provides additional sources of revenue. On the other hand, despite unprecedented expenditure on health budgets, disparities between access to, and use of, health care by the rich and poor have increased. Medicalisation of society has served to reinforce existing disadvantage, which is evident in the large expenditures on "elective" surgery and IVF. The organisation of medicine and of health care, more generally, has social, economic and political consequences.

While social and ethical questions about the practice of medicine have arisen throughout its history, with some strong advocates for addressing these questions, attention to them has been marginalised, at best, especially as biomedicine has become so all-embracing. As Porter points out:

the power to do good is double-edged. The fear today is that a "can do, will do" mentality will prevail at the frontiers of research, clinical medicine and surgery, regardless of wider ethical responsibilities. And the biomedical model can be myopic, searching ever-more microscopically for disease but often omitting the wider picture of populations, environments and health. (2003, p. 98)

Similarly, Magner calls for a broader focus than such narrow conceptions of disease:

Understanding the tensions that derive from changing patterns of health, disease, and demography, and the differences in patterns found in the wealthy nations and the developing nations requires familiarity with history, geography, ecology, and economics, as well as knowledge of medicine and science. (1992, pp. 364–365)

A Biomedical Model of Medicine

The shifts in the practice of medicine outlined above have been possible by virtue of, or in response to, the model of medicine that came to dominate over time in the west, namely, a biomedical model. Prevailing social and material conditions, coupled with political and economic imperatives, have created a situation where a biomedical model has thrived and dominated over other models of medical practice, especially during the last century. This model continues to be evident among contemporary medical practitioners (Burroughs et al., 2006; Coulter, 2002; Germov, 2005b; Stålsby Lundborg et al., 1999), as well as those aspiring to practise medicine (Camargo & Coeli, 2006; Dall'Alba, 1998, 2004), although it is not the only view of medicine in evidence.

The biomedical model has features that draw on developments over time during the history of western medicine. Like the germ theory, it is based on a notion that each disease or ailment can be traced to a single cause that affects the body in predictable ways through identifiable biological processes. According to this view, disease can be localised to particular parts of the body, such as specific organs and tissues, although some diseases can spread from their initial location to other parts of the body. In this model, the body is regarded as a form of machine consisting of interconnected parts, a view harking back to the 14th century. The biomedical model is a somatic model of disease, so mind and body are regarded as separate entities (See Chapter 2 for a critique of this dualism). The physical body is the primary concern in the biomedical model, in line with an agreed division between science and the Church dating from the 14th century. As noted above, increasing concern with somatic disease in medicine has shifted focus from caring for the person who is ill to diagnosing and treating the diseased or "inadequate" body, while adopting an "objective" attitude.

As the brief history of medicine above indicates, the biomedical model is a relatively recent development and is only one of several possible models that could have become prevalent. For example, recognition that diet, hygiene and standard of living all play major roles in health and disease could have lead to a preventative or public health focus for medicine. However, recognition of the provisional character of the biomedical model is lost on many contemporary medical practitioners. As Elliot Mishler points out, the assumptions on which the biomedical model is based:

> are so deeply interwoven with ways of thinking and working in medicine that health professionals tend to forget that it is a conceptual model, a way of thinking about the world. That is, the biomedical model is treated as *the* representation or picture of reality rather than understood as *a* representation. Like other conceptual models, the biomedical model defines, classifies, and specifies relationships among events in particular ways. (1981b, p. 1)

In other words, assumptions on which the biomedical model is based are so interwoven with the practice of medicine that they "are not assumptions that one thinks about, but rather are assumptions from which one thinks and acts" (Anderson, 1995, p. 413). The common "reality"—based on an instrumental view—is at risk of being accepted as the only reality when we do not think deeply and critically about its broader consequences (Heidegger, 1998/1967, p. 171; 1993; see also Chapters 2 and 4).

In a provocative paper in 1977, the medical practitioner, George Engel, argues the biomedical model has become not only a model of disease, but also an unquestioned dogma. While identifying a range of inadequacies of the biomedical model, he notes several reasons for resistance to change:

> The power of vested interests, social, political, and economic, are formidable deterrents to any effective assault on biomedical dogmatism.... The enormous existing and planned investment in diagnostic and therapeutic technology alone strongly favors approaches to clinical study and care of patients that emphasize the impersonal and the mechanical. (1977, p. 135)

In putting forward his argument, Engel quotes a fellow medical practitioner who argues in a similar vein that "the Medical establishment is not primarily engaged in the disinterested pursuit of knowledge and the translation of that knowledge into medical practice; rather in significant part it is engaged in special interest advocacy, pursuing and preserving social power" (Holman 1976, p. 11 cited in Engel, 1977, p. 135; see also Coulehan, 2005). These arguments are consistent with points made in Chapter 2 about claims to knowledge and status of professions.

While the biomedical model is dominant in medicine and continues to exert substantial influence over other health professions, as we have seen above it is by no means universally accepted. The literature is replete with critiques of the biomedical model by medical practitioners (for example, Burroughs et al., 2006; Camargo & Coeli, 2006; Charon, 1989; Engel, 1977;) and social scientists or humanities scholars (for example, Germov, 2005b; Mishler et al., 1981; Montgomery Hunter, 1991; Toombs, 1993). Below we consider some of the limitations of this model, including the inadequate notion of disease upon which it is based, the constraints it places on medical care and its neglect of the social, cultural and material contexts of medical practice.

Before doing so, it should be acknowledged that a biomedical model has a benefit for patients who favour it or do not see an alternative. As Robert Anderson points out: "a major benefit of the traditional medical model is the opportunity for patients to turn over the anxiety inherent in being ill to a physician. Being cared for by a compassionate and competent physician can be an extremely rewarding experience" (1995, p. 414). However, this medical model guarantees neither compassion nor competence and is more likely to undermine both, as discussed below. Moreover, there is considerable evidence that most patients do not want to be treated as passive and dependent upon medical practitioners in the way a biomedical model requires. Instead, they want "a patient centred approach, with communication, partnership, and health promotion" (Little et al., 2001, p. 468; see also Coulter, 2002). Where efforts by patients to seek such partnership in the care of their health are met with resistance or defensiveness, the professional-patient relationship risks being undermined. In other words, where patients or clients in service provision are not treated as partners or collaborators, a relationship of mutual trust cannot be established (Schembri, 2005). In this way, over-stating the agency of the professional misses the point of service provision.

The Notion of Disease

If we were to limit our critique to considering a biomedical model of disease on its own terms, this model can be seen to be inadequate for contemporary medical practice. This is because a person may not be ill despite biological signs of disease and, conversely, someone can be ill without biological signs. Even when the "same" biological signs are present, such as the presence of specific bacteria in the body, the symptoms of disease can vary and people can experience their impact on health or well-being in different ways.

As we noted above, some diseases simply do not follow a simple cause-effect model, with progression through predictable biological processes, on which the biomedical model came to be based when the germ theory of disease gained ascendancy. While acknowledging advances made through the biomedical model, Engel calls into question the adequacy of such a view of disease:

> What do require scrutiny are the distortions introduced by the reductionistic tendency to regard the specific disease as adequately, if not best, characterized in terms of the smallest isolable component having causal implications, for example, the biochemical; or even more critical, is the contention that the designation "disease" does not apply in the absence of perturbations at the biochemical level. (1977, p. 131)

This notion of disease overlooks the substantial unexplained variance in the diagnosis of disease (Camargo & Coeli, 2006; Mishler, 1981b). Moreover, in a detailed study of medical practice in different specialisations, Annemarie Mol (2002) demonstrates that practitioners not only enact medical practice in different ways, but the construction of disease varies in line with those varying enactments. In the longitudinal study of Karolinska medical students, we see a similar pattern (see Chapter 7). The biomedical view of disease is, then, an oversimplification. In some instances, it simply fails to account for the disease process. Malnutrition, hypertension and depression are cases in point. A person's life situation can also have substantial influence on the onset and course of a disease, as is evident for asthma, diabetes and stress-related illnesses.

In addition, the point at which a person reports feeling ill or is given the status of patient is not only dependent on clinical data (symptoms) or laboratory data (biological signs), but also upon social and cultural patterns of disease and its interpretation. For example, low body weight or hyperactivity may be seen as pathological for someone belonging to a particular social group or culture, while expected and accepted in a different context. As well, signs or symptoms that are considered normal for the elderly may be regarded as pathological in a young person. Biological processes, as well as the practice of medicine, are always embedded within social, cultural, historical and material contexts. There is no simple cause-effect relationship that can be identified through scientific neutrality. The biomedical model, then, does not fully account for disease and its alleviation. Illness and its treatment is much more complex than the biomedical model would have us believe:

> A great gulf exists between the way we think about disease as physicians and the way we experience it as people. Much of this separation derives directly from our basic assumptions about what illness is. Our medical world view is rooted in an anatomicopathologic view of disease that precludes a rigorous understanding of the experience of illness. What we need to remedy this problem is not just the admonition to remember that our patients are people, but a radical restructuring of what we take disease to be. (Baron, 1985, p. 606)

Constraints on Medical Care

In re-thinking the notion of disease, it follows that what constitutes medical care also needs to be re-thought. With its emphasis on finding cures for acute disease, the biomedical model is inadequate for patients who are chronically ill or dying (Anderson, 1995; Toombs, 1993). As Kay Toombs points out:

> It is important to note that the manner in which illness is conceived has a profound impact on the notion of "healing," and thus on the way in which the end of the patient-physician relationship is defined.... If the end of the medical encounter is defined solely in terms of diagnosis and cure of "disease," the suffering of those with chronic illness seems intractable. The focus on "cure" suggests that the physician has little to offer the person who is incurably ill. (1993, pp. 111–112)

Within a biomedical model, aspects of medical care that are non-biomedical become marginalised in a way that undermines care of the patient (Engel, 1977, p. 131). For example, Jack Coulehan points out that:

> physicians enter their patients' [hospital] rooms as infrequently as possible; and when they do enter, they listen to these patients as little as possible. Instead, they usually have an agenda in mind—a procedure to perform or a parameter to check. (2005, p. 894)

A biomedical model overlooks the impact on the healing process of the relationship between a person who is ill and a medical practitioner or other health professional providing assistance. The importance of this relationship was recognised early in the history of care of the sick, particularly given that comfort and care were largely what medical practitioners were able to provide—ineffective treatments notwithstanding—until the 20th century. The comparatively recent dominance of the biomedical model has lead to preoccupation with finding cures and lifestyle remedies, with enormous associated expenditure, in a manner that has progressively moved away from care of the sick. This model also downplays or overlooks preventative and non-medical ways of dealing with ill health.

The reductionist focus of the biomedical model is based upon an instrumental view of reality and human being (see Chapters 2 and 4), with the consequence that the lived experience of ill health is overlooked in accounts of disease and its treatment (Anderson, 1995; Baron, 1985; Engel, 1977; Toombs, 1993). As Engel argues:

> Planning for systems of medical care and their financing is excessively influenced by the availability and promise of technology, the application and effectiveness of which are often used as the criteria by which decisions are made as to what constitutes illness and who qualifies for medical care. (1977, p. 135)

As a consequence of an instrumental view of human being, medicine can fail to care for the sick or relieve suffering:

> The relief of suffering, it would appear, is considered one of the primary ends of medicine by patients and lay persons, but not by the medical profession. As in the case of the dying, patients and their friends and families do not make a distinction between physical and non-physical sources of suffering in the same way that doctors do. (Cassell, 1982, p. 640)

Not only can medicine fail to relieve suffering, but through focusing on biomedical knowledge of the physical body at the expense of medical care of the person, medical practitioners can cause suffering: "this [mind-body] dichotomy itself is a source of the paradoxical situation in which doctors cause suffering in their care of the sick" (Cassell, 1982, p. 640).

Kathryn Montgomery Hunter argues that such an approach cannot lead to adequate medical care: "Indeed, an isolating, 'scientific' approach to a diseased organ or limb cannot of itself include or lead to reliable therapy. To move toward ameliorating the patient's condition, the part must be recontextualized, considered again as a part of the whole." The "whole" to which she refers is "the prompt, attentive care of the patient" (1991, p. 10). A way forward is to adopt an approach "that takes human experience as seriously as it takes anatomy" (Baron, 1985, p. 606). In a similar vein, Rita Charon argues "we need to conceptualise in human terms what it means to doctor, what it means to be with sick people in ways that help them. It is no longer enough, more and more people are convinced, to offer only medicines and surgeries" (1989, p. 150). Where being with sick people in this way does not occur, dis-ease related to disturbances to our usual ways of being in the world is not addressed. Drawing on Heidegger's notion of "being-at-home" in our everyday world (1962/1927, p. 176), Kay Toombs points out:

> the experience of illness represents a distinct way of being in the world, a way of being that is typically characterized by a loss of wholeness and bodily integrity, a loss of certainty and concurrent apprehension or fear, a loss of control, a loss of freedom to act in a variety of ways, and a loss of the hitherto familiar world. (1993, p. 97).

This lived experience of ill health is neglected in accounts of disease and its treatment within a biomedical model (Anderson, 1995; Baron, 1985; Engel, 1977; Svenaeus, 1999; Toombs, 1993). A consequence is the loss of opportunities for medical care to contribute to restoring a sense of "at-homeness" that characterises health and well-being (Svenaeus, 1999; Toombs, 1993).

Not only is the patients' lifeworld overlooked, but also that of medical practitioners. There is a gaping discrepancy between the biomedical model—with its proferred image of rational, objective "scientists"—and the human challenges of medical practice. This model leaves medical practitioners largely unsupported professionally in dealing with the challenges they encounter. In a study of experienced medical practitioners, Ulla Holm (1993) reports many have difficulty dealing with some of the human interactions in their own practice (see also Coulehan, 2005, p. 896). Lack of support in dealing with this difficulty may be related to higher than average suicide rates among medical practitioners (see, for example, Juel et al., 1999; Schernhammer, 2005; Torre et al., 2005). In a study of nursing students, Ester Mogensen (1994) points to the key role that experienced practitioners play (or fail to play) in assisting students who are learning to deal with stressful or emotionally difficult situations within healthcare. Learning to address the complexity of these challenges is typically not a priority in medical education programmes or in continuing education for medical practitioners. It does not fit well with the image of the rational, objective scientist but, rather, poses a threat to this image (see also Coulehan, 2005).

Voices of disquiet about the dominance and inadequacy of the biomedical model (for example, Baron, 1985; Burroughs et al., 2006; Camargo & Coeli, 2006; Cassell, 1982; Charon, 1989; Donnelly, 1996; Engel, 1977; Mishler et al., 1981; Montgomery Hunter, 1991; Svenaeus, 1999; Toombs, 1993) have gained momentum to the extent there is a counter-movement for reinstating a "patient-centred" model of medicine and of healthcare, more generally (for example, Anderson, 1995; Balint, 1964; Carpenter, 1993; Coulter, 2002; Little et al., 2001; Szasz & Hollender, 1956). Not only is this movement seeking to redress a narrow focus on disease of the physical body, but also its proponents argue this can only be achieved through autonomy for, and collaboration with, those who are ill. As seen previously in the history of medicine, there is some resistance to these efforts to challenge and change the status quo. As Angela Coulter notes:

> Some critics see attempts to promote a more patient-centred approach as peripheral to the serious business of treatment and care, an unnecessary and burdensome addition to the long list of demands made on health professionals. Others dismiss it as mere political correctness, a temporary fashion that can be ignored. Yet others fear it will be too costly, believing that recognising patients' autonomy and taking account of their preferences will increase the demand for scarce resources to unsustainable levels. (2002, p. 120)

She goes on to argue that:

> these objections miss the point altogether. Far from being peripheral, the development of a more active role for the patient and citizen will be fundamental to securing the future of public healthcare. It is the only way to ensure its affordability, acceptability and sustainability over the long term. (p. 121)

Moves towards placing patient care at the centre of healthcare have meant increased attention to how medical practitioners relate to patients. Alongside these moves has been expanding access to information by patients, shifting commercial pressures and opportunities for medical practitioners, increased calls for accountability among medical practitioners, and growing recognition of the need for health professionals to learn to work together in interprofessional teams. As John Bligh points out, these changes "have put pressure on doctors to rethink and take stock of what being a medical professional is and what it means" (2005, p. 4). This has lead to efforts to define or identify what makes up "medical professionalism", which has also been described as personal and professional development. While debates continue about what constitutes professionalism in the practice of medicine (for example, Coulehan, 2005; Cruess & Cruess, 2008; Hilton & Slotnick, 2005), it is often regarded as including attributes such as "ethical practice; reflection/self-awareness; responsibility for actions; respect for patients; teamwork, and social responsibility" (Hilton & Slotnick, 2005, p. 58). Sean Hilton and Henry Slotnick consider that the first three of these refer to "personal (intrinsic) attributes", while the remaining three are "cooperative attributes of professionals" (p. 60). Following Aristotle, they also propose "practical wisdom" as a defining characteristic of professionalism (p. 58), although it is unclear how they see practical wisdom as relating to the attributes of professionalism they identified from the literature. They are quite unusual in the medical and medical education literature in regarding professionalism not as a trait but a state to be achieved and maintained, although this appears to be somewhat in tension with their emphasis on attributes to be acquired.

In response to the changing contexts in which medicine is practised around the globe and concern that the commitment of medical practitioners to patient welfare was being eroded, the American Board of Internal Medicine Foundation, the American College of Physicians-American Society of Internal Medicine Foundation and the European Federation of Internal Medicine (2002) collaborated in preparing a document entitled *Medical Professionalism in the New Millennium: A Physician Charter*. This document has received widespread attention and support, prinicipally in the western world (see Blank, Kimball, McDonald, & Merino, 2003). In this charter, the contract that medicine has with society is regarded as based on medical professionalism. In contrast to much of the debate on professionalism that focuses on specific attributes, three key principles of professionalism are identified: (a) primacy of patient welfare in which the interests of the patient are to be served, (b) respect for patient autonomy, such that medical practitioners are honest with patients and enable them to make informed decisions, and (c) promoting social justice to fairly distribute resources and eliminate discrimination in health care (p. 244). Derived from these principles are ten commitments that medical practitioners are to make in order to uphold the social contract between medicine and society, such as commitment to professional competence, patient confidentiality and improving quality of care.

In line with this charter on professionalism, Jordan Cohen (2006) defines professionalism as "the means by which individual doctors fulfil the medical profession's contract with society" (p. 608). Cohen identifies what he regards as contemporary threats to professionalism, including a human tendency towards self-interest rather than others' welfare, financial and other temptations available to medical practitioners from pharmaceutical companies and elsewhere, the intrusion of commercial ethics and imperatives into the doctor-patient relationship, and unprofessional behaviour by other medical professionals that goes unsanctioned. While threats such as these are of current relevance, they also echo those evident throughout the history of medicine, although the form they take has changed over time to some extent.

Alongside efforts to identify what constitutes medical professionalism, medical education programmes are seen to have a key role to play in developing such professionalism in preparation for the challenging and changing contexts that medical practitioners encounter (for example, Archer, Elder, Hustedde, Milam, & Joyce, 2008; Cohen, 2006; Cruess & Cruess, 2008; Gordon, 2003). None of the various attributes and principles considered to make up professionalism is entirely new to medical programmes. The teaching of communication skills, ethics, empathy, teamwork and so on have been part of many medical education programmes over an extended period of time (see, for example, Brown, 2008; Gordon, 2003; Holm & Aspegren, 1999), although in some instances they have come to be regarded as more central to medical practice than they were previously. While medical education is seen to have a key role in developing professionalism, teaching and assessing competency in professionalism is increasingly a requirement in medical programmes (see, for example, Archer et al., 2008; Cohen, 2006). The various points of view on what constitutes professionalism, as well as difficulties in explicitly teaching and assessing professionalism, present challenges to these efforts.

An additional challenge is that professionalism is learned not only through the formal or planned curriculum, but also the informal or "hidden curriculum" (Archer et al., 2008; Cohen, 2006; Gordon, 2003. See Snyder (1970) for elaboration of the notion of the hidden curriculum). The recognition of the impact of the hidden curriculum and the culture of medicine on learning of professionalism has prompted the argument that teaching and assessing professionalism will be to little effect unless this culture is addressed in the practice of medicine and in medical education (Cohen, 2006; Coulehan, 2005; Gordon, 2003). Jack Coulehan argues that:

> today's culture of medicine is hostile to altruism, compassion, integrity, fidelity, self-effacement, and other traditional qualities. Hospital culture and the narratives that support it often embody a set of professional qualities that are diametrically opposed to virtues that are explicitly taught as constituting the "good" doctor. (2005, p. 892)

While it is possible to question whether such a nostalgic view of medicine ever pervaded the practice of medicine (see the brief history above), Coulehan's point that tensions between the culture of medicine and what is explicitly taught in medical education deserves critical scrutiny (see also Chapter 6). He argues, further, that:

> While the explicit curriculum focuses on empathy, communication, relief of suffering, trust, fidelity, and pursuing the patient's best interest, in the hospital and clinic environment these values are largely pushed aside by the tacit learning of objectivity, detachment, self-interest, and distrust—of emotions, patients, insurance companies, administrators, and the state. (p. 894)

Coulehan argues that the current approach to professionalism in which exercises or courses explicitly teach professionalism with required competencies that students must demonstrate "does not alter the tension or conflict between tacit and explicit values" (p. 897). Moreover, he considers that current approaches to teaching and assessing professionalism fail to address the tension between self-interest and altruism. For this reason, he argues that the professionalism movement will fail as it is "too simple, too neat, too flimsy, and doesn't engage the problems it is designed to address" (p. 892). He argues that in an effort to make professionalism more quantifiable, the professionalism movement "may use skills and practices as surrogates for virtue" (p. 893).

As Coulehan implies, attributes that are seen to make up professionalism, such as communication, ethics and so on, have typically been treated as separate attributes or skills to be learned in preparation for the practice of medicine. Such reductionist tendencies arguably contribute to some of the difficulties experienced in developing medical professionalism. Jill Gordon (2003) and Ray Archer and colleagues (2008) argue for the need to develop professionalism across the curriculum, not as a separate set of skills. Arguments for professionalism that extends beyond separate attributes or skills and permeates the curriculum can be seen as pointing toward the kind of ontological turn argued for throughout this book. Rather than conceiving professionalism in terms of such attributes or skills, emphasis is needed on the interrelation between the various aspects of medical practice. For instance, communication or empathy would be learned not as separate skills or attributes, but in such a way that their centrality for skilful medical practice is clearly evident. Extending Nel Noddings' argument, each of the "attributes" of medical professionalism commonly identified in the literature is arguably "a way of being in relation, not a set of specific behaviors . . . or an individual attribute" (1992, p. 17). This would mean they would be developed in a way that contributes to the process of becoming attuned and responsive medical practitioners: epistemology in the service of ontology (see Chapter 4).

While efforts towards promoting professionalism and patient-centred health care in the practice of medicine are important and laudable, they have not achieved the status or attention directed to what is considered the core of medicine, that is, biomedical knowledge. Moreover, the impact of these efforts has not been sufficient to call into question, in any substantial way, the biomedical notion of disease or a focus on disease as an individual phenomenon. Locating disease in the individual carries with it the risk of biological determinism—that individuals are biologically predisposed to particular diseases—or victim blaming (Sontag, 1983, p. 61)—that individuals have failed to care for their health—while overlooking the demonstrated impact on health and disease of social, cultural, historical and material conditions. The importance of these conditions highlights the social responsibilities of the medical profession. While *Medical Professionalism in the New Millennium* identifies social responsibilities of medicine as one of three key principles, the flow-on effects on medicine and medical education have yet to be fully realised.

Medicine as Social Practice

Not only is disease embedded in social, cultural, historical and material contexts, but so, too, is the practice of medicine. As Montgomery Hunter (1991) and Mishler (1981a, 1981b; Mishler et al., 1981) make clear, "medicine is active interpretive work through which a particular social reality is constructed" (Mishler, 1981a, p. 162). Nicholas Rose elaborates this notion, as follows:

> The persons and populations with which medicine concerns itself do not merely exist, sickly and mutely awaiting its attention: they are formed by differentiation. Medical thought and medical practice always exist in relation to other forms of thought and practice.... An analytic of medicine thus needs to examine the divisions within which its objects are formed, *the lines of differentiation* which define certain persons, groups, sites, locales as appropriate for medicine and others as not. (1994, p. 57)

Contrary to an idealised version of the biomedical model, these lines of differentiation are contested within contemporary medical practice (see, for example, Anderson, 1995; Burroughs et al., 2006; Camargo & Coeli, 2006; Donnelly, 1996), as has also been the case during the history of medicine. However, this contestation is not simply a conceptual debate, but has practical consequences for the health care that is received, as well as who receives care at all (Engel, 1977; Mishler, 1981a, 1981b; Mol, 2002; Rose, 1994). This means that:

> clinical practice is based on and guided by sociocultural values and assumptions, organized and regulated by social norms and institutional requirements, and socially consequential in its effects on the rights and responsibilities of those labeled as sick and assigned the social role of patient. (Mishler, 1981a, p. 162)

In other words, the practice of medicine can be seen as "a system of rules for making symptoms into illnesses, and for transforming persons into patients" (Mishler, 1981b, p. 12). It also operates as a form of social control, for example, approving absence from work or financial compensation following injury for some, while denying it to others.

Chapter 6
Interplay Between Traditions and Being Professionals

> *The concerns of our own time about the direction of medical*
> *study—the need to "humanize" physicians in an increasingly*
> *technological age, the lack of student experience in dealing*
> *with normal patients in an ambulatory [outpatients] setting,*
> *the estrangement of hospital and medical school, the fear that*
> *medical training has become too specialized, the complaint*
> *that students learn too much of the science of medicine and*
> *too little of its art—only echo the historic tensions.*
>
> (Bonner, 1995, p. 348)

Against the background of the history of medicine and critical examination of the biomedical model in the previous chapter, this chapter explores some ways in which the traditions of practice for medicine play out for those learning to be medical practitioners in the contemporary western world. Through this investigation, we see that contemporary medical programmes can "echo the historic tensions", in the words of the quote above. As we saw in Chapter 1, this is also the case for other professional education programmes. While we take the medical education programme at Karolinska Institute as an empirical example, the challenges that are explored in this chapter can be seen to have parallels in many other professions. These challenges include power relations between professionals and clients, emotional demands of practice, and the gendered character of professional practice (see also Chapter 2).

When the empirical study involving Karolinska students was conducted, just over half the medical students were female. Approximately one-third of Sweden's medical practitioners were educated through this programme, while today 25% are educated there. The Karolinska medical programme has similarities to medical programmes elsewhere and to professional education programmes beyond medicine. These programmes are typically organised around the idea that knowledge and skills are to be acquired and applied, in line with the normative curriculum (see Chapter 3). At the time of the empirical study, the Karolinska medical programme followed a classic normative design, beginning with courses providing "basic knowledge", followed by courses in which knowledge was to be applied, for instance in clinical contexts. Most of the clinical courses incorporated observation of, or participation in,

G. Dall'Alba, *Learning to be Professionals*, Innovation and Change in Professional
Education 4, DOI 10.1007/978-90-481-2608-8_6,
© Springer Science+Business Media B.V. 2009

94 6 Interplay Between Traditions and Being Professionals

clinical practice. Professional education programmes commonly include some form of supervised practicum of this kind in which aspiring professionals are monitored, to varying extents, by more experienced professionals. Even in less conventional curriculum designs, the purpose of these practicum periods is usually seen in terms of providing opportunities to apply knowledge and skills in practice, as in the normative curriculum. The scope of the practicum varies from one field to the next and across social and cultural contexts.

At the time of the empirical research presented here, the statement of aims for the Karolinska medical programme identified a range of personal qualities and dispositions to be developed, areas of biomedical knowledge relating to diagnosing and treating diseases and their symptoms, as well as knowledge about developing a productive doctor-patient relationship and cooperating with other professionals relating to healthcare. Conventional pedagogy was prevalent during the medical programme, emphasising acquisition of biomedical knowledge and skills, primarily through lectures, laboratory work, practical skills classes, clinical seminars, and observations of, and involvement in, clinical practice. Problem based learning tutorials had been introduced in some courses within a conventional curriculum design for the programme. This conventional design began with two pre-clinical years, including courses on topics such as cell biology, anatomy and physiology. One semester of clinical preparation followed, including medical history taking, physical examination and communication skills. The subsequent three years of clinical study were organised in the form of courses on geriatrics, psychiatry, epidemiology, paediatrics, gynaecology and obstetrics, and so on. On completion of the programme, the students were required to undertake a 21-month internship prior to being eligible for registration as medical doctors. The period of internship is outside the scope of the longitudinal study presented here, although research on the internship period would be a valuable extension to this study (see, for example, Luke, 2003).

On entry to the medical programme, the 13 students in the longitudinal study varied in age (from 19 to 26 years), gender (7 women and 6 men), and procedures by which they had entered the medical programme. Admission procedures included a national university entrance examination or grades in high school, while some entered through "local admission" based on a written motivation for studying medicine as well as an interview with medical practitioners and a psychologist. In addition, when entering the programme, the students varied in their understanding of what medical practice involves, which had been investigated for their whole cohort in a related study (Dall'Alba, 1998). In brief, in this earlier study, medical practice was understood in diverse ways, as: (a) helping or saving lives; (b) diagnosing or treating using required procedures; (c) locating the problem and informing the patient; (d) diagnosing and treating the problem, while interacting in a supportive way: (e) seeking a way forward with the patient; or (f) enabling the patient to better deal with his or her life situation.

During the Karolinska medical programme, the students not only learned to negotiate the demands of the various courses in which they participated, but also to construe the world in medical terms:

> Entry into the world of medicine is accomplished not only by learning the language and knowledge base of medicine, but by learning quite fundamental practices through which medical practitioners engage and formulate reality in a specifically "medical" way. These include specialized ways of "seeing", "speaking" and "writing". (Good, 1994, p. 71).

In other words, the students began to learn ways of being medical practitioners in the context of routines and traditions of medicine. They learned to incorporate those routines and traditions into contemporary medical practice, carrying forward the past into the present. While routines and traditions of practice frame what we do and who we are as professionals, they also provide openings in ways of being professionals. There is scope, then, for both routine and creativity.

By learning to engage in professional practice in ways that meet the requirements of the profession and the broader society—while at times bending, circumventing and calling into question some of those requirements—aspiring and experienced professionals participate in forming and, perhaps, transforming practice. They may comply with some aspects of professional practice, while challenging other aspects. There were many instances where Karolinska students complied with established ways of practising medicine. At other times, they critically reflected upon the practice of medicine, particularly as it was presented to them during the medical programme. Their capacity to critically reflect in this way provided them with opportunities for developing their ways of being medical doctors. For example, some of the Karolinka students adopted a biomedical approach in learning to practise medicine, while others incorporated biomedical components into a broader perspective that they considered more adequately met the needs of patients, as Chapter 7 illustrates. Challenges and tensions relating to reproducing and renewing practice come to the fore in the issues raised below. These challenges and tensions highlight the way in which preparation for professional practice is not solely a cognitive or individual enterprise, but also entails the formation of professional ways of being in interplay with prevailing traditions of practice. Learning professional practice includes, then, both continuity and transformation.

As noted in Chapters 2 and 4, any practice is not singular, but can be enacted and embodied in a range of ways. These various ways of enacting practice may be in tension and even in competition with each other, as noted above. For example, the dominant biomedical focus of medicine usually sits uncomfortably with collaborating with patients about their health. Not only do aspiring professionals learn to engage in practice, but they must also learn to negotiate the complexity of different, and potentially competing, ways of enacting practice. As they do so, their development as professionals does not follow a linear path, but unfolds over time along various development trajectories, as Chapter 7 illustrates. This variation in development trajectories challenges a notion of uni-directional movement towards entry into practice (see Chapter 2; see also Dall'Alba & Sandberg, 2006), as though there were a unitary practice. Below we consider some of the challenges and tensions faced by the Karolinska students in learning to become medical practitioners against the background of traditions of practice for medicine.

Disease in Patients' Lives

As noted in Chapter 5, a central feature of the relationship between patients and medical practitioners is the way in which disease is conceptualised and enacted. For some of the Karolinska students in the longitudinal study, disease was to be found in specific parts of patients' bodies, where it could be located and treated. The lives in which disease was embedded were only of relevance insofar as they impacted upon the disease or its treatment. Hence, disease was decontextualised from the lives of patients in such a way that patients were reduced to diseases or sets of symptoms to be diagnosed and treated. This way of enacting disease aligns with a biomedical model and neglects patients' lifeworld. During consultations with patients, these students focused on medical history taking and physical examination. For example, in a specialist neurology clinic in a large metropolitan hospital, Lennart consulted with Barbara, who had suffered from migraine over a period of 30 years. Afterwards he described the approach he'd taken, as follows:

> *I started by asking a few open questions. Then you go more into what problems they're having and try to get them to describe that. And yes, and then, then you start asking more—well if you know something about the area, you can say— then you try to ring in and ask, like, so-called differential diagnosis questions about, for example, headache: If it's in the morning, [or] not in the morning, if it gets worse during the day and if it comes like an attack and things like that.* (1st semester of 5th year, p. 32)

After taking notes on Barbara's medical history during the consultation, Lennart had issued several instructions to her during a physical examination, only rarely giving her a brief indication of the purpose of his requests. He described the physical examination he carried out, as follows:

> *Then [after the medical history taking] I then took, since it was neurology, I then did, well a physical examination with neurological questions. It's, it was a battery of questions with different things we've learnt during the course and that we've had, gone through. Yeah, on the first days of the course you went through with a doctor, what you're supposed to do and that. And it's a bit of gymnastics almost, a bit at the start. You have to walk backwards and forwards in the room and things like that. Walk on your toes, walk on your heels. Then stretch out your arms and that. To see how, how the nerve system is functioning. And then you examine other, these nerves and things like that. The eye's functioning and that. Other reflexes and feeling and things like that.* (pp. 33–34)

Once he had completed the medical history taking and physical examination, he rounded off the consultation, as follows:

Lennart: *Mm. OK. What you want most of all from this is that you want an X-ray taken?*

Barbara: *Yes, that's most of all what I want. And then I don't know how it is then to take, if you want to keep taking this many [brand of headache tablet] and that, then. How it is*

Lennart: *in the long term, yes.*

Barbara: *if they have side-effects or if you can just keep munching them.*

Lennart: *Mm. OK. Yes, good. I think I'm satisfied here, so we need to wait a little while and then we can see the doctor as well as [other] medical students*

Barbara: *Mm*

Lennart: *in another room. So you can wait out in the waiting room in the meantime. Fine, thanks.* (pp. 24–25)

As the consultation and his account of it show, Lennart focused on medical history taking and physical examination for the purpose of reaching a diagnosis. He did not address Barbara's questions near the end of the consultation, even to the extent of reminding her she would be able to pose the questions to an experienced medical practitioner. Instead, he remarked that he was satisfied, although he did not consider whether Barbara was also satisfied with the consultation to this point.

Max, too, demonstrated a similar view of medical practice, identifying tensions it created during consultations with patients:

The basic thing is to uncover and cure and ease sicknesses. And then I've understood that it's very much about things that are on the margin of what is sickness . . . and a lot that falls outside [of sickness] which you have to deal with. . . . There are many social problems . . . that are about the social situation and personality of the person . . . that you can't diagnose, but they have lots of other underlying problems that you can see are probably at the root of it all. . . . They fall outside what you think is actually the doctor's role. (final semester, pp. 29–31)

Knowledge about diseases and their symptoms allowed Lennart to focus on identifying and treating disease, while Max also adopted a similar focus in sorting patients' health problems into those that belonged to medical practice and those that did not.

Enacting medical practice in ways that decontextualise disease from patients' lifeworld is also evident among students in the remainder of the cohort at the beginning and end of the medical programme (Dall'Alba, 1998, 2004), as well as among experienced medical practitioners (Stålsby Lundborg et al., 1999). In both groups, there is some variation in the extent of this decontextualisation, ranging from focusing squarely on diagnosing and treating disease, to interacting with patients in a supportive way while reaching a diagnosis and treatment plan. As noted above, however, most patients do not want to be regarded *as* their disease or ailment. Maurice Merleau-Ponty points to a discrepancy when personhood is overlooked in this way:

In so far as I have a body, I may be reduced to the status of an object beneath the gaze of another person, and no longer count as a person for him. . . . Saying

*that I have a body is thus a way of saying that I can be seen as an object and
that I try to be seen as a subject.* (1962/1945, p. 167)

Other Karolinska students interacted with patients in ways that did not bring
about this discrepancy, as they saw disease as afflicting not only patients' physical
bodies, but their lives. In medical consultations, these students were concerned to
elicit an account of a disease or ailment that included its impact on those lives.
This was seen as necessary for assessing symptoms and proposing treatment, in
line with the critique of the biomedical model described above. Ingrid illustrated
such a view when discussing treatment implications. She sought to assist patients
with health problems in ways that took into account each patient's situation and
expectations:

*It's a matter of taking care of the patient, in the patient's way.... Even if
two people come in with exactly the same symptoms and the same sickness
profile, you might treat them differently, depending upon their expectations
and motivation about what should be done. That's my view. You don't only
take care of the heart or whatever.... You might do it in different ways that
suit the patient best.... What I'm striving for is not to bluster in and have
made up my mind from the start, but try to find out what the patient's goal is.*
(2nd semester of 3rd year, pp. 13–14)

Kay Toombs (1993) makes a related distinction between medical history and clinical
narrative. She describes medical history as concerned with the kinds of information targeted in checklists provided to the medical students, including occurrence of
symptoms, their duration, previous sicknesses and so on. This form of history taking
framed Lennart's consultation with Barbara above. A clinical narrative, on the other
hand, "is the story of the illness from the patient's point of view" (p. 103), including
both the pattern of symptoms and their impact on the patient's life.

Those medical students who broadened their enactment of medical practice to
incorporate the embeddedness of a disease or ailment in patients' lives also interacted with patients in ways that did not reduce them to a disease or set of symptoms.
For example, Ingrid described the way she carried out physical examinations, as
follows:

*From what I've noticed, I usually always talk while I'm examining [the
patient]. So I don't only feel the stomach and stand there completely silent,
like, but I try to talk or ask questions while I'm doing something and say what
I'm doing. And, for me, that somehow feels quite good.*

Interviewer: *Mm. Why do you think it feels better to, for example, tell them
what you're doing and talk with them a little as you go?*

*Partly because then it also feels as though you're involving the patient in what
you're doing. So if I'm going to, for example, test a reflex under the foot, then
I want to tell the patient that this feels a bit uncomfortable. It's a pain reflex
I'm going to test. So then it isn't just an object that's lying in front of me*

and I'm going to find out what's wrong with it. It's not, like, a Volvo but a person, who naturally wonders what I'm doing. (2nd semester of 3rd year, pp. 24–25)

As these examples show, a focus on diagnosing and treating disease continues to be in evidence among aspiring medical practitioners, as does a focus on caring for the person who is ill. Tension between these two ways of enacting practice has long been evident in the practice of medicine, as noted previously.

Power Relations Between Medical Practitioners and Patients

Over time, the specialised knowledge of medical practitioners and the social status this knowledge afforded them has invested power in these practitioners when compared with patients. This power relation can be compounded by patients' ill health. Echoing Elliot Mishler's argument (1981a, p. 162) that "patient" is a social role, Lotta pointed out the position of dependence in which patients are placed when seeking assistance from medical practitioners: "You have such a role as a doctor, you have such power over patients. It isn't until I tell you you're sick that you're sick. And you have to have a lot of respect and humility about that. What an incredible position of dependence the patient ends up in" (1st semester of 5th year, pp. 59–60). This power relation has historically given rise to tension among medical practitioners who have varied in the way they relate to patients, as well as between patients and medical practitioners.

The power and control exercised by medical practitioners is increased when patients are reduced to physical objects or sets of symptoms, which may be one reason the biomedical model continues to dominate medical practice. However, there is a sense in which patients are not entirely powerless in these situations. As they become increasingly informed about a range of health conditions, patients can question or challenge medical practitioners' knowledge. These practitioners are also reliant upon patients' efforts to achieve improved health. When patients do not follow prescribed treatments or they seek assistance elsewhere, they undermine the authority of medical practitioners.

Efforts towards collaborating with patients in the care of their health, such as patient-centred health care, attempt to achieve balance in these power relations. These efforts increase the likelihood health care will be provided that is built on care for the other. In other words, it is a form of care that seeks not to dominate, but to support patients in achieving improved health and well-being. Richard Sennett (2003) argues for the importance of autonomy for patients as they have knowledge and experience about their illness or ailment that is necessary for its treatment. For Sennett, autonomy means "accepting in others what one doesn't understand about them. In so doing, the fact of their autonomy is treated as equal to your own" (p. 262).

Exposure of Patients During Physical Examination

An issue arising for the medical students that related to power over patients concerned the exposure of patients' bodies when they were being examined. The students examined patients' bodies in ways that could bring discomfort or pain, as well as placing patients in a potentially exposed position. This was particularly the case at the beginning of the clinical period when the students were most inexperienced and also during more intimate forms of contact with patients. On the other hand, the medical students were initially unaccustomed to dealing with this kind of physical closeness or intimacy in professional practice, so it potentially involved some degree of discomfort for them, as well. For instance, Karl described feeling tense in anticipation of learning to do gynaecological examinations: "It was unexpectedly tense somehow. That's what I thought, we all thought that. We thought it felt a bit demanding, in any case the guys, I think" (2nd semester of 5th year, p. 2).

Max described an incident during a ward round in the first clinical period when five people, including medical students and doctors, came to a patients' bedside in a hospital ward. He experienced the situation as uncomfortable on account of the exposed position of the patient:

> She was lying in bed and then we come in and stand around her, looking down, and then she had to undress and [pause]. Then you can feel that [pause] it's almost impossible to maintain integrity there because there are many of us. You're [laughs] standing up and she was a woman and most of us were men and she had to undress and that.... It was noticeable that she thought, I thought I saw anyway, that she felt embarrassed by it and I don't think it's at all odd, either [laughs]. In actual fact, you had these [pause] feelings most strongly just when you'd first come out to the clinic. (2nd semester of 3rd year, p. 16)

Over time, the students became progressively more accustomed to situations in which patients' bodies were exposed during examination, although they were sometimes critical of how experienced medical practitioners handled these situations:

> I've also experienced, on an ultrasound, where they, where the patient has climbed down from the gynae [gynaecology examination] chair and is there about to get dressed. Then they [the doctor] suddenly starts talking about what they've found. So the poor woman is standing there in her shirt, like, that [only] comes down to about here and is going to get the result of the examination. And the doctor, and I think that, like, um, and sure, we're stressed or you want to get on with the work, you can't manage to stand and wait ten minutes, or five minutes, three minutes, while someone gets dressed to then tell them about it. But I don't know, then I feel uncomfortable as a medical student standing there beside them, and you're also supposed to stand and talk with some person, stand and look a person in the eye who doesn't have her pants on.... I think it's demanding. You have to, you, all of us, we have to handle, like, our ideal about things like this in our own way and, for me, I think it's important you don't behave like that.... But it can be really demanding

*during this course when I feel that maybe the doctors who are more blunted
to this situation, I think maybe don't really show consideration.* (Elisabet, 2nd
semester of 5th year, pp. 57–59)

Situations such as these provide additional examples of the inadequacy of an "objective", scientific approach to medical practice, which fails to take sufficiently into
account the need to respect patients and aspiring medical practitioners as persons.
These situations also provide evidence of tensions that arise between adopting such
an approach and caring for those who seek medical assistance.

Emotional Demands of Medical Practice

Not only could medical students experience the exposure of patients' bodies as
uncomfortable, but the emotional demands of medical practice also presented challenges, such as the death of children or advice to patients that there were no remaining treatments available for terminal illnesses. Given the demanding nature of some
of the situations medical students encounter, it might be expected efforts would be
made to be alert to helping students deal with these situations. In contrast, several
students pointed out there were rarely opportunities during the medical programme
to talk through difficult experiences with medical practitioners or other health professionals (see also Coulehan, 2005). Ingrid observed:

*If something terrible happens, there isn't really anyone to talk to about it
actually. I know I was in a consulting room, there was a father of a 40 year old
who had a terminal illness and was dying. He [the father] went in and talked
with the doctor and she told him they'd given up hope and she'd be surprised
if he [the son] lasted until Christmas. And the father was devastated and I felt,
too, that I was close to tears. And I don't know, it's more that you comment
when he's gone out that it feels difficult. But it isn't anything that comes up
for discussion anywhere. That's the kind of thing you talk about with other
medical students. There isn't room for it [in the medical programme], it isn't
really set up that way.... You feel, how are you going to deal with this if it's
a child, how are you going to be able to do that? ...Maybe you're not mature
enough to deal with these tragic situations.* (1st semester of 4th year, p. 32)

Ingrid wondered whether her difficulty in dealing with these demanding situations
was due to her lack of maturity, but the teaching staff and medical programme bore
some responsibility for helping students learn to deal with situations such as these.
In a few instances, students reported efforts by medical staff to discuss demanding
situations the students had encountered in clinical situations. Kristina described a
situation she had experienced when a small baby was rushed into the emergency
paediatric department:

*Just as I was about to go at nine o'clock, to go off duty, the alarm sounded. And
it was clear it was a little girl with a heart condition and so I thought I'd stay.
And so we all ran to the emergency room and so there was this Hans, that's*

the doctor's name, and he was very, very calm and collected and . . . he saw to it that everyone was ready and that the staff who were needed were there. And then this child came who was already dead. And we all understood when they came with the little girl that it was over, which meant it wasn't as desperate, maybe. It was, like, you could let go of it all a bit. But all prescriptions were followed to do what could be done, trying cardiopulmonary resuscitation there and giving the required medicine and that, and then stopping after a number of minutes according to all the rules there are, ethical and moral rules that are written and that.

And then, and through the whole thing, I think it was 20 minutes of trying to get the child going, and the whole time it's very calm in the room and everyone doing what should be done, I have no function at all. I'm the one standing on the periphery watching and that's what's difficult. Because if I'd had a function to fill it might have been a bit easier. But I didn't, I was just there. And then I went home after that.. . . But I found it consoling afterwards that is was so calmly handled and paradoxically, in some odd way, that it was already over [from the start], and that.

And then when I came back, because I was on duty again in emergency in the morning on the day after, then they rang me . . . and said that when things like this happen we have a support group that meets. If you're interested we can talk about it, about what's happened. And it was like this, that I had talked quite a lot with the intern who was also there [the night before] and I didn't think I needed it then, so I said, "No thanks". But then later on . . . I was on a placement where I came across him again, that doctor, and he almost took me by the ear and sat me down in a room that was partitioned off and just told me what had happened afterwards, what had been found in the postmortem and that. Because he presumably wanted to catch up with me, like, and hear how it had been or just tell me collegially as a doctor what had happened.. . . But it was a difficult thing [to witness]. It raised very many, yeah, feelings.

Interviewer: *Yes, sure, I can imagine that. But did you think it was good that you had the chance to talk with the intern immediately after it had happened?*

Yes, it was good, yes, and very objective. In this branch, the things you experience emotionally are spoken about very little. It's spoken about in an objective way, because the rest

Interviewer: *So was that what you talked about?*

Yes, mostly, actually, and yeah a bit that it was difficult. Like, we said it was very sad and that. But more than that you don't go into in these discussions, but you keep it on a very objective level because otherwise you might break apart as a person. I don't know.

Interviewer: *But these feelings are there all the same, I can imagine.*
Yes

Interviewer: *How can you work through them yourself, then,*
Yes, exactly.

Interviewer: *when you come across something like that? It sounds demanding.*

Yes, it's really demanding. I think that's the danger of this job, that you can end up there. But I asked him, too, when he'd taken me by the ear and sat me down, when he asked me a bit about how it had gone and how I was there in the room and how it felt and that. So I told him a bit about what I thought was good, that it was so calm and it was done so well. And in the end I asked him, when his pager had already rung so he was actually already on the run again, because it's like that all the time, they never have any time those people. So I asked him, "But what do you do? You see this sometimes and have to keep track of everything and talk with the parents. How do you deal with all that?" . . . And he said, "We talk it through together as colleagues, Christer and I, the one who was there, too, he was on duty then. We've talked about it a lot afterwards. And that network, you have to take care of it and protect it because that's where you pick yourself up again." When you experience these difficult things, I can imagine that. So I think it's dangerous if you feel alone in that kind of work.

Interviewer: *Yes, sure.*

Because then you have to bear a lot yourself, when you aren't able to, yeah, talk about it. . . . Because people breeze past so much, too, in this line of work. So there's just so many people. And we hop around and stream from one place to the next so we never manage to deepen our contacts, more than with each other in our course, without feeling really odd about even asking the question at all. (2nd semester of 5th year, pp. 18–24)

Kristina thought her lack of place and function in the situation made it difficult to deal with what she had experienced. She clearly still had difficulty describing this experience later in the semester.

When they experienced emotionally demanding situations, some students felt it necessary to protect themselves by maintaining distance from patients and their problems, which is not to be confused with adopting an appropriate professional approach. This distancing from patients is an additional consequence of an "objective" approach to medical practice, which has been central to the rise of the biomedical model. In a study of nursing students, Ester Mogensen (1994) notes some health professionals also use distance and busyness to protect themselves, while the work culture tends to promote this strategy. Maintaining distance in this way signals to students that addressing the emotional demands of practice is to be avoided:

> The instrumental work culture operates also as a practical defence, in this case for the nurse, against the anguish she meets in everyday healthcare. . . . The possibility of learning about and from these meetings seems to a great extent to depend on the student's own initiative. If the students see the nurse avoids this kind of dialogue, they don't gain any preparedness to take initiative themselves. A pattern such as this, which here is the consequence of social learning, can be difficult to break. The message can be interpreted as: "You don't spend time on that (dialogue with the patient), it isn't our primary task, there isn't time for it, someone else can take care of it". . . . To assume an air of busy efficiency—or not be able to make the change from a stressful moment to a calmer one—can be a means for health professionals to protect themselves. (p. 158)

When students witness avoidance of dealing with emotionally demanding situations, opportunities to work through, and learn from, these situations are denied them. Several of the medical students remarked on the action-focused culture in surgery clinics. Given surgery is intrusive into patients' bodies in ways that can be life-threatening and can also produce pain, sometimes for extended periods, it is perhaps not surprising that the busy efficiency noted by Mogensen is particularly evident there. The prevalence of men in this speciality may also contribute to a heightened reluctance to address the emotionally demanding nature of these situations. Several studies have shown a stronger emphasis by women than men on connecting with others, rather than remaining detached (for example, Belenky, Clinchy, Goldberger, & Tarule, 1986; Holm & Aspegren, 1999; Newton, Barber, Clardy, Cleveland, & O'Sullivan, 2008; Stålsby-Lundborg et al., 1999), although there are also differences within these two groups.

As the examples above show, the students encountered a range of situations in which a distant, objective approach was in tension with caring for people who were sick, as well as with taking due care of themselves as aspiring medical practitioners. Most often, the students were not given assistance in negotiating tensions such as these as part of the medical programme. The prevalence of an objective approach to the practice of medicine meant students did not receive the support they needed in dealing with the complexity and challenges of medical practice. However, it is unlikely medical staff will provide such support and opportunities for learning if they have difficulty dealing with these situations themselves, as research suggests (Holm, 1993). The higher suicide rates among medical practitioners compared with the rest of the population (Juel et al., 1999; Schernhammer, 2005; Torre et al., 2005) also signal a need to critically assess the extent to which these professionals are adequately prepared for, and supported in, the demands of their work. Jack Coulehan argues that:

> Physicians are particularly vulnerable to anxiety, loneliness, frustration, anger, depression, and helplessness when caring for chronically or terminally ill patients. They often try to cope with these emotions by suppressing or rationalizing them. The more effectively physicians reverse this process by developing self-awareness, the more likely they will have the resources to connect with, and respond to, their patients' experiences. (2005, p. 896)

In contrast to a distant, objective approach, several of the medical students felt some degree of engagement with patients' concerns was necessary to understanding their situation and coming to an agreement about appropriate treatment. So engagement of this kind was seen as a central component of medical practice. Female medical students more commonly expressed this view than did male students, in line with research on connecting with others, as noted above. In a similar vein to the students who expressed such a view, Rita Charon argues that "the physician's effectiveness increases with empathy, and empathy springs from the ability to imagine the patient's point of view" (1989, p. 137; see also Anderson, 1995; Baron, 1985; Cassell, 1982; Engel, 1977; Holm & Aspegren, 1999; Newton et al. 2008; Toombs, 1993). Similarly, in a study of experienced nurses, Patricia Benner points out that when the experiences of a patient are foreign to the nurse, understanding comes by letting patients "teach the nurse what it is like to be in their shoes" (1984, p. 68). She notes, further, that those who were identified by colleagues as expert nurses "repeatedly described a committed, involved relationship" (p. 164). Similarly, medical practitioners who gained a reputation among the Karolinska medical students for being particularly skilful and were most admired by them consistently demonstrated this kind of relationship with patients, as well as with students. Rather than distancing themselves from patients as a protection from demanding situations, close engagement can provide health professionals with resources for dealing with those situations:

> Distancing techniques protect nurses from the pain in the situation, but they also prevent them from taking advantage of the resources and possibilities that come through engagement and participation in the patients' and families' meanings and ways of coping. (Benner, 1984, p. 164)

Suzanne Rosberg (2000), too, provides rich accounts of the way in which some physiotherapists draw upon resources such as these when they engage with patients in an involved, committed way. These studies provide examples of being with others (see Chapter 2) in ways that value, rather than neglect, their personhood. Collectively, these studies challenge assumptions about the need to maintain distance in providing healthcare. They also suggest ways forward in more adequately addressing the emotional demands of professional practice.

Being with People Who Seek Help

The examples of medical encounters above demonstrate that being with others is a key aspect of practice, as well as of learning to become professionals. Several of the students described how they became aware of the complexity of dealing with patients through encounters with them, rather than through explicit attention to this issue during the medical programme:

> *[From the medical programme] you've got a lot of knowledge, that isn't to be ignored. You've got medical knowledge. That's important. Then ... yes, then you've had to learn a bit about how to hand, like not learnt but got a bit of direction on how to be when you're with people, people who need help, people who are upset or angry or sick and so on because, you've been able to practise it in any case. You've like, no-one has, it's not something you've been taught or been given direction on in some way. But it's something you've seen and learnt, made mistakes and learnt and made mistakes again and learnt, more or less like that.* (Monica, 1st semester of 5th year, p. 33)

In his final semester, Gunnar also reflected on how his understanding of medical practice had shifted over time through encounters with patients:

> *What I thought in the beginning was just, like, it was that you'd just learn a lot of things and then you'd meet a patient and then you'd, like, have all the data in your head and spit out a diagnosis. Very airy fairy, of course. And then you'd treat and then the patient would be fine, I think. That was, yeah. So I had absolutely no idea about ... that different patients have different expectations about how a doctor should be.* (p. 29)

The awareness that develops through encounters with patients about their needs is a further challenge to the adequacy of a biomedical model. Moreover, it calls into question a focus on epistemology during medical education, at the expense of learning "how to be when you're with people who need help" during encounters that are a central part of professional practice.

Social Distancing in Medical Practice

A need to learn to be with others who seek help was evident when some medical students and experienced practitioners interacted with patients who differed markedly from themselves. Historically, wealthy patients have received better access to health care, as noted in the previous chapter. In a study of social work students, Jan Fook and colleagues identify a phenomenon they refer to as "social distancing", which involves "the distancing of people or groups seen as socially different.... This social distancing can be termed a type of 'othering' where workers become more sympathetic to or identify with those of similar social standing to them" (2000, pp. 153–154). This may be exacerbated by the tendency of medical students in some programmes to socialise mostly with other medical students (for example, Blakey, Blanshard, Cole, Leslie, & Sen, 2008). Like social workers, most medical practitioners and students are middle class, while medical students are typically in early adulthood, although patients are usually considerably more diverse. The phenomenon of social distancing was sometimes evident among the Karolinska medical students when they talked about patients. For example, Karl described a period in the medical programme when he thought the work with patients was "awful and dirty and tragic and so on. Lots of old people" (1st semester of 5th year, p. 49).

Some students recognised the challenges of relating to patients who differed from themselves, such as alcoholics or the elderly. Others pointed out the most vulnerable patients were often most at risk of not receiving the care they needed. For example, Lotta thought the handling of a Finnish alcoholic by experienced medical practitioners "wasn't the least bit patient-focused" (1st semester of 5th year, p. 12). Similarly, Monica related an example of a patient with serious health problems who did not receive the care she needed: "She became ill immediately after her husband had died and ... everyone thought it was sure to be psychological" (1st semester of 4th year, p. 16). The social distancing some of the students pointed out raises questions about the quality of care provided to those from another social class, culture, age and gender from the practitioners and students themselves, demonstrating an "objective" approach to the complexities that medical practice entails is an illusion.

Gender and Access to Medical Practice

In the history of medicine, not only has patients' access to medical care depended upon who they were, but so, too, has aspiring medical practitioners' access to education and opportunities in medical practice (see Chapter 5), as continues to be the case today. Several of the medical students in the longitudinal study raised the issue of the impact of gender on access to medical practice, either during medical education or for a subsequent choice of medical speciality (see also Newton et al., 2008). For instance, Karl felt female students were able to form a different contact with female gynaecologists and obstetricians than was the case for male students:

I had a feeling, and I've also talked about it with others, mostly guys, that it got a bit, that with a female-dominated course leadership, you're talking about women's issues and so it easily becomes more personal about women's diseases and their chat between the girls and the female course coordinators. That it often got to be a bit like a sewing circle, where viewpoints and ideas and questions from the male side of the course were seen as laughable or more that it was just a placement. (Karl, 2nd semester of 5th year, pp. 9–10)

At the same time, he found it easier to talk with female than male gynaecologists:

There were two women doctors in charge of the ward where I was, and yeah, they were very easy to get along with somehow. And quite careful to, or careful to explain. If you asked a question you got a reply.... I think sometimes it's much easier to communicate with a woman than with a man because, yeah, there's a different tolerance for, yeah, you don't necessarily have to be so correct in your manner with a woman. It's more, it can be more relaxed.... There's more room to, yeah, joke is maybe to go too far, but a bit, a bit more tolerance for person, to be your own personality. (Karl, 2nd semester of 5th year, p. 15)

Kristina, too, raised the issue of gender during the gynaecology and obstetrics course. She expressed apprehension that, as an inexperienced medical student, she may not be able to meet the expectations of female midwives during a placement in a maternity ward:

I remember I was scared about that in the beginning. I thought, God, that huge crowd of only women, you know, I thought, it can be a bit, it's only women really who are midwives. And I thought, yeah, and they know so well and midwives are so practical and they're no-nonsense and effective and I felt, a female medical student who comes there and is fumbling and that, but it went well.... They gave really good supervision.... So there wasn't suddenly a cold, off-putting look, but they expected you'd get involved and stand there fumbling with the needle and things like that. So it went well. It went well. (2nd semester of 5th year, p. 26)

Other students described what they perceived to be barriers to selecting particular medical specialities in their choice of career following the medical programme. For instance, Erik expressed concern that what he perceived to be decreasing numbers of male gynaecologists could discourage male medical students from entering this field. He reinforced gender stereotypes in accepting that surgery was not attractive as a field for women, but he considered gynaecology could be of interest to men if there were more male gynaecologists:

In ten years if there isn't a single male gynaecologist and no male nurse and no, like, then it can be a really big problem for medical students to come at all. Because then it can feel even more unnatural for men.
Interviewer: *Yes, sure, sure. Both for the patients and medical students, presumably.*

Yes, yes.

Interviewer: *Is this the same situation a little, but in the opposite direction, for surgery? How is it there where female surgeons are concerned?*

Yeah, there are a few more women there.
Interviewer: *There are?*

It is male-dominated, it is. But there aren't those psychological aspects there anyway. It's more, it has more to do with what kind of work you choose. Or it's a bit more macho to be a surgeon so there aren't so many women who are attracted to it. But gynaecology is actually really interesting. It's a very varied field.... Just the, it's a lot of surgery and lots more besides. It's not only gynae examinations. That's quite a small part of the whole thing, in actual fact. (2nd semester of 5th year, pp. 9–10)

Contrary to stereotype, Monica showed interest in surgery as a possible career, but she felt this was not encouraged by the male surgeons:

I like the fact that you actually, yeah literally, tangibly can see what the problem is and do something about it. And just the fact that you actually can have patients who are sick or have some problem and fix it. Put it in plaster or operate.
Interviewer: *You want to see the result immediately?*

Mm. So I think that's positive. I think bones are fun, actually. I think it's exciting. Skeleton, there's a lot that's, it's very easy to think it's just dead tissue but there's a lot that's like, a lot complicated in its own way [inaudible]. So I think it was fun. But we'll have to see how it goes. Because orthopaedics is a bit difficult.... First of all, it's very popular. But the problem, too, is that there are very few female doctors there. Extremely few. It's one of the specialties where there are very, yeah, very few women and there's a simple explanation for that, it's quite hard and heavy work. It's hard to perform a reduction, like to set bones in place [and secure them surgically] and like, but it isn't only that. It easily happens that it just continues the same as before. If there have always been men, then it's more difficult for women to come in.
Interviewer: *Do you think it's been difficult for you to come in?*

Yeah, I do, . . . Yeah, it, it has been. But that's something you know and that you expect when you come to that clinic.
Interviewer: *How do they treat the girls differently?*

No, well, I've been incredibly enthusiastic. I've gone on duty, like, six extra times and I've been there the whole time. I, like, they, I've shown my enthusiasm and my interest in all possible ways. I've studied extra, I, and it, you notice as

*long as you're there as an interested medical student it's just really great. But
as soon as you express, like, that this is something I would like to do in the
future, then it immediately becomes, then the atmosphere changes.*

Interviewer: *Uh huh, how do you mean?*

*Yeah, it mm, it's becomes like, they, there's a distancing in some way. Or it has
felt as though people haven't interacted with me in the same way any longer.
In the beginning it was: "Oh, do you want to come to the operation? Come
on, come and do this and this and this." But then, when they see it's more than
that, that you're interested more than just these four weeks, then it gets a bit.
But we'll see how it goes in the future. Yeah, I mean the only thing I want is
that they give me a fair chance.* (2nd semester of 4th year, pp. 3–5)

Being given a fair chance in selecting and pursuing a career after five-and-a-half
years of undergraduate medical studies followed by a 21-month internship seems
a reasonable expectation. Monica's account provides a counter-argument to the
stereotype that students of one gender or another are simply not interested in some
medical specialties. It also shows that students continue to experience barriers to
their engagement in, and choice of, medical specialty in ways that undermine the
inclusiveness and breadth of the profession. These barriers work against a climate
that would promote critical reflection and open possibilities for other ways of being
professionals.

Medical Practice as Service Provision

Resisting or excluding some aspiring professionals from entry to a profession in
ways not associated with their suitability or merit suggests maintaining the status quo is given precedence over provision of service to society. In the relatively
high status profession of medicine, vested interests in the status quo can be strong,
although medicine is not alone among professions in this respect. Not only does
maintaining the status quo divert focus from the service to be provided by the profession, but so, too, does emphasis on acquisition of biomedical knowledge and
skills in medical education programmes. In other words, focus is shifted away from
promoting the health and well-being of patients. A substantial number of students
in the Karolinska cohort were not assisted to achieve understanding of this purpose
in their practice of medicine (Dall'Alba, 2004).

Learning to achieve high quality service provision arguably presents a central
challenge to students and professional education programmes. Where these programmes fail to enhance ways of being professionals in line with this purpose, they
fall short of their mandate. Studies of experienced medical practitioners (Mishler,
1984; Stålsby Lundborg et al., 1999; Toombs, 1993), university teachers (Dall'Alba,
1993) and engineers (Sandberg, 1994, 2000) demonstrate that such a lack of focus
on the purpose of the enterprise extends well beyond medical students. Taken
together, these studies suggest an urgent need to critically examine the focus and
practices of professional education programmes.

Chapter 7
Learning Professional Ways of Being

Here's my life, steel-stitched at one end into my mother's belly,
then thrown out across nothing, like an Indian rope trick.
Continually I cut and retie the rope. I haul myself up, slither
down. What keeps the tension is the tension itself—the pull
between what I am and what I can become. The tug of war
between the world I inherit and the world I invent. I keep
pulling at the rope. I keep pulling at life as hard as I can. If the
rope starts to fray in places, it doesn't matter. I am so tightly
folded, like a fern or an ammonite, that as I unravel, the actual
and the imagined unloose together, just as they are spliced
together—life's fibres knotted into time.

(Winterson, 2001, p. 210)

This chapter extends the examination of learning to become professionals begun
in previous chapters, by more closely examining what is learned about practising as professionals during preparation for professional practice. More specifically,
the development of professional ways of being is explored over time during the
medical programme at Karolinska Institute. Formal programmes of preparation for
professional practice are typically periods of substantial change towards becoming
professionals. These changes not only include increasing experience of, and familiarity with, knowledge, routines and procedures relating to professional practice, but
also transformation and shifting awareness of the self, as professional. As noted in
Chapter 4, learning to become professionals has both epistemological and ontological dimensions, which is illustrated through case studies below. It involves not only
what we know and can do, but also who we are becoming.

As conceived here, professional ways of being are never formed once and for all,
but are concerned with this process of becoming. They are enacted and embodied
in the way we go about everyday activities that constitute professional practice.
Through these activities, we produce and reinforce our practice as professionals,
while being transformed over time through our engagement in practice. The development of professional ways of being includes, then, both continuity and transformation. In the quote that opens this chapter, Jeanette Winterson describes such
interplay as "the pull between what I am and what I can become. The tug of war
between the world I inherit and the world I invent". This process of becoming continues throughout our professional lives and is interwoven with the rest of our lives
in various ways.

G. Dall'Alba, *Learning to be Professionals*, Innovation and Change in Professional
Education 4, DOI 10.1007/978-90-481-2608-8_7,
© Springer Science+Business Media B.V. 2009

Professional ways of being are both individual and intersubjective, as we noted in Chapter 4. While it is possible to describe the development of professional ways of being for individuals over time, this development is derived from, and contributes to, intersubjective traditions of practice for the profession in question, as noted in Chapter 2 and elaborated in Chapter 6. For instance, the development of ways of being medical practitioners that is illustrated in the present chapter occurs in the context of traditions of practice for medicine that were described in Chapter 5. The form this development takes is shaped by the profession and its practice, as well as by the broader society impinging on this practice. However, professional practice is not singular or static, as noted in Chapter 2, but takes multiple forms and undergoes changes over time (see also Billett, 2001; Dall'Alba & Sandberg, 1996; Chaiklin & Lave, 1993; Knorr Cetina, 2001; Lamiani et al., 2008; Mol, 2002; Toulmin, 1976). It is precisely this complexity that students encounter and must deal with as they learn to become professionals (see Introduction to Chapter 1).

The case studies reported here are drawn from the longitudinal study in which 13 Karolinska medical students were interviewed individually towards the end of each semester during the clinical component of the medical programme (semesters 6–11; see Chapter 6 for further details on the programme). Each of the students was interviewed, then, on six occasions during a three-year period, with the exception of one student who was interviewed five times and could not be contacted near the end of the programme. The longitudinal study was carried out as part of research on a whole medical student cohort (Dall'Alba, 1998, 2004). Connected with the interviews, students were observed in consultation with patients each semester that this was possible. During some semesters, or the later part thereof when interviews occurred, the students did not consult with patients, although they may have observed consultations. In a small number of instances, it was not appropriate to have an observer present, such as during consultations with persons with severe psychiatric disorders.

Prior to observing each student in consultation with patients, approval to carry out the research was sought from the clinical director for the department in question and then from the medical practitioner who would be responsible for the student on the day of the visit. In most instances, these medical practitioners were open to, and often curious about, research that involved observing the students and their own interaction with them. In a few cases, however, there was some nervousness about observation of their practice. Before each patient consultation, the students requested consent to the presence of a researcher who would observe their practice and audio-record the consultation. All these requests were granted, with one patient first raising questions about the purpose of the observations. The consultations took place in teaching hospitals and health clinics where students would typically be accompanied by medical staff for at least part of a consultation, so patients and family members were aware of the likelihood additional adults may be present.

When consultations were being observed, efforts were made to focus on what the students were doing in an attempt to reduce any associated discomfort patients might experience. As well, observations were made while standing behind the student and to the side, to allow a clear view of what the student was doing, but at a distance from the patient. This was important given the observations occurred in situations where patients could feel exposed or vulnerable, especially during intimate physical examinations or when patients were unwell. It was also an attempt to avoid obstructing the students as they carried out their activities. For the most part, patients and students seemed primarily concerned with interacting with one another or with experienced medical practitioners when they entered into consultations. However, when responding to a student's or medical practitioner's questions, some patients included me in the conversation, such as through eye contact. On one occasion, during a consultation between an elderly woman and a young male student in a hospital gynaecology clinic, when the student briefly left the room the patient turned to me and said she was pleased to have another woman in the room during the gynaecological examination.

All interviews with students in the study included discussion about what had occurred during specific patient consultations, whether or not these had been observed. In this way, the conversations related to the students' engagement in, and observations of, medical practice. In particular, we discussed how the students had engaged with and experienced these consultations. With some guidance through questioning, the students described what they had done during specific consultations, what they had observed, how they felt the consultation had progressed and what they were attempting to do during the consultation. These discussions were situated within students' accounts of the courses and activities in which they had been involved during the semester in which the interviews took place. Our conversations then turned to the medical programme and its role in the students' development as medical practitioners. For instance, students identified what they had learned from the semester of study in which they were participating, challenges they had encountered, how they were developing towards becoming medical practitioners and ways in which the medical programme could more effectively support their learning.

The interviews and consultations were audio-recorded and transcribed verbatim, with written observations made during consultations. Interactions were also observed between the medical students and health professionals, including with medical practitioners who supervised the students during consultations. Observational notes were made of these interactions and the situations in which students found themselves during clinical visits. Based on the interviews and observations of students in consultation with patients over the duration of the clinical component of the programme, their development trajectories were analysed. The development trajectories that were investigated in the longitudinal study are the focus of this chapter.

Development Over Time: Unfolding Professional Ways of Being

Over the three years in which the interviews with students and observations of patient consultations occurred, the students gained relevant knowledge, learned to carry out medical procedures and solve medical problems, as well as moving progressively closer towards becoming medical practitioners, with the challenges and interrelationships this demanded. As they developed greater fluency and confidence with a broad range of medical routines and procedures, the part these routines and procedures were seen to play varied with the students' ways of enacting medical practice. Max van Manen (1999) makes a similar point about the way teaching techniques are used in teaching. All the medical students in the study, for example, learned to obtain information from patients about the problem or ailment for which they were seeking medical assistance. The students initially used a checklist of key questions to patients with which they were provided. For instance, they asked about the circumstances under which the patient's symptoms had first occurred, their duration, previous illnesses, whether the patient was regularly taking any medication, consumption of alcohol, whether the patient smoked and so on. Over time, the students' reliance on, and use of, this checklist varied, as they gained confidence in obtaining the information they sought.

More importantly, there was variation among the students in their style of questioning or discussion and, in particular, in the part the information obtained was seen to play within the medical consultation. For some students, obtaining the necessary information largely took the form of a question-and-answer sequence about symptoms, with a focus on diagnosis and subsequent treatment. In other cases, the discussion included not only symptoms but, to varying degrees, also their impact upon the patient's everyday activities (see also Chapter 6). Elliot Mishler (1984) has described similar differences in talk during patient consultations. He distinguishes the "voice of medicine" from the "voice of the lifeworld", noting it is unusual for medical practitioners to take account of the patient's lifeworld (see also Stålsby Lundborg et al., 1999).

Paralleling the differences in focus they adopted during consultations, medical practice took various forms when enacted by the students, demonstrating development of distinctly different ways of being medical practitioners during the programme. Paradoxically, among some students the programme promoted a biomedical focus on diseases and symptoms, while, to varying extents, others developed more complex, inclusive ways of being medical practitioners, incorporating the relevant experience of both patient and medical practitioner. These differences among students in the longitudinal study are consistent with those evident for the whole cohort (see Chapter 6; see also Dall'Alba, 1998, 2004). The complex, inclusive ways of enacting medical practice are arguably more consistent with—but some extend beyond—the stated aims of the programme, which included a range of personal qualities and dispositions, biomedical knowledge about diseases and symptoms, and productive doctor-patient relationships. In addition, these more inclusive ways of engaging in medical practice are closer to developments internationally towards patient-centred health care (see Chapter 5).

Not only was variation in ways of being medical practitioners evident among the students in the longitudinal study and in the wider cohort, but there were also patterns evident over time as the students sought to learn ways of being medical practitioners that were acceptable to themselves and others. A striking feature of the students' descriptions of, and reflections on, their developing practice of medicine is the integration of *what* they learned with *who* they were becoming. The two are intertwined in the students' accounts.

Among the students, the development of professional ways of being along differing trajectories over time was delimited—but not determined—by their understanding of medical practice when they embarked on clinical studies. Their ways of being medical practitioners unfolded over time. Further evidence of a similar form of unfolding as students learn in higher education settings can be seen in previous research (Beaty, Dall'Alba, & Marton, 1997), although this conceptualisation was not part of the earlier study. Conceptualising the development of professional ways of being as unfolding along trajectories contrasts starkly with a notion of accumulating knowledge and skills in an additive or linear fashion (see Chapter 3). Implicit in the notion of unfolding along development trajectories is that transformation does not occur only in a specific direction over time; many trajectories are possible (see also Dall'Alba & Sandberg, 2006).

Not only does the development of our ways of being unfold over time, but this process is always embedded within a web of interrelationships through entwinement with our world (see Chapter 2). For medical students and experienced practitioners encountering patients, such a web of interrelationships includes the health care system, its procedures and its function in relation to citizens' health. The practice of medicine refers and belongs to this web of interrelationships. Interpreting medical encounters within this web of involvement gives rise to ways of being medical practitioners that are continually reinforced and renewed for both individual professionals and the profession as a whole.

Two cases are used below to demonstrate this unfolding of professional ways of being along different trajectories, beginning when the students embarked on clinical studies. For example, for Karl medical practice involved selecting among a range of solutions to a patient's problem that the health care system has to offer, as well as informing the patient when no solution was available. In this approach, the health care system was taken as the frame of reference and the patient's problem matched against available solutions. In contrast, for Lotta a health problem or ailment was embedded within and impacted upon the patient's life, which needed to be addressed in dealing with the health issue. The task at hand involved taking the patient's life situation as the frame of reference and working with each patient to find a solution that worked. The selection of two illustrative cases carries with it a risk the cases can be seen as setting up a duality relating to practice, such as good/bad, uncaring/caring and so on. Setting up such a duality is not the purpose of outlining these cases here. Rather, they are included to illustrate continuity and transformation as professional ways of being unfold and take shape along different development trajectories during a professional education programme. These cases illustrate only two of a range of development trajectories that were evident during this study.

Case 1: Karl

Karl spent his childhood and adolescence in a small town south-west of Stockholm. After completing his schooling, he spent 12 months living in a Continental European country, studying the language and culture. He then studied economics in southern Sweden before entering the medical programme at the age of 24. Karl applied and was accepted through both a university entrance examination and local admission procedures, although he wasn't certain about his choice of medicine as a career until well into the programme. While remaining interested in economic questions, he had decided to study medicine as he considered it would be more stimulating in the longer term with a broader range of career options, reducing the risk he might "get stuck in a little office somewhere" (final semester, pp. 55–56). During consultations, Karl was pleasant with patients, while sometimes a little distracted or unfocused, as he himself pointed out. In the first clinical semester during his third year in the medical programme, he talked about being uncertain how to proceed in patient consultations:

> *You haven't really thought things through at the start. You don't have clear ideas about what's wrong with the patient. You can't target your medical history taking and direct your examination really. You do quite a broad examination. You examine, listen, look, and feel all over the place....It's the same with the questions [to patients].* (2nd semester of 3rd year, p. 9)

His focus was diseases and symptoms, with a view to diagnosis and treatment. He later came to regard paying attention to patients as a means to diagnosis and treatment. When discussing his development as a medical practitioner, Karl placed emphasis on the facts he was learning that enabled him to diagnose and treat diseases according to a scientific model. In later semesters, he also included the need to "be your own person" and "make your own decisions". In several semesters, he spontaneously raised the issue of empathy, initially indicating he was concerned at his lack of empathy with patients, then later indicating he had made progress through observing a few doctors who were exceptional in showing empathy to patients even after many years of medical practice.

In the first clinical semester, Karl examined and talked with a 48 year old man, Lars, who was lying on an examination table in a hospital room. Lars had been brought by ambulance to the hospital with chest pain the night before. While Lars described the pain and his anxiety when it had continued, Karl sought information about the symptoms:

> Lars: *It was as though someone stood on me about here [indicating an area on his chest]*
>
> Karl: *Did it feel as though you were straining to breathe?*
>
> Lars: *Yeah, I breathed, I tried to take deep breaths like this to, I wasn't really straining, but it was sort of, yeah you could say it was straining. But I was given oxygen the whole time [once the ambulance arrived], but, but it was like as though it wasn't enough, you know. Do you know what I mean? I actually wanted more oxygen.*
>
> Karl: *Yes, yes. Did you feel, did you think about how fast your heart was beating? Was it beating quickly? Did it feel as though it was thumping normally?*
>
> Lars: *Yes, it started to. But not in the beginning so then I took it quietly, but then I felt it wasn't easing. I thought it would ease like it did on*

Saturday.... But then when it didn't ease, I started taking deep breaths. Then I broke out in a cold sweat and I felt, I noticed my wife getting anxious and everyone else around me and then, then my heart rate went up again. But I didn't really think it felt worse from that. My pulse was high, they said when they came, 170 over, what was it? 90 or something like that

Karl: *That was blood pressure.*

Lars: *yeah, when they came. And I normally have low blood pressure....*

Karl: *Have you felt something like this before when you've exerted yourself?*

Lars: *I felt it during the day, it was there from the beginning. I didn't feel anything on Sunday and I even played bandy a bit in the park with the young kids, but I didn't feel anything then. Other than that I could feel a little bit of a burning feeling. Like yesterday when I went for a walk at work and I thought I'd breathe properly and that. So off I went and I went up a hill at the back. And when I was going up the hill, I was a bit short of breath and then I felt it, I recognised the feeling,*

Karl: *Mm*

Lars: *ah, it's, now it's back again. There's obviously something that isn't right, because I'm not so unfit. Even if I haven't been exercising lately, I'm not so unfit that I can't go up a hill, you know.*

Karl: *You don't usually, do you usually exercise?* (pp. 31–32)

Consistent with his focus during the consultation, in the interview that followed, when Karl talked about the practice of medicine, he placed emphasis on investigating symptoms to reach a diagnosis and treat patients:

Interviewer: *What do you think is central to the work of a medical doctor?*

Central to the work of a doctor? It's this investigating the diseases to reach a diagnosis and just as much it's presumably treating it, following up the result of the treatment. They follow from each other. It's the quite active parts that are central ... Firstly, that's what the patients are looking for, to get help with. Secondly, that's what you've educated yourself to be able to do or thought you'd be able to. That's what all the investigations and things are aiming towards.... In one way or another, the goal is to work out what to do, to treat different ailments.

Interviewer: *Mm, mm. What do you think are the most important things you've learnt in the medical programme so far?*

That's a bit difficult. They overlap.... The most important is probably physiology and pathology and then the practical application of it here [in the clinic]....

Interviewer: *Can you explain that a little?*

I think, for example, that physiology looks quite concretely at how organs function and how oxygen exchange works, how systems are built up, how they work. Pathology looks at how things can go wrong when something doesn't work. And then this [clinical] medicine course develops how you should, what methods you can use to work out further what's wrong. You have to have physiology as your base, like the way to think and then you investigate and then you reach an answer. It's those, it feels as though those are the most important parts. (pp. 47–50)

In Karl's descriptions of medical practice, the role played by the medical practitioner is clearly in focus, as it also is in the interview extracts below. The "active parts" he identifies as central to medical practice are active for the medical practitioner, not necessarily for the patient.

During the interview, Karl raised the issue of lack of empathy and feeling impatient with patients. He used the example of an 80 year old man he had examined who had been admitted to the hospital with chest pain early in the morning a few days beforehand:

He was quite anxious. He complained a lot, had pain everywhere, had been operated on here and there. He had cramps and was grumbling a bit. He was that sort, kind of. It wasn't only that he had chest pain, he had pain in his knee and his legs and his stomach and reflux. . . . I got quite impatient, actually [but] I think he felt quite well treated. . . . We were able to communicate. I was able to get the ques, the answers I wanted. Or I could ask the questions I wanted answers to. I got responses quite well and then we could even talk a little, a little less formally, too. You could behave quite correctly, or how can you put it? a little more, it seemed as though you attended to the patient a little more than you do sometimes. Sometimes you're pressured and uninterested and tired of all the complaining and nagging.

Interviewer: *Mm mm. You are sometimes?*

Yes, you sure are. It's an awful development, I hope it changes. But I really feel impatient and lacking in empathy for the patient. You just stand there and look. It can be incredibly dramatic, like a cardiopulmonary resuscitation and things like that, and you just stand and watch, quite unmoved. . . . It's starting to be the case that you distance yourself a little too much. It's

Interviewer: *Is this a development you've noticed this semester?*

Yes, maybe it was especially noticeable then because you meet patients so much, but already at the beginning of pathology and onwards when you do post-mortems the whole time, then I think, then you start to close off. (pp. 23–27)

Earlier in the interview, Karl demonstrated this distancing from the patient when describing how he had taken a bone marrow sample from an elderly patient:

You prick a hole in the pelvis so it makes a cracking sound. First you've given an injection [local anaesthetic]. . . . It gave me a real kick. I was on a high the whole afternoon. . . .

Interviewer: *How was it that you got such a kick?*

It's quite, you do the whole process. . . . First you've found the right place then you give the injection, then you prick the needle through the bone and it's a feeling you're really unfamiliar with. Then you suck it up. . . . There are several steps you look after yourself. . . . This is maybe the most advanced thing a medical student is allowed to do during this course. And you only get to do it if you're lucky and are with the right doctor and the patient turns up. It's in the same class maybe as puncturing a knee or a joint on an arthritic patient, which is a bigger, a bit more advanced. It can go wrong a bit.

Interviewer: *How did it go in this case?*

It went OK. . . . I didn't get much bone marrow, so I had to do it again. I think the process was right. It can be really difficult. It was quite an elderly person, so it can be difficult to get to the bone marrow in that investigation.

Interviewer: *So you were on a high all afternoon?*

Just about. I think it's important, not just because you learn a lot and it's difficult in some way, but to have done it, a "test" like that, and others have done things that are difficult and so you get self-confidence that "I can do that". (semester 6, pp. 3–4)

Mastering various medical procedures is, understandably, seen by the students as an achievement and contributes to their increasing confidence in becoming medical practitioners. However, a focus on diagnosis and treatment reduces the patient to a set of symptoms and diseases. It carries a risk that the person who is the patient is overlooked, as Karl's comments about lack of empathy indicate.

In interviews with Karl and observations of his interactions with patients, it is evident that patients provide the means by which Karl can become a medical doctor; they are there for him, rather than the reverse. Given Karl is a student in a medical programme, he can be expected to have an interest in his own development towards becoming a medical practitioner. However, it might be argued that a central aspect of learning to be professionals is recognising that professions provide a service to society, as noted in the aims for the programme (see also Chapter 6). This is a primary reason societies invest considerable resources in educating professionals. There is a tension, then, between the learning needs of students who aspire to be professionals and the need to provide a service to society. This tension was evident in various ways throughout the study. When Karl later began to pay attention to the patient, this did not involve major transformation in his way of being a medical doctor, as we see below. However, given Karl had begun to attend to the patient, there may be scope for such transformation in the future.

About eighteen months later, early in his fifth year of the medical programme, Karl was feeling some anxiety about whether he could manage his future career as a medical practitioner. At the same time, he was encouraged by his observation that when he consulted with patients, he was almost always on the right track. Being on the right track continued to be primarily about diagnosis and treatment, although Karl acknowledged this was somewhat at odds with patients' views:

People often have strong ideas about how a doctor should be or not be. And you should behave in a certain way. . . . You have to remember there's a lot to gain through positive contact with patients and behaving in the correct way and doing things well. But, but that's not actually what's central. It's medicine that's central and the actual problem and how you can solve it. But a lot of that happens behind the scenes, and you need to see how it happens. And [maybe] the patient feels untreated, even though there have been hour-long discussions, and maybe X-rays and team meetings, and you've talked with colleagues and various specialists have had input on different parts. You see a lot more of that if you're involved in it. And then the picture you get is that that's what's essential. That's where most of the work happens, not in the room with the patient, which are usually short meetings. And in those meetings, a lot has to be evaluated. The results of the treatment have to be evaluated maybe or the symptoms have to be evaluated. And which are the important ones? What does this suggest? And then choosing the right method of examination. Then the part about positive contact with yeah, listening and so on, I think it takes a back seat. It, it becomes an increasingly smaller part of what the work is about. . . . No-one is just born a good doctor. You have to go through, you have to learn raw facts. And that's where I think there's a discrepancy between what you thought before and what people, in general, think and what you think later. (pp. 46–47)

Karl then reflected that his focus on medicine—or, more accurately, biomedical aspects of medical practice—was being directed over time in this way by the medical programme. He then raised again the notion of empathy with patients:

On the other hand, and I think we talked about this last time, too, your view of the patient changes from in the beginning being very empathetic and I think there was a period when I saw the patient as just a phenomenon. And it wasn't the person you saw behind it then. You didn't care so much about what they felt and it was maybe a kind of defence mechanism. You thought it was awful and dirty and tragic and so on. Lots of old people. You'd had enough of it in some way. But I think, and I really hope, that that picture is becoming more nuanced. And a little more to get back to really seeing that it's a person and take time to listen and take, never forget you have to take those people into account.

Interviewer: *And you said, too, when you described what the work of a doctor involves, that you gain from treating patients in a reasonable way and so on. What do you think you gain from that?*

. . . If I win their confidence, then maybe they'll do what I say. And then my treatment will be better and they feel better, too. So it, plus it's often described as the problem when there are formal complaints made. It's misunderstanding that's at the bottom of it. It's dysfunctional communication that's definitely the grounds. Although it's a bit of a crass view, but that would be why. (pp. 49–50)

The reason Karl gives for taking patients into account closely parallels that put forward in an article in *Academic Medicine*:

> Empathy is one of the most highly desirable professional traits that medical education should promote, because empathic communication skills promote patient satisfaction and adherence to treatment plans while decreasing the likelihood of malpractice suits. (Newton et al., 2008)

So, once again, we see Karl is not atypical in his view.

In his final semester, as Karl approached the end of the five-and-a-half year programme, he continued to place emphasis on the biomedical aspects of medicine, but he again mentioned listening to patients, both to what they ask and possibly what they tell. As his way of being a medical practitioner unfolded over the course of the programme, his inclusion of listening demonstrates that ways of being are open to possibilities. As new aspects of practice become revealed through experience, they can be incorporated into our ways of being, provided we are sufficiently open to their inclusion. Often, however, rather than substantially transforming us, new aspects are incorporated with little change to our ways of being. For instance, listening to patients enabled Karl to obtain the information he needed for diagnosis and treatment or to provide patients with answers to their questions. It did not transform the way he practised medicine in any substantial way. Karl continued to emphasise biomedical aspects of the practice of medicine, highlighting the agency of the medical practitioner while the patient was cast as an information source:

> *A good doctor is, partly, is skilled . . . within medicine, who clearly has very much the whole process from physiology to medicines, or however you can describe it. Who has an overall picture of that. Who also has a feeling for what's likely, can judge likelihood. You can call it a feeling for that, but also a little facts: What produces this? It can be this or that. Preferably someone who also works from facts, you know: These facts point to this, can it be that? . . . Who doesn't get stressed and try to do too much, include too much in an investigation. Keeps this in mind when he's forming a judgement. Being a good doctor also means that he or she is able to listen to what people say, what they're actually asking and possibly telling you. And be able to get that out, or get out the responses that are needed to take the medical history and things like that. And be able to say clinically what it is. Keep track of the tests and examinations. But at the same time be so self-assured that they can be their own person towards the people around. (pp. 45–46)*

Karl summarised what he had been saying, as follows:

> *[A good doctor is someone who] must be skilful, is able to capture what's important, and preferably achieve results, of course. Can't be full of prestige . . . be their own person (p. 47).*

When elaborating on the need to be your own person, Karl noted that his development was also influenced by interactions outside the medical programme, especially through encountering prejudice towards medical doctors:

[There are] conflicts with other people, very often debate and you often get questions that are, that provoke you in a way, [they're] prejudiced in some way. Often heaps of ideas and examples about treatment mistakes by other people that you didn't have anything to do with. . . . Every time you say what you do . . . it leads to some kind of reaction that in some way forces you to, forces you at least to take a position. (pp. 39–40)

Karl's unwillingness to take responsibility for the actions of other medical practitioners, while understandable, appears to be somewhat in tension with his desire to become an accepted member of the medical profession, which has a reputation for closing ranks around its members when they are under scrutiny.

When looking back over his development from the beginning to the end of the medical programme, Karl reflected, as follows:

Well, I feel like the same person that I was then [at the beginning of the programme]. . . . You see with the same perspective almost. But I think a lot has happened. I think I have, I feel quite confident within medicine, a bit independent, ready to take the step, ready to have people come to me, given I've done this medical programme and I can start to work, even if I'm a long way from being able to do much, but that's the way it is anyway. . . . Both because you get a bit older but also you've done what you wanted and grown into the role a bit. (pp. 38–39)

He then elaborated on the process of change he had experienced, again raising the tension between engagement and distance from patients:

During the medical programme you meet patients, you see awful things. You study, you learn. You learn to understand a scientific way of thinking that you didn't have from the beginning. I think that's a big part. Yeah, that part and then a look at how people think and a bit more understanding for how other people think. . . . Partly the empathetic, you can understand that a person suffers from a situation that you might think is not so bad, or you can, you try to put yourself in that person's situation a bit. And also learn not to put yourself in, or take it with you too much or become too involved. . . . You constantly have new experiences in this branch. . . . Sometimes I think you have, it's been tough. You have to perform, you really have to get something done under time pressure and you have to be alert and that, and so anyway it might be difficult to be there. You might come in contact with people whose fate is a heavy burden, but you distance yourself from it. And there's also a kind of, you ought to get involved in this maybe, but you don't. (pp. 40–41)

In further describing the change process, Karl pointed to the importance of support from other medical students. In contrast, he seemed to have difficulty providing support to some patients, admitting to being impatient in cases when he considered there was nothing he could do:

I think, what I think helps is that you're with other students in the same situation. You know that. You learn to relate to each other. I think everyone has something they have trouble dealing with. . . . [For me] things that aren't engaging are difficult, that aren't anything, that aren't hopeful, so you can't do anything. It's, like, uneventful and you have to get involved in some way, otherwise, otherwise I can't muster any interest or I can't achieve anything. I think that's negative. Because that's often the way it is with medicine patients and, yeah, most of all maybe some of them with a heap of extra things that have to be organised so it can work and it's part of your role. (pp. 42–43)

Karl felt, though, that through the medical programme he was becoming more open-minded over time:

The question of how you've changed as a person, that's extremely difficult. It's really difficult to have any real idea about. . . . It's a certain way of thinking. . . . When I was a bit younger I thought, you just think it was black and white. I think the medical programme has done a lot to show there's very rarely yes or no, or black or white. . . . Partly there's such a big variation between different individuals and then during a period of time, in one hospital something is done in a particular way, and it works there. Then you come somewhere else: "You can't do that. . . . We do it this way." Then you see, ah ha, presumably it works both ways. (pp. 43–45)

In sum, with his focus on symptoms and diseases for the purpose of diagnosis and treatment, albeit with some acknowledgement of the patient, Karl can be seen as a prototype of this medical programme, and many other such programmes elsewhere. Based upon the descriptions of the programme provided by the students and discussions with a broad range of those teaching in the programme, Karl's view matched the focus of the programme, in its implementation or enactment. This view is consistent with the prevalent view of medicine in the literature (for example, see Anderson, 1995; Coulehan, 2005; Engel, 1977; Germov, 2005a; Sacks, 1985; Svenaeus, 1999; Toombs, 1993; Toulmin, 1976). As we see in Karl's case, the programme had not yet fully addressed the tension between focusing on diagnosis and treatment, while also taking the patient into account. The patient has been incorporated into the programme without a substantial shift in focus.

Similarly, the development of Karl's way of being a medical doctor parallels changes at the collective level of the profession in the sense that societal demands for more patient-focused healthcare have often been incorporated into existing ways of enacting the practice of medicine. In other words, although increased attention must now be paid to the patient, this requirement is typically incorporated into prevalent ways of being medical practitioners, rather than bringing about substantial transformation within the profession, as research on experienced medical practitioners shows (for example, Stålsby Lundborg et al., 1999). However, not all students in the longitudinal study unquestioningly adopted a primarily biomedical focus (see Chapter 6 for examples), reflecting a similar tension in the practice of medicine among the broader profession. While acknowledging the importance of biomedical dimensions of medical practice, some of the students considered a biomedical focus to be incomplete, as demonstrated by Lotta in case 2 below. The development of

ways of being medical practitioners for students like Lotta followed trajectories
that differed from that for Karl and those who shared his way of being a medical
practitioner. Instead, a re-interpretation of medical practice is evident for some of
the students that we also see among some experienced medical practitioners (see, for
example, Burroughs et al., 2006; Camargo & Coeli, 2006; Donnelly, 1996; Stålsby
Lundborg et al., 1999).

Case 2: Lotta

Lotta was raised and went to school in Stockholm, then spent six months in a European country learning the language, before entering the Karolinska medical programme through the local admission process. She was 18 years old when she entered
the programme, a little younger than most in her cohort. Despite her relatively
young age, among the group of 13 students Lotta was one of the most reflective
and constructively critical about medical practice, and about her own development
as a medical practitioner. Her way of practising medicine was also uncommon in
this group in the extent to which she incorporated both medical and patient perspectives. While completing the clinical semesters of the medical programme, Lotta
had noticed a gap between the clear-cut way in which biomedical knowledge is
presented in books and lectures, and the often more diffuse and complex problems
patients brought to her. As noted in Chapters 1 and 3, Donald Schön (1983, 1995)
has called this gap into question in his critique of the separation of knowledge
acquisition and application. As Lotta sought to develop her way of being a medical
practitioner, the discrepancy between textbook knowledge and practice seemed to
provide food for thought.

   When discussing her development as a medical practitioner, Lotta emphasised
the importance of the contact she had with patients. This interaction was also central to her interest in studying medicine and her choice of specialisation on grad-
uating from the medical programme. Lotta considered the programme provided
opportunities to interact with a broad range of patients, as well as providing the
medical knowledge for assisting patients to deal with their ailments. Throughout the
longitudinal study, she talked about the importance of relating the necessary medical
knowledge to patients' life situations. She sought to understand patients' perspectives and considered this central to the skilful practice of medicine, as do a range of
others (Baron, 1985; Burroughs et al., 2006; Charon, 1989; Coulter, 2002; Donnelly,
1996; Montgomery Hunter, 1991; Svenaeus, 1999; Toombs, 1993).

   During consultations, Lotta began by asking the patients how they were and what
they wanted help with. The course the conversation then took depended upon issues
the patients raised, with Lotta asking questions to clarify their problem or ailment.
In the first clinical semester, during her third year, Lotta had a consultation with a
65 year old widow, Ester, in a hospital medicine clinic. Ester had diabetes and, on
the advice of her general practitioner, was reluctantly considering insulin injections.
Lotta talked with Ester about her sugar levels, blood pressure, medication, previous
ailments, illnesses in her family and home situation. Ester admitted to having some

difficulty keeping track of all the detail of her previous ailments. When discussing Ester's diabetes, Lotta asked about her diet. At this point, Ester began talking about the death of her husband several years earlier. This issue was then incorporated into the conversation about Ester's health:

> Lotta: *How has it been, taking care of your diabetes where food and things are concerned? Do you think it's going well?*
>
> Ester: *Well, it's quite tedious cooking just for one. It comes down to that....*
>
> Lotta: *Mm, I understand it's boring cooking when there's no-one to offer it to. I feel the same way.*
>
> Ester: *It's difficult.*
>
> Lotta: *You have to find someone to invite for a meal* [laughing]
>
> Ester: [laughs] *But you get so lazy, so you think that's troublesome, too. I miss my husband, you know, you're [used to being] two. [Now] You'd have to prepare a meal and be pleasant and you don't really have the energy for all that at once.*
>
> Lotta: [laughing] *No, it's good to have a husband you don't have to be pleasant to!*
>
> Ester: [laughs] *It's difficult being alone.*
>
> Lotta: *I understand that.... Was it a while ago he passed away?* (pp. 43–45)

In an interview after the consultation, Lotta again demonstrated her efforts to understand Ester's health problem within the context of its impact on her life. She reflected on the importance of interaction with patients, as follows:

> *When you talk with them, you find out a lot, if they've become worse or better or what the problem is. In older medical records, like now, there isn't much that seems right. [She gives examples from the consultation.] The patient doesn't even remember these [health problems reported in the records]. Everyone doesn't see things in the same way ... the patient says one thing, but the doctor thinks you should write something different. That's how I see what happens. [Pause] It went quite well. Her [sugar] levels were a little high, she may have had some discomfort from sweating and difficulty sleeping, and wanted to do something about that, but at the same time she was fearful of starting [insulin] injections. It always feels awful, it's a big step for a diabetic.... It said in her medical records that they tried to change her diet so she was given advice about nutrition, but it hasn't gone so well. The problem isn't that she doesn't know what she should eat, but it's tedious to have diabetes. There's a lot to think about and you have to have some understanding about that. Then you have to make judgements about complications and what kinds of problems they have.* (pp. 62–63)

Later in the interview, Lotta emphasised the importance of patient contact for medical practice. She also noted, though, that the medical programme had primarily given her theoretical knowledge:

Interviewer: *What do you think is central to the work of a medical doctor? What's central to the work of a doctor for you?*

It's patient contact. That's what feels most enjoyable and attracts me most. At the same time it wouldn't be fun to just meet patients all day every day, but that's what everything revolves around.... I'd like to see some continuity, meeting the same patient over a period of time, so you develop a relationship and come to know each other....

Interviewer: *Mm, OK. What do you think are the most important things you've learnt in the medical programme so far?*

Well, the most important [pause] in some way the most important has to be theoretical knowledge. The rest is difficult to learn...for the most part you have to work out for yourself how you should act [laughing]...but if you don't have a base in theoretical knowledge you can't do anything. (pp. 71–72)

Just over 18 months later, early in her fifth year of the medical programme, Lotta again spoke about the need to take the point of departure from patients, identifying their problems or ailments and finding a way forward within the context of their lives. Lotta felt the patients were in focus in courses that semester and she was particularly receptive to what she could learn about being a skilful medical practitioner. By her own accounts, Lotta's experiences during the semester had a substantial impact on her development as a doctor. Prior to the interview, she had done four weeks of a psychiatry course, including periods in an open psychiatric ward and a clinic for alcoholics. One of the things that impressed Lotta during the course was observing the way doctors, psychologists, social workers, occupational therapists and physiotherapists worked together in teams, bringing their varied expertise to bear on a patient's problem, as well as supporting each other when working with demanding patients. She contrasted this with lack of clarity and guidance during the medical programme about "how a doctor should be" (p. 29) when compared with other health professionals. She considered this lack of clarity and direction created difficulties for learning to be medical practitioners.

Another feature of the psychiatry course that made an impression on Lotta was that it highlighted "the whole person, how everything is related to everything else" in a way she considered relevant for all branches of medicine (p. 10). She had learned to see:

another side of human beings...I could see the whole person, both the psychological and physical. And not just an arm or only a liver, as tends to be the case, particularly in specialised hospitals that have different sections for all the organs....I felt the whole person was so important. (p. 5)

When elaborating, Lotta explained the medical relevance of emphasising the whole person in the context of their lives:

We usually say [in the medical records] whether they're unemployed or if they have, or what kind of work they do maybe, but I think it's broader than this. To know whether they're getting on well, if they're generally happy, if they're in good spirits or if anything feels difficult just now. It's a question of how they can deal with an illness in all this and also to judge how relevant the symptoms are. If someone comes in with stomach pain and you know they're going through a difficult divorce and the children are getting up to things, you can't dismiss the symptoms, but you need to keep all this in mind. (p. 20)

Lotta remarked, though, that it would be difficult to put forward an approach highlighting the whole person in the other hospital wards and clinics, where the emphasis was on individual organs. She gave the example of a Finnish alcoholic who came in drunk to the hospital and there was no-one who could understand Finnish there at the time. He had been sent to the psychiatry clinic but didn't want to go and complained of hip pain, so he was sent to the orthopaedics clinic. There Lotta examined him and thought he seemed sensitive to touch over the kidneys, not far from the area where his hip pain was:

> *I said to the doctor, "I think he seems sensitive to touch over the kidneys. Can't we take a lab test to check it?" But he thought, "No, because if he had kidney pain he should be referred to the medical clinic. And so it wasn't here in orthopaedics that they should do the test".... He thought the patient should instead be sent to psychiatry. And then I said, "Should we write something in the referral to psychiatry about this?" "No, because then they'll wonder why we haven't done anything about it." And I felt this wasn't the least bit patient-focused, while he thought ... that if you get a referral you respond to the issue and you don't put forward other theories and you don't do anything but that.... Unfortunately, that's how it works in large teaching hospitals. You only check what your section deals with.... And I think it will be changed, it will become more patient-focused and the doctors will run around instead of the patients being sent here and there.* (pp. 12–13)

Consistent with her continuing emphasis on patients' perspectives, Lotta emphasised the health problems or ailments for which patients wanted help. In making this point, she related an example about a doctor who misunderstood why a patient had come:

> *A young woman came who had a little area on her back that was very painful ... and it was clear that it was a little nerve ending that was affected in some way. And the doctor told her that's just what it was: "So you don't need to be anxious." But the girl wasn't there because she was anxious. She was there because it was painful and she wanted help, while the doctor was very pleased she could state it wasn't dangerous. And I felt that she didn't understand the patients at all, what they wanted. But that's most central to what you're there for.... Why is the patient there and what does the patient want from me?* (p. 18).

Lotta's critical reflections about medical practice show her recognition of the need to provide a service to patients. When reflecting on her development during the medical programme, Lotta felt her view of what was central to medical practice hadn't changed, but she had learned a lot about how to be this kind of doctor. She elaborated the importance of an emphasis on taking the point of departure from each patient for her unfolding way of being a medical practitioner:

> *I want all the patients who come to me to feel a little better when they leave, irrespective of in what way they feel better, as well as feeling they've at least been able to put forward their problem. Then if I can do anything about it I've at least shown I understand. And I think a doctor's task is to treat those diseases that can be treated, that's central. But then you also have to try to have the whole patient feeling better. . . . But if someone comes in with pneumonia, then I give them penicillin. And I see my task as knowing when it's pneumonia, when it's something else and how I can determine what it is and what medicine I'll give. That's my task. And my task is also to inform the patient about what will happen and who will do what, and what kind of follow-up there will be and what they can do, the role they can have and how it can influence the course of events. And to see they feel understood and they can influence how we proceed, so it isn't just someone in the hospital deciding about them. . . . You have to have the patient with you, otherwise it doesn't work to go against them. And I feel my role is to take all patients seriously. . . . Every visit to the doctor is important for the person who comes. You have such a role as a doctor, you have such power over patients. It isn't until I tell you you're sick that you're sick. And you have to have a lot of respect and humility about that. What an incredible position of dependence the patient ends up in. And even if it isn't a serious illness but is mild, for someone who's never been sick it's a big problem. Just starting from where the patient is at and not from me as doctor who sees a lot of suffering every day. . . . That's what makes you a good doctor, in my view, that you start from each patient.* (pp. 57–60)

During this and subsequent semesters, Lotta also talked about the part each medical specialty plays in the practice of medicine, as it relates to helping patients with problems they bring. As noted above, she expressed some frustration at the way in which the point of departure in large teaching hospitals tends to be the medical specialty, not the patient. Not only did she consider her patients' health problems within the context of their lives, more broadly, but she also talked about her efforts to balance her own working life with her life outside work.

In her final semester, after almost five-and-a-half years in the medical programme, Lotta continued to emphasise the need to take the point of departure from patients, identifying their problem or ailment in the broader context of their lives. She clearly demonstrated this focus in a health clinic early in the week, in consultation with a middle-aged woman, Karin, who was in pain after an operation. After Karin limped in to the consultation room and sat down, Lotta asked her what the problem was:

Karin: *On September 13 [about a month beforehand], I had a hysterectomy*
Lotta: *Mm*

Karin: *and I haven't been well since then. And now there's only a week left of my sick leave.*

Lotta: *Mm*

Karin: *And I've been in pain the whole time and only taken [non-prescription painkiller] but it doesn't help with this horrible pain.*

Lotta: *Mm mm*

Karin: *And last ... Monday I rang the doctor and wanted to know the test results, if there was any cancer left or not, but the results weren't ready.*

Lotta: *Mm*

Karin: *And I was to ring yesterday, which I did. Last Monday I told them I was in pain, I have, it's swollen around the scar. I think so anyway. And it's, it's sore and I can't sleep properly, I haven't been able to sleep the whole time*

Lotta: *Mm*

Karin: *so I'm exhausted.*
Lotta: *Yes, I understand. Why were you operated on?*

Karin explained there were abnormal cells that were pre-cancerous and so she had to have a hysterectomy.

Lotta: *Mm, but is the scar itself painful now?*

Karin: *No, it's all this [indicating an area across the lower abdomen], this whole area. I can't sleep properly and I can't turn over and I can't walk and I can't sit for long periods. Everything is difficult.*

Lotta: *Yes, I understand. Were you given a time to go back to, was it [name of local] hospital?*

Karin: *Yes, I should go this Friday. Then on Monday I'm supposed to go back to work.*

Lotta: *You won't be able to.*

Karin: *But if I have to wait until Friday like this, [tearfully] I'm exhausted.*
Lotta: *Yes, I can see that.*

Lotta asked Karin additional questions about the pain, her use of painkillers, and whether she had contacted the hospital to arrange an earlier appointment.

Lotta: *And have you been in this much pain the whole time? Or how has it felt since the operation?*

Karin: *It's slightly better, but not much better, only slightly. But the restriction of movement is about, yeah, it's been like this since I was in hospital. It was as though no-one listened and really looked at how I was feeling. I tried to tell them I wasn't up to leaving, but I had to go anyway.*

Lotta helped Karin onto the examination table and carefully examined the painful area, clarifying where the pain was located. She then asked an experienced doctor to come in while Karin was on the examination table. All three agreed the gynaecology clinic at the hospital should be contacted and asked to allow Karin to come in as soon as possible. At this point, Karin said:

> *You've listened to me anyway.* (p. 25) *Thanks for listening to me.* (p. 27)

After the consultation, Lotta described the encounter, as follows:

> *She was a little desperate, completely exhausted after what she's been through. And she thought she wasn't well treated at the hospital, either. All the same, she was pleased to be going back there now. I felt a little that now we're send- ing her to the people she was already disappointed with. . . . I tried to think whether it could be something else: her stomach, urine, but it was exactly above where she'd been operated on. So the thought was whether there might have been some bleeding and that was why she was like this. Otherwise there isn't so much more we can do here because gynae has to take care of it. So it was more that it felt really important to listen to her because she felt no- one had done that up to now. . . . When she first came in, the doctor had only said she had some pain, so when she came in I thought she had pain in her joints. . . . I thought she might have had rheumatism or something when she limped in. But then she said immediately she'd had an operation and that was why she was in pain and she was healthy otherwise. So it went very quickly to understand the problem. . . . My task was to work out what her problem was and what I could do about it. . . . I could see how she felt when she came in and also when she tried to climb up here [on the examination table] . . . and then I felt, in this case, I needed to take particular care to help out and try to treat her well because she felt she'd been so badly treated previously. . . . I felt the only thing I could offer her was support, so I felt it was especially important. . . . She had two problems really. One, that she was in pain and, two, that no-one believed she was in pain and was prepared to do anything about it. You can say, one main problem and a secondary problem. You have to try to solve the problems you can. . . . I think she felt better when she left than when she came.* (pp. 28–39).

Lotta then reflected on what she was trying to achieve as a medical practitioner, again raising the importance of identifying the patient's problem and how she could help:

> *When you're providing healthcare, it's such an advantage that it gives so much when you listen to someone. It was, it gave her so much that I listened and understood and that felt good. It feels that you make a contribution, otherwise you can feel: "This was a patient who I couldn't do anything for. I'll just send her on to the hospital." Because I could have done that, but then I wouldn't have done anything positive. . . .*
>
> Interviewer: *I'm trying to understand, when we talked about what your task is you talked about working out what her problem was and listening.*
>
> *Mm.*
>
> Interviewer: *But how, for example, this listening you talked about now, how does it relate to working out the problem?*

Mm.

Interviewer: *How do you see that? You say it has to be there, but how is it part of the same task?*

But if you listen, you find out about all the problems.

Interviewer: *Mm.*

I think you get that as part of it. She was able to talk for a long while before I interrupted her or anything. So, then you often have time to think up better questions as well.... I think everything came out when she talked: that she was in pain, no-one had listened to her. She said that several times: "No-one was listening to me." So I don't need to bring that out in some way.... Then do a proper examination, listen carefully and explain clearly so you're working together, you need to sell the solution to the patient, see if they have a better one. (pp. 44–47)

In sum, in her practice of medicine, Lotta draws upon medical knowledge and procedures, thinks through health problems with a view to solving them, as well as talking and interacting collaboratively with patients. Medical knowledge and knowledge about working with patients are both central to her way of being a medical practitioner. Her embodiment of this knowledge is a crucial part of the way she acts towards patients and is a medical practitioner, as the examples above demonstrate. This is not to suggest there can be no inconsistencies in Lotta's way of practising medicine but, rather, the point to be made is that knowing, acting and being are interrelated in professional ways of being. One of these aspects does not precede or cause another; they are interrelated in constituting who we are as professionals.

A Synthesis: Karl and Lotta Learning to be Professionals

As Karl and Lotta learned to practise medicine, their development trajectories followed differing paths based on their unfolding ways of being medical practitioners, as was also the case for the remaining students in the longitudinal study. There is, then, not a single development path towards becoming professionals, even for one profession (Dall'Alba & Sandberg, 2006). Moreover, through interaction with others and reflection on practice, questions and challenges arise that may cut across and even displace an unfolding development trajectory. For example, Karl initially focused on disease and symptoms for the purpose of diagnosis and treatment. During the medical programme, the importance of taking patients into account was featured, which introduced some tensions and challenges for Karl's way of practising medicine. His efforts to address these challenges and tensions influenced the path his development subsequently followed. On the other hand, taking account of the patient was already integral to Lotta's practice of medicine, so featuring it in the medical programme reinforced and extended the development of her way of being a medical practitioner.

The cases involving Karl and Lotta also demonstrate that, as professional ways of being unfold over time, they do not necessarily become more attuned to the profession in question. For instance, Karl expressed concern that his empathy with patients declined during the medical programme, although empathy is arguably critical to skilful medical practice (Baron, 1985; Charon, 1989; Newton et al., 2008; Toombs, 1993). Several of the remaining medical students in the study also commented on experiencing decreasing empathy with patients as the medical programme progressed. Their experience also parallels decreasing empathy among students in other conventional medical programmes (see, for example, Holm, 1985; Newton et al., 2008).

In Karl and Lotta's practice of medicine, we also see "sediments of earlier historical modes, as well as buds or shoots of its possible future" (Engeström, 1993, p. 68). For instance, we see the biomedical model expressed in attention to diagnosis and treatment, while we also see, to varying extents, awareness of the need to take patients into account. A biomedical model came to be dominant during the 20th century, with increasing awareness of patients as collaborators in the care of their own health from the later part of that period and into the 21st century (see Chapter 5). The tension in the students' accounts between a biomedical focus and a broader focus that includes patients' experience of their illness or ailment in collaborating with them about their health parallels a tension within contemporary medicine. Medical students such as Karl and Lotta attempt to negotiate tensions such as this, so that learning to be medical practitioners is both individual and social. Moreover, students such as Lotta and experienced medical practitioners who recognise the inadequacy of a biomedical model can show a way forward for the practice of medicine. As Patricia Benner points out, it need not be "a question of choosing *either* science *or* practical wisdom, but rather how to relate the two" (2001, p. viii).

The cases above, featuring Karl and Lotta, demonstrate that learning to be medical practitioners involves much more than learning about diseases, symptoms, routines and procedures. It involves not only much more than this, but something other than this. It involves integration of knowing, acting and being medical practitioners. This process is always incomplete, so professional ways of being continue to unfold over time, even for experienced professionals. When professional education programmes adopt an epistemological focus on knowledge and skills acquisition, they fall short of facilitating the integration of these knowledge and skills into ways of being professionals (Dall'Alba, 2004).

Part IV
Implications for Professional Education

Chapter 8
Designing Professional Education: Where to from Here?

Forget your perfect offering.
There is a crack in everything.
That's how the light gets in.

(From the song, *Anthem*, by Leonard Cohen)

The introductory chapter of this monograph called for re-thinking professional education programmes and the learning therein. It was argued that such re-thinking is necessary due to an intensified pace of change in our contemporary world and a deepening crisis of confidence in the professions that spills over into professional education. Moreover, an argument has been developed throughout the book that the way we currently educate professionals is limited in scope and inadequate in preparing them for the challenges of professional practice in our changing world. An alternative way forward has been proposed that would mean an ontological turn for professional education programmes, centred on developing professional ways of being (see also Dall'Alba & Barnacle, 2007). This proposed alternative is consistent with transformation from student to professional that is assumed to flow from professional education programmes. Not only is it consistent with this transformation, but also a focus on developing professional ways of being strives to explicitly promote and enhance such transformation. While contributing to processes of becoming professionals in this way is a heavy responsibility, it accords with society's expectations of professional education programmes.

In contrast, the critical examination of professional education programmes in previous chapters has shown that these expected transformations are typically not the focus of the design and implementation of these programmes. Instead, knowledge and skills are generally in focus even though, while necessary, these are not sufficient for transformation as professionals. Moreover, as Chapter 7 demonstrates, the knowledge and skills that are gained can largely be incorporated into existing ways of being professionals, rather than contributing to more substantial transformation where this is required. The empirical evidence presented in previous chapters suggests the variation in unfolding professional ways of being among aspiring professionals is not fully addressed in conventional professional education programmes.

G. Dall'Alba, *Learning to be Professionals*, Innovation and Change in Professional Education 4, DOI 10.1007/978-90-481-2608-8_8,
© Springer Science+Business Media B.V. 2009

As these programmes typically are not directed to professional ways of being, this is not surprising. As a result, professional practice is enacted in distinctly different ways, some of which arguably fall short in fulfilling the purpose of the profession in question. When continuing professional development activities make less than the desired impact on the performance of professionals, it is likely this occurs for similar reasons, namely, that these activities do not address ways of being for the professions in question (see also Webster-Wright, 2006).

Preparing aspiring professionals to deal with the flux and fluidity that follows from an intensified pace of change requires not only providing them with relevant knowledge and skills, but also addressing who they are becoming as professionals (see also Barnett, 2005). It involves enabling them not only to learn knowledge, routines and procedures, but also to develop and take informed stands on enacting the professional practice to which they aspire, including on the significance and role of that practice in society (see Chapter 4). The challenges of professional practice demand no less. As long as professional education programmes fall short of enhancing—rather than simply assuming—this broad, deep transformation towards becoming professionals, a crisis of confidence in professional education is likely to continue.

Where do we go from here in designing professional education programmes that promote and enhance professional ways of being for specific professions? As the extract from Leonard Cohen's song above suggests, the cracks and chinks that become evident in our usual ways of educating for the professions can open possibilities for acting and being otherwise: "That's how the light gets in". The limitations and tensions we identify in professional education programmes can afford opportunities for growth. However, innovation will not be achieved without deep, critical thought and sustained effort. It is necessary we seize opportunities for innovation and improvement if they are not to be lost to us.

In a spirit of looking forward, towards enhanced professional education, this chapter distils some key principles for educating professionals from the foregoing critical examination of professional education programmes and empirical research on learning to be professionals. Its purpose is to point a way forward for innovation in professional education, as well as identifying areas of research that could support this process. The specific way in which each of the broad principles below has relevance and meaning for particular professional education programmes will depend upon the nature of the professions to which the programmes are directed, as well as the part those professions are to play within the broader society. The way in which these principles play out in practice for specific professional education programmes will need to be interrogated in the context of designing, implementing and evaluating those programmes. This chapter adopts, then, a broad brush approach to looking outward and forward from current practice and research on professional education.

Beyond Knowledge and Skills in Professional Education

The previous chapter demonstrated that students in professional education programmes, such as Karl and Lotta, learn knowledge, routines and procedures that are part of professional practice, but they employ those knowledge and skills in various ways and to differing ends. Their development does not follow a uni-directional trajectory from novice to professional, based upon knowledge and skills acquisition (see also Dall'Alba & Sandberg, 2006). Instead, they enact professional practice in distinctly different ways, both during and at the end of the "same" professional education programme. When the results of this longitudinal study have been discussed with teachers across a range of fields, such as in business, dentistry, engineering, information technology, medicine, physiotherapy, psychology, speech pathology and teacher education, they see parallels in their own experiences with students.

The longitudinal study provides further evidence that we cannot expect to simply transfer knowledge and skills relating to professional practice to aspiring professionals. Instead, they construct, enact, and embody the knowledge and skills they encounter to varying extents and in a range of ways, both individual and shared, as discussed in Chapters 2 and 4. This important point is overlooked when knowledge and skills acquisition is the focus of curriculum design. In addition, such a focus neglects the difficulties students encounter when they are left with the challenging task of integrating knowledge and skills into professional practice (see Chapter 3). If aspiring professionals are to be assisted in integrating knowledge and skills into their practice, this integration must receive explicit attention in curriculum design and implementation in a manner that is recognised and valued by them. In order that aspiring professionals will value the knowledge, routines and procedures they are learning, the relevance and significance of those knowledge and skills for the practice in question must be made clear to them. In other words, the ways in which particular knowledge, routines and procedures are integral to being medical practitioners, teachers, architects and so on must be made explicit. Research that explores how students learn knowledge, routines and procedures in ways that inform their unfolding professional ways of being, as well as obstacles to this learning, would be beneficial in supporting this process.

Overcoming a Theory/Practice Gap in Curriculum Design

Associated with a focus on acquisition and subsequent application of knowledge and skills, the empirical material presented in Chapters 6 and 7 demonstrates the persistence of a theory-practice gap in curriculum design, which was highlighted by Donald Schön (1987; see also Chapters 1 and 3). Like many other professional education programmes, students in the Karolinska medical programme were expected to acquire theory from lectures, textbooks, seminars, laboratory classes and so on, then to apply this theory in practice contexts. Knowledge was typically presented to students in ways that were more clear-cut than the complexities of practice they encountered. How students were to relate this knowledge to the varied array of practice settings and patients they encountered was generally not made clear to them. As previous chapters demonstrate, this gap posed difficult challenges to students, presenting barriers to the integration of their knowing, acting and being. Rather than facilitating the development of professional ways of being, then, this curriculum design presented some obstacles.

As theory is only possible through, and in relation to, the embodied way in which we engage with our world (see Chapter 2), it can help to make practice intelligible for students, as well as enabling them to question and enhance their practice. This is only likely to occur when we "bring to life theory in practice and practice in theory" (Darling-Hammond, Hammerness, et al., 2005, p. 399), rather than presenting theory and practice as separate entities. Moreover, learning can be enhanced through "multiple opportunities to experience and study the relationship of theory with practice" (ibid, p. 401). Curriculum design can provide opportunities for experiencing and exploring these interrelationships, for example, through course readings that address the relationship of theory to practice, reflective exercises directed to engagement in practice, and focused dialogue with others that foregrounds the relationship of theory with the practice students are experiencing. Informal forms of learning that professionals find beneficial (see, for example, Cheetham & Chivers, 2005; Webster-Wright, 2006, in press) also need to be encouraged and nourished through creating a climate of learning and inquiry throughout professional education programmes. These various opportunities can enable aspiring professionals to learn to develop their practice in ways that remain relevant after they complete professional education programmes. They provide a means of preparing aspiring professionals for the challenges of practice in a changing world. Research that examines ways of exploring the interrelationship of theory with practice, and of promoting a climate of learning and inquiry in professional education programmes could provide insights that would be of benefit to this learning.

Professional Education as Preparation for Practice

A key principle of professional education is that it must be directed to preparing professionals for the challenges of contemporary practice. The design, enactment and evaluation of professional education programmes need to maintain such a focus; a largely ad hoc process is unlikely to provide appropriate preparation. Adopting such a focus means involving aspiring professionals in continual inquiry directed to engagement in practice, so they learn about practice while engaging in that practice (Ball & Cohen, 1999; Schön, 1987). As noted previously, such engagement in inquiry implies neither a functional fit between preparation and practice, nor geographically locating all parts of professional education programmes in the practice settings to which the programmes relate. Instead, it clearly targets learning for practice beyond the university context, through examining key questions and issues related to engaging in the practice of a particular profession. This includes exploring questions and issues that arise during professional practice, as well as critically examining current ways of practising and the enduring significance of the profession for society. For example, in preparing to practise medicine, this would include critical analysis of the way in which a focus on diagnosing and treating disease downplays both the importance of preventing disease within whole populations (Germov, 2005a) and caring for those with chronic or terminal illness (Toombs, 1993).

Thoughtful, informed inquiry that targets engagement in professional practice recognises the need for aspiring professionals to develop skilfulness in their practice, but also to develop a capacity to be reflexive about that practice, not only as individuals but also at the collective level of the field or profession. Such critical examination of practice and the profession is dependent upon openness to recognising current strengths, challenges and limitations, perhaps especially those that align less well with the image the profession prefers to present of itself. Adopting an informed, critical stance on and in professional practice is necessary for the enhancement of practice and for taking seriously the service role of the profession to society. While there is growing interest in how a critical, reflective approach can be fostered among students and experienced professionals (for example, Barnett, 2004; Boud et al., 2006, Brockbank & McGill, 1998, 2006; Bulman & Schutz, 2008; Ghaye, 2005; Knott & Scragg, 2007; Kyburz-Graber, 2006; Moon, 1999, 2008; Schön, 1987), there is a need for further research that addresses how such an approach can promote skilfulness and reflexivity in professional practice.

Herman Stein puts forward an argument about educating for the practice of social work that can be extended to other professions, as follows:

> Education at its best raises questions about what might be changed in the world of practice and characteristically generates at least an element of skepticism about the validity of current patterns and functions in [professional] work. The practice world, on the other hand, generally seeks personnel prepared for its tasks and socialized to its subcultures, and sometimes has its own significant innovations which are not yet reflected in the training centers. The struggle between conservatism and innovation takes place as much within the practicing milieux of [professional] work as it does within the field of [professional] education. (2003, p. 100)

To the extent that strong vested interests, among either practising professionals or those teaching in professional programmes, attempt to exclude such critical analysis, the education of professionals will be diminished. Both practising professionals and professional education programmes have important contributions to make in enhancing the education of professionals.

Addressing Ambiguity in Professional Practice

While the main purpose of professional education is to contribute to preparation for contemporary practice, the various ways of practising within specific professions (see, for example, Borko et al., 1997; Mol, 2002; Sandberg, 2000; Stålsby Lundborg et al., 1999) pose challenges for learning to be professionals. As we saw in Chapters 6 and 7, the variation in ways of practising medicine among Karolinska medical students paralleled those in the broader practice of medicine. Some of these differences exist side by side, while others can lead to conflict (Mol, 2002). As aspiring professionals inevitably encounter a range of ways of being professionals, it is important this ambiguity is addressed, so they are not left unassisted to contend with perhaps one of the most perplexing aspects of learning professional practice.

Of particular importance is that they learn to recognise this ambiguity and learn to deal with it to the extent necessary for engaging in professional practice.

As noted in Chapter 4, it is important to point out here that promoting professional ways of being that are appropriate for the service role of particular professions is not equivalent to seeking "identical products" from professional education programmes. The ambiguity associated with alternative meanings and ways of being can never be resolved once and for all. Nor would this be desirable, as this ambiguity opens possibilities for renewing practice as new contingencies emerge. Research that identifies differing ways of being professionals and of dealing with this ambiguity can be of value for both students and those teaching in professional education programmes.

This ambiguity can also be used for positive purposes during professional education, such as in troubling taken-for-granted assumptions about a profession or its practices. As Karl came to realise when confronted with differences in medical practices, there can be more than one way that works. When encountering ambiguity, aspiring professionals can come to experience the familiar or everyday in new ways, or be confronted with aspects of their practice that are questionable. Calling into question and re-shaping assumptions about what it means to practise medicine, to teach or to apply the rule of law, can open new possibilities, or other ways of being. Examining practice anew in this way can contribute to transforming ways of being professionals. It can contribute to the process of "turning around" aspiring professionals in a way that is directed to, and attuned with, the professional practice in which they are learning to engage.

Integrating Ontology and Epistemology in Professional Education

As professional practice incorporates our knowing and how we act, as well as who we are as professionals, each of these aspects must be developed in relation to the others, if professional education programmes are to live up to their mandate. In other words, if these programmes are to enhance professional ways of being that are attuned with the service role of the profession, they must adopt such a focus. For most aspiring professionals, such transformation is unlikely to occur despite, or simply as a by-product of, professional education programmes that fail to adopt such a focus. Developing ways of being that are attuned with a particular profession is clearly no minor task, but it is unlikely to be achieved across student cohorts if an ontological dimension of becoming professionals is overlooked.

In the design of professional education programmes and their enactment in practice, the interrelation of ontology and epistemology needs to be explicitly addressed if these programmes are to contribute positively to processes of becoming. Addressing this interrelation provides a means of developing a coherent curriculum that integrates knowing, acting and being the professionals in question, thereby reducing the pitfalls of a fragmented curriculum (see Chapter 3). For instance, developing a capacity to care as "a mark of personhood" (Noddings, 1992, p. 24; see also

Chapter 4) provides a means of integrating ontological and epistemological aspects of becoming professionals. Developing such a capacity includes being ethical and respectful of the other in providing a service. A capacity to care has relevance for all professions by virtue of their service role in society. Aspiring professionals need to develop necessary knowledge, routines and procedures for entering into appropriate caring relations with those to whom they provide a service; ontology and epistemology are both implicated. For example, accountants need to develop knowledge and skills in accounting in order to provide ethical accounting services that respect the needs of their clients. Teachers need knowledge and skills for entering respectfully and ethically into pedagogical relations that enhance the learning of their students.

Highlighting the integration of ontology and epistemology in key features of practice can contribute to the enhancement of professional ways of being, while also providing a framework for the design of professional education programmes that takes such learning seriously. Implementation of these programmes can be evaluated and improved on the basis of this framework. Research on key features of practice for particular professions and the interrelationships of those features can assist in developing such a framework. Moreover, research on how such features and their interrelationships are experienced and learned could contribute to revising frameworks of this kind and improving the practice to which they refer.

Professional Education as a Process of Becoming

While the development of professional ways of being necessarily incorporates ontological and epistemological dimensions, this process of becoming is never complete (see Chapters 4 and 7). Through facing the uncertainty and openness of the process of becoming in which they are engaged, aspiring professionals can contribute to addressing and shaping this process. Professional education programmes can provide valuable opportunities to thoughtfully interrogate possible ways of being professionals, as well as supporting the efforts of aspiring professionals to embody and enact the kind of professional practice for which they strive. For example, class discussions and feedback during practicum placements can focus on ways of being professionals as these unfold over time, while course readings can draw attention to key issues and questions relating to the profession that arise during such placements. Karolinska medical students in the longitudinal study suggested that discussions about their practice of the kind in which we engaged during the research were of benefit to their learning, including their reflections on consultations with patients, their development over time as medical practitioners, and challenges and rewards of professional practice. Several of these students suggested dialogue of this kind should be included for all students within the medical programme.

In order to promote the development of professional ways of being, it is important that professional education programmes provide opportunities and space for aspiring professionals to take a stand on what is being learned and who they are becoming. This includes taking an informed stand on the professional practice to which they aspire. It also includes developing informed self-awareness that enables them to evaluate their own practice, recognising strengths as well as areas in need of improvement. As it matters to them who they are becoming, they desire to be adequate to the task in their own and others' eyes (see Barnacle, 2005; Knorr Cetina, 2001).

Opportunities to evaluate their practice in the light of the stands they are forming on the profession and its practice can provide openings for moving forward in the process of becoming professionals. For example, Lotta and other medical students questioned the adequacy of the prevalent enactment of medical practice for responding to patients' health needs. This opened possibilities for ways of being medical practitioners that more adequately took account of experiences with patients. In negotiating their own ways of practising medicine, these students may have been inspired by emergent versions of practice already in evidence. The availability of role models with whom students can identify, as well as other learners with whom to discuss their points of view, are important to this process. Negative role models also provide students with opportunities to take a stand on who they are becoming as professionals. As we saw in Chapters 6 and 7, there was sometimes tension between the medical practice the students observed and ways of being medical practitioners they sought to develop. Professional education has a key part to play in informing and shaping the stands students take (see also Vu & Dall'Alba, 2008). The contribution of these programmes to this process is sorely in need of research.

As noted in Chapter 4, informing and shaping the stands aspiring professionals take raises important ethical questions about whose standards and judgements are to be adopted. There is no easy or final answer to these questions, but they must be periodically raised and debated in open and thoughtful ways if a nurturing pedagogical relation based on care for the other is to be established and maintained. As the curriculum can act as an instrument of power, it must be used carefully and with discretion.

Challenging and Supporting Learning to be Professionals

If education is to contribute constructively to a process of becoming, "the teacher has to let the pupil learn rather than impose learning upon her" (Bonnett, 2002, p. 241; see also Chapter 4). As Richard Sennett notes, when change is imposed from without, it is unlikely to bring about transformation: "Subjected to change, people do not feel themselves changing. They do not become more self-conscious in ways that open them up to others" (2003, p. 241). In contrast, as Michael Bonnett points out, "A Heideggerian account sees learning as a highly demanding and participatory affair which requires the full engagement of the learner and is certainly not something that could be instilled from without through a heavily didactic approach" (2002, p. 241). If they are to participate fully in the learning process as collaborators, not simply recipients of knowledge and skills, learners need some autonomy. As Elisabet noted, they need to be progressively given responsibility in order to "try out [their] wings a little, to see how far they hold" (2nd semester of 5th year, p. 131).

Participating in learning to become professionals requires engagement, commitment and risk. Aspiring professionals need to be challenged and supported in deepening their commitment and dealing with risk. This is particularly the case in light of the transformations involved in becoming professionals, which can be experienced as challenges to the self and familiar ways of being. Providing support in negotiating uncertainty, anxiety and resistance, while bringing forth the passion, excitement and satisfaction of becoming the professionals that students seek to become is of central importance. Bonnett describes this challenging and support as "empathetic challenging":

> from out of her sensitivity to the concerns of the learner and the potential of the domain with which he is attempting to engage, the teacher can suggest, challenge, provoke in ways that both respect the integrity of this engagement and deepen and refine it. Also, through the judicious revealing of her own sense of what is important, problematic, analogous, fascinating, a source of wonderment, she can exhibit—to the extent that she is authentic—what an honest engagement might mean and how it becomes integrated into a human life, making a difference to what is seen and felt. In such a relationship, no *one* initiates the work, is wholly responsible for it, controls it. (2002, p. 241)

This pedagogical relationship has a strong ethical dimension that relies on mutual commitment (see also Noddings, 1992): while students must commit to the process of becoming professionals, teachers have a key role in challenging and supporting them in this process. Research on the formation of such a pedagogical relationship and its significance for enhancing professional ways of being has the potential to reinforce and strengthen efforts towards empathetic challenging.

Developing Attuned Responsiveness to Professional Practice

Preparing aspiring professionals for practice means promoting the development of professional ways of being that continue to be attuned and responsive to the emergent challenges of practice (see Chapter 4). As we are inextricably entwined with and oriented towards our world, knowing and learning are constituted in and through the web of interrelationships of which we are a part. Attuned responsiveness to others and things that constitute professional practice can be developed through this orientation towards the world. It is a practical manifestation of the capacity to care which, it was argued above, is a central feature of professional practice through the service role of professions. As we saw in Chapter 4, developing attunement and responsiveness enhances a sense of agency and provides a focus for efforts towards becoming skilful professionals.

Developing attuned responsiveness could provide an overarching and practical focus for professional education programmes that is consistent with developing professional ways of being. Such a focus could be the basis for programme design, enacting the curriculum, and evaluating the achievements and limitations of these programmes. Not only is attuned responsiveness relevant and appropriate to unfolding ways of being among aspiring professionals, but teachers, too, must be attuned and responsive to this learning if they are to contribute to promoting it. This is Bonnett's empathetic challenging outlined above. Research on the implications of a focus on developing professional ways of being through attuned responsiveness could provide insights to guide these efforts into the future.

Concluding Remarks

This monograph has argued for an ontological turn in professional education programmes in order that these programmes directly address their purpose in preparing aspiring professionals for the challenges of contemporary professional practice. As long as these programmes continue to focus primarily on knowledge and skills, they will fall short of living up to this mandate. Instead, there is a need to reconfigure professional education as a process of becoming, whose key purpose is developing professional ways of being, rather than simply knowledge and skills. Knowledge and skills would be developed in ways that contribute to this process of becoming professionals.

The argument made here for an ontological turn in professional education is grounded in Martin Heidegger's notion of being-in-the-world and Maurice Merleau-Ponty's concept of the lived body. Being-in-the-world highlights our entwinement with others and things in our world, while the concept of the lived body extends this notion through identifying the body as the medium for embeddedness in and engagement with our world. These concepts make a radical break with mind/body or subject/object duality, thereby overcoming a conventional separation into mind (or cognition), body and world. An extended concept of the lifeworld that draws upon being-in-the-world and the lived body provides an integrated framework for exploring professional practice. It brings together epistemology and ontology, or what we know and can do with who we are (becoming). If professional education programmes are to enhance processes of becoming, the interrelation of epistemology and ontology is to be nurtured and sustained. In learning to become professionals, knowing, acting and being are integrated into professional ways of being that unfold over time in interplay with traditions of practice. Professional education must open and interrogate possibilities for being professionals within, and despite, existing constraints. It must enhance learning among aspiring professionals in ways that free them in, and for, becoming.

Shifting focus from knowledge and skills to the development of professional ways of being that are attuned and responsive to professional practice can be seen to have far-reaching implications for aspiring professionals, teachers and professional education programmes. The cracks and chinks we find in current professional education programmes can be the beginning of a better future:

> The past produces the resources for multiple futures, for open pathways, for indeterminable consequences, as well as for those regularities and norms that currently prevail.... This means that the future, possible futures have the inexhaustible resources of the past, of that realm of the past still untouched by the present, to bring about a critical response to the present and ideally to replace it with what is better in the future. (Grosz, 2004, p. 253)

The changes proposed here for an ontological turn in professional education can only be fully accomplished if they occur in parallel with related changes in the broader society. This is because professional education does not take place in isolation, but is of, and for, the society in which it is embedded. However, changes to professional education can contribute to encouraging and sustaining such transformation in society. The two can nourish each other.

References

ABIM Foundation, ACP-ASIM Foundation, European Federation of Internal Medicine (2002). Medical professionalism in the new millennium: A physician charter. *Annals of Internal Medicine, 136*, 243–246.

Alexander, S., & Boud, D. (2001). Learners still learn from experience when online. In J. Stephenson (Ed.), *Teaching and learning online: Pedagogies for new technologies* (pp. 3–15). London: Kogan Page.

Alvesson, M. (2001). Knowledge work: Ambiguity, image and identity. *Human relations, 54*(7), 863–886.

Anderson, R. M. (1995). Patient empowerment and the traditional medical model: A case of irreconcilable differences? *Diabetes Care, 18*, 412–415.

Antepohl, W., Domeij, E., Forsberg, P., & Ludvigsson, J. (2003). A follow up of medical graduates of a problem-based learning curriculum. *Medical Education, 37*, 155–162.

Archer, R., Elder, W., Hustedde, C., Milam, A., & Joyce, J. (2008). The theory of planned behaviour in medical education: A model for integrating professionalism training. *Medical Education, 42*, 771–777.

Arnman, R. (2004). *Doctors' experiences of work related moral problems: Responsibility without clear boundaries.* Stockholm: Karolinska University Press.

Arnold, M. (2003). On the phenomenology of technology: The 'Janus-faces' of mobile phones. *Information and Organization, 13*, 231–256.

Balint, M. (1964). *The doctor, his patient and the illness.* London: Pitman Medical.

Ball, D. L., & Cohen, D. K. (1999). Developing practice, developing practitioners: Toward a practice-based theory of professional education. In L. Darling-Hammond & G. Sykes (Eds.), *Teaching as the learning profession: Handbook of policy and practice* (pp. 3–32). San Francisco: Jossey-Bass.

Barnacle, R. (2005). Research education ontologies: Exploring doctoral becoming. *Higher Education Research and Development, 24*, 179–188.

Barnett, R. (1992). What effects? What outcomes? In R. Barnett (Ed.), *Learning to effect* (pp. 3–18). Buckingham: SRHE; Open University Press.

Barnett, R. (1994). *The limits of competence: Knowledge, higher education and society.* Buckingham: SRHE; Open University Press.

Barnett, R. (1997). *Higher education: A critical business.* Buckingham: SRHE; Open University Press.

Barnett, R. (1999). Learning to work and working to learn. In D. Boud & J. Garrick (Eds.), *Understanding learning at work* (pp. 29–44). London: Routledge.

Barnett, R. (2000). *Realizing the university in an age of supercomplexity.* Buckingham: SRHE; Open University Press.

Barnett, R. (2004). Learning for an unknown future. *Higher Education Research and Development, 23*, 247–260.

Barnett, R. (2005). Recapturing the universal in the university. *Educational Philosophy and Theory, 37*, 785–797.

G. Dall'Alba, *Learning to be Professionals*, Innovation and Change in Professional
Education 4, DOI 10.1007/978-90-481-2608-8_BM1,
© Springer Science+Business Media B.V. 2009

Barnett, R., & Hallam, S. (1999). Teaching for supercomplexity: A pedagogy for higher education. In P. Mortimore (Ed.), *Understanding pedagogy and its impact on learning* (pp. 137–154). London: Paul Chapman Publishing.

Baron, R. J. (1985). An introduction to medical phenomenology: I can't hear you while I'm listening. *Annals of Internal Medicine, 103*, 606–661.

Barrows, H. S. (1996). Problem-based learning in medicine and beyond: A brief overview. In L. Wilkerson & W. H. Gijselaers (Eds.), *Bringing problem-based learning to higher education: Theory and practice* (pp. 3–12). San Francisco: Jossey-Bass.

Barrows, H. S., & Tamblyn, R. M. (1980). *Problem-based learning: An approach to medical education*. New York: Springer.

Bauman, Z. (2004). Liquid sociality. In N. Gane (Ed.), *The future of social theory* (pp. 17–46). London: Continuum.

Beaty, E., Dall'Alba, G., & Marton, F. (1997). The personal experiences of learning in higher education: Changing views and enduring perspectives. In P. Sutherland (Ed.), *Adult learning: A reader* (pp. 150–165). London: Kogan Page.

Belenky, M.F., Clinchy, B.M., Goldberger, N.R., & Tarule, J.M. (1986). *Women's ways of knowing: The development of self, voice, and mind*. New York: Basic Books.

Benner, P. (1984). *From novice to expert: Excellence and power in clinical nursing practice*. San Francisco: Addison-Wesley.

Benner, P. (2001). *From novice to expert: Excellence and power in clinical nursing practice* (2nd ed.). Upper Saddle River, NJ: Prentice-Hall.

Benner, P., Tanner, C. A., & Chesla, C. A. (1996). *Expertise in nursing practice: Caring, clinical judgment, and ethics*. New York: Springer.

Berger, P. L., & Luckmann, T. (1966). *The social construction of reality*. Harmondsworth: Penguin.

Billett, S. (2001). Knowing in practice: Reconceptualising vocational expertise. *Learning and Instruction, 11*, 431–452.

Billett, S., Fenwick, T., & Somerville, M. (Eds.). (2006). *Work, subjectivity and learning: Understanding learning through working life*. Dordrecht: Springer.

Blake, N., Smeyers, P., Smith, R., & Standish, P. (2000). *Education in an age of nihilism*. London: Routledge Falmer.

Blakey, H., Blanshard, E., Cole, H., Leslie, F., & Sen, R. (2008). Are medical students socially exclusive? A comparison with economics students. *Medical Education, 42*, 1088–1091.

Blank, L., Kimball, H., McDonald, W., & Merino J. (2003). Medical professionalism in the new millennium: A physicians' charter 15 months later. *Annals of Internal Medicine, 138*, 839–841.

Bligh, J. (2005). Professionalism. *Medical Education, 39*, 4.

Bonner, T.N. (1995). *Becoming a physician: Medical education in Britain, France, Germany, and the United States, 1750–1945*. New York; Oxford: Oxford University Press.

Bonnett, M. (2002). Education as a form of the poetic: A Heideggerian approach to learning and the teacher-pupil relationship. In M.A. Peters (Ed.), *Heidegger, education and modernity* (pp. 229–243). Lanham MD: Rowman; Littlefield.

Borko, H., Davinroy, K. H., Bliem, C. L., & Cumbo, K. B. (2000). Exploring and supporting teacher change: Two third-grade teachers' experiences in a mathematics and literacy staff development project. *Elementary School Journal, 100*, 273–306.

Borko, H., Mayfield, V., Marion, S., Flexer, R., & Cumbo, K. (1997). Teachers' developing ideas and practices about mathematics performance assessment: Successes, stumbling blocks, and implications for professional development. *Teaching and Teacher Education, 13*, 259–278.

Boshuizen, H. P. A., & Schmidt, H. G. (1992). On the role of biomedical knowledge in clinical reasoning by experts, intermediates and novices. *Cognitive Science, 16*, 153–184.

Boud, D., Cressey, P., & Docherty, P. (Eds.). (2006). *Productive reflection at work: Learning for changing organizations*. New York: Routledge.

Boud, D., & Garrick, J. (Eds.). (1999). *Understanding learning at work*. London; New York: Routledge.

Boud, D., & Solomon, N. (2001a). Future directions for work-based learning: Reconfiguring higher education. In D. Boud & N. Solomon (Eds.), *Work-based learning: A new higher education?* (pp. 203–227). Buckingham: SRHE; Open University Press.

Boud, D., & Solomon, N. (2001b). Repositioning universities and work. In D. Boud & N. Solomon (Eds.), *Work-based learning: A new higher education?* (pp. 18–33). Buckingham: SRHE; Open University Press.

Boud, D., & Solomon, N. (Eds.) (2001c). *Work-based learning: A new higher education?* Buckingham: SRHE; Open University Press.

Boud, D., Solomon, N., & Symes, C. (2001). New practices for new times. In D. Boud & N. Solomon (Eds.), *Work-based learning: A new higher education?* (pp. 3–17). Buckingham: SRHE; Open University Press.

Bourdieu, P. (1977). *Outline of a theory of practice*. Cambridge: Cambridge University Press.

Bowden, J., & Marton, F. (1998). *The university of learning: Beyond quality and competence*. London: Kogan Page.

Bowman, W. (2004). Cognition and the body: Perspectives from music education. In L. Bresler (Ed.), *Knowing bodies: Moving minds* (pp. 29–50). Dordrecht: Kluwer Academic.

Bresler, L. (Ed.) (2004). *Knowing bodies, moving minds: Towards embodied teaching and learning*. Dordrecht: Kluwer Academic.

Breton, G. (1999). Some empirical evidence on the superiority of the problem-based learning (PBL) method. *Accounting Education, 8*, 1–12.

Brockbank, A., & McGill, I. (1998). *Facilitating reflective learning in higher education*. Buckingham: SRHE; Open University Press.

Brockbank, A., & McGill, I. (2006). *Facilitating reflective learning through mentoring and coaching*. London; Philadelphia: Kogan Page.

Brown, B. A., Harte, J., & Warnes, A. (2007). Developing the healthcare workforce: A comparison of two work-based learning models. *Education + Training, 49*, 193–200.

Brown, J. (2008). How clinical communication has become a core part of medical education in the UK. *Medical Education, 42*, 271–278.

Bulman, C., & Schutz, S. (Eds.). (2008). *Reflective practice in nursing* (4th ed.). Oxford; Malden, MA: Blackwell.

Burroughs, H., Lovell, K., Morley, M., Baldwin, R., Burns, A., & Chew-Graham, C. (2006). 'Justifiable depression': How primary care professionals and patients view late-life depression? a qualitative study. *Family Practice, 23*, 369–377.

Camargo, K.R., & Coeli, C.M. (2006). Theory in practice: Why "good medicine" and "scientific medicine" are not necessarily the same thing. *Advances in Health Sciences Education, 11*, 77–89.

Carpenter, C. (1993). The experience of spinal cord injury: The individual's perspective—implications for rehabilitation practice. *Physical Therapy, 74*(7), 614–628.

Carter, K., Cushing, K., Sabers, D., Stein, P., & Berliner, D. (1988). Expert-novice differences in perceiving and processing visual classroom information. *Journal of Teacher Education, 39*, 25–31.

Casey, C. (1999). The changing contexts of work. In D. Boud & J. Garrick (Eds.), *Understanding learning at work* (pp. 15–28). London; New York: Routledge.

Cassell, E. J. (1982). The nature of suffering and the goals of medicine. *New England Journal of Medicine, 306*, 639–645.

Castells, M. (1996). *The rise of the network society* (Vol. 1). Massachusetts; Oxford: Blackwell.

Castleton, G., Gerber, R., & Pillay, H. (Eds.) (2006). *Improving workplace learning: Emerging international perspectives*. New York: Nova Science.

Cavanaugh, S.H. (1993). Connecting education and practice. In L. Curry, J. F. Wergin, & Associates (Eds.), *Educating professionals: Responding to new expectations for competence and accountability* (pp. 107–125). San Francisco: Jossey-Bass.

Chaiklin, S. (Ed.). (2001). *The theory and practice of cultural-historical psychology*. Aarhus: Aarhus University Press.

Chaiklin, S., & Lave, J. (1993). *Understanding practice: Perspectives on activity and context.* Cambridge: Cambridge University Press.

Charon, R. (1989). Doctor-patient/reader-writer: Learning to find the text. *Soundings, 72,* 137–152.

Cheetham, G., & Chivers, G. (2005). *Professions, competence and informal learning.* Cheltenham, UK; Northampton, MA: Edward Elgar.

Chi, M., Feltovich, P., & Glaser, R. (1981). Categorization and representation of physics problems by experts and novices. *Cognitive Science, 5,* 121–152.

Clark, A. (1998). Where brain, body, and world collide. *Daedalus, 127,* 257–280.

Clark, A. (2001). Reasons, robots, and the extended mind. *Mind and Language, 16,* 121–145.

Cohen, J.J. (2006). Professionalism in medical education, an American perspective: From evidence to accountability. *Medical Education, 40,* 607–617.

Cole, M., & Engeström, Y. (1993). A cultural-historical approach to distributed cognition. In G. Salomon (Ed.), *Distributed cognitions: Psychological and educational considerations* (pp. 1–46). Cambridge: Cambridge University Press.

Collier, G. L. (2004). A comparison of novices and experts in the identification of sonar signals. *Speech Communication, 43,* 297–310.

Contu, A., & Willmott, H. (2003). Re-embedding situatedness: The importance of power relations in learning theory. *Organization Science, 14,* 283–296.

Coulehan, J. (2005). Today's professionalism: Engaging the mind but not the heart. *Academic Medicine, 80,* 892–898.

Coulter, A. (2002). *The autonomous patient: Ending paternalism in medical care.* London: TSO.

Cruess, S. R., & Cruess, R. L. (2008). Understanding medical professionalism: A plea for an inclusive and integrated approach. *Medical Education, 42,* 755–757.

Dall'Alba, G. (1993). The role of teaching in higher education: Enabling students to enter a field of study and practice. *Learning and Instruction, 3,* 299–313.

Dall'Alba, G. (1998). Medical practice as characterised by beginning medical students. *Advances in Health Sciences Education, 3,* 101–118.

Dall'Alba, G. (2002). Understanding medical practice: Different outcomes of a premedical program. *Advances in Health Sciences Education, 7,* 163–177.

Dall'Alba, G. (2004). Understanding professional practice: Investigations before and after an educational program. *Studies in Higher Education, 29,* 679–692.

Dall'Alba, G. (2005). Improving teaching: Enhancing ways of being university teachers. *Higher Education Research and Development, 24,* 361–372.

Dall'Alba, G. (2009). Learning professional ways of being: Ambiguities of becoming. *Educational Philosophy and Theory, 41,* 34–45.

Dall'Alba, G., & Barnacle, R. (2005). Embodied knowing in online environments. *Educational Philosophy and Theory, 37,* 719–744.

Dall'Alba, G., & Barnacle, R. (2007). An ontological turn for higher education. *Studies in Higher Education, 32,* 679–691.

Dall'Alba, G., & Sandberg, J. (1996). Educating for competence in professional practice. *Instructional Science, 24,* 411–437.

Dall'Alba, G., & Sandberg, J. (2006). Unveiling professional development: A critical review of stage models. *Review of Educational Research, 76,* 383–412.

Darling-Hammond, L., Hammerness, K., Grossman, P., Rust, F., & Shulman, L. (2005). The design of teacher education programs. In L. Darling-Hammond & J. Bransford (Eds.), *Preparing teachers for a changing world: What teachers should learn and be able to do* (pp. 390–441). San Francisco: Jossey-Bass.

Darling-Hammond, L., Pacheco, A., Michelli, N., LePage, P., Hammerness, K., & Youngs, P. (2005). Implementing curriculum renewal in teacher education: Managing organizational and policy change. In L. Darling-Hammond & J. Bransford (Eds.), *Preparing teachers for a changing world: What teachers should learn and be able to do* (pp. 442–479). San Francisco: Jossey-Bass.

Davies, B. (2003). Death to critique and dissent? The policies and practices of new managerialism and of 'evidence-based practice'. *Gender and Education, 15,* 91–103.

Davies, B. (2005). The (im)possibility of intellectual work in neoliberal regimes. *Discourse: Studies in the Cultural Politics of Education, 26*, 1–14.

de Ruyter, D., & Conroy, J. (2002). The formation of identity: The importance of ideals. *Oxford Review of Education, 28*, 509–522.

Dochy, F., Segers, M., Van den Bossche, P., & Gijbels, D. (2003). Effects of problem-based learning: A meta-analysis. *Learning and Instruction, 13*, 533–568.

Donnelly, W.J. (1996). Taking suffering seriously: A new role for the medical case history. *Academic Medicine, 71*, 730–737.

Downie, R.S., & Charlton, B. (1992). *The making of a doctor.* Oxford: Oxford University Press.

Dreyfus, H. L. (1991). *Being-in-the-world: A commentary on Heidegger's being and time, division 1.* Cambridge, MA: MIT Press.

Dreyfus, H. L., & Dreyfus, S. E. (1986). *Mind over machine: The power of human intuition and expertise in the era of the computer.* New York: Free Press.

Duin, N. & Sutcliffe, J. (1992). *A history of medicine: From prehistory to the year 2020.* London; Sydney: Simon & Schuster.

Ellström, E., Ekholm, B., & Ellström, P. (2008). Two types of learning environment: Enabling and constraining a study of care work. *Journal of Workplace Learning, 20*, 84–97.

Engel, G. (1977). The need for a new medical model: A challenge for biomedicine. *Science, 196*, 129–136.

Engeström, Y. (1993). Developmental studies of work as a testbench of activity theory: The case of primary care medical practice. In S. Chaiklin & J. Lave (Ed.), *Understanding practice: Perspectives on activity and context* (pp. 64–103). Cambridge: Cambridge University Press.

Engeström, Y. (2005). *Developmental work research: Expanding activity theory in practice.* Berlin: Lehmanns Media.

Engeström, Y., & Kerosuo, H. (2007). From workplace learning to inter-organizational learning and back: The contribution of activity theory. *Journal of Workplace Learning, 19*, 336–342.

Engeström, Y., & Miettinen, R. (1999). Introduction. In Y. Engeström, R. Miettinen, & R. Punamäki (Eds.), *Perspectives on activity theory* (pp. 1–16). Cambridge: Cambridge University Press.

Engeström, Y., Miettinen, R., & Punamäki, R. (Eds.). (1999). *Perspectives on activity theory.* Cambridge: Cambridge University Press.

Eraut, M. (1994). *Developing professional knowledge and competence.* London: Falmer Press.

Evans, N. (2001). From once upon a time to happily ever after: The story of work-based learning in the UK higher education sector. In D. Boud & N. Solomon (Eds.), *Work-based learning: A new higher education?* (pp. 61–73). Buckingham: SRHE; Open University Press.

Flyvbjerg, B. (1992). *Rationalitet og magt. Det konkretes videnskab,* Bind 1 (*Rationality and power: The science of the concrete,* Vol. 1). Copenhagen: Akademisk Forlag.

Fook, J., Ryan, M., & Hawkins, l. (2000). *Professional expertise: Practice theory and education for working in uncertainty.* London: Whiting and Birch.

Foucault, M. (1973/1963). *The birth of the clinic: An archaeology of medical perception* (A. M. Sheridan Smith, Trans.). London: Routledge.

Foucault, M. (1980). *Power/knowledge: Selected interviews and other writings, 1972–1977* (C. Gordon, Trans.). Brighton; Sussex: Harvester Press.

Freire, P. (1970). *The pedagogy of the oppressed.* New York: Herder & Herder.

Fuller, A., & Unwin, L. (2004). Young people as teachers and learners in the workplace: Challenging the novice-expert dichotomy. *International Journal of Training and Development, 8*, 32–42.

Furlong, J. (2000). Intuition and the crisis in teacher professionalism. In T. Atkinson & G. Claxton (Eds.), *The intuitive practitioner: On the value of not always knowing what one is doing* (pp. 15–31). Buckingham; Philadelphia: Open University Press.

Gadamer, H. (1994/1960). *Truth and method* (2nd ed.). New York: Continuum.

Garrick, J., & Kirkpatrick, D. (1998). Workplace-based learning degrees: A new business venture, or a new critical business? *Higher Education Research and Development, 17*, 171–182.

Germov, J. (2005a). Challenges to medical dominance. In J. Germov (Ed.), *Second opinion: An introduction to health sociology* (3rd ed., pp. 290–313). South Melbourne, VIC: Oxford University Press.

Germov, J. (Ed.). (2005b). *Second opinion: An introduction to health sociology.* South Melbourne, VIC: Oxford University Press.

Ghaye, T. (2005). *Developing the reflective healthcare team.* Oxford & Malden, MA: Blackwell.

Gibbs, P.T. (2004). *Trusting in the university: The contribution of temporality and trust to a praxis of higher learning.* Dordrecht: Kluwer Academic.

Giorgi, A. (1990). Phenomenology, psychological science and common sense. In G. R. Semin & K. J. Gergen (Eds.), *Everyday understanding: Social and scientific implications* (pp. 64–82). London: Sage.

Giorgi, A. (1994). A phenomenological perspective on certain qualitative research methods. *Journal of Phenomenological Psychology, 25,* 190–220.

Gonzalez, M. (2001). Learning independently through project work. In M. Walker (Ed.), *Reconstructing professionalism in university teaching: Teachers and learners in action* (pp. 170–180). Buckingham: SRHE; Open University Press.

Good, B. (1994). *Medicine, rationality and experience.* New York: Cambridge University Press.

Gordon, J. (2003). Fostering students' personal and professional development in medicine: A new framework for PPD. *Medical Education, 37,* 341–349.

Gray, J. G. (1968). Introduction. In M. Heidegger (Ed.), *What is called thinking?* (pp. xvii–xxvii). New York: Harper & Row.

Grosz, E. (1994). *Volatile bodies: Toward a corporeal feminism.* St Leonards, NSW: Allen & Unwin.

Grosz, E. (2004). *The nick of time: Politics, evolution and the untimely.* Crow's Nest, NSW: Allen & Unwin.

Hearn, J. (1982). Notes on patriarchy, professionalization and the semi-professions. *Sociology, 16,* 184–202.

Heidegger, M. (1962/1927). *Being and time* (J. Macquarrie & E. Robinson, Trans.). New York: SCM Press.

Heidegger, M. (1996/1927). *Being and time* (J. Stambaugh, Trans.). Albany: State University of New York Press.

Heidegger, M. (1968). *What is called thinking?* (T. F. D. Wieck & J. G. Gray, Trans.). New York: Harper Row.

Heidegger, M. (1993/1954). The question concerning technology (D. F. Krell, Trans.). In M. Heidegger (Ed.), *Basic writings* (2nd ed., pp. 311–341). London: Routledge.

Heidegger, M. (1998/1967). Plato's doctrine of truth (T. Sheehan, Trans.). In W. McNeill (Ed.), *Pathmarks* (pp. 155–182). Cambridge: Cambridge University Press.

Hilton, S. R., & Slotnick, H. B. (2005). Proto-professionalism: How professionalisation occurs across the continuum of medical education. *Medical Education, 39,* 58–65.

Holm, U. (1985). *Empathy in the doctor-patient relationship: A theoretical and empirical analysis.* Stockholm: Almqvist och Wiksell International.

Holm, U. (1993). *Lakares vardag: En studie av den psykiska arbetsmiljon (Medical doctors' work day: A study of the psychological work environment).* Uppsala, Sweden: Uppsala University Press.

Holm, U., & Aspegren, K. (1999). Pedagogical methods and affect tolerance in medical students. *Medical Education, 33,* 14–18.

Holmström, I., Sanner, M., & Rosenqvist, U. (2004). Swedish medical students' views of the changing professional role of medical doctors and the organisation of health care. *Advances in Health Sciences Education, 9,* 5–14.

Hung, S. (2003). Expert versus novice use of the executive support systems: An empirical study. *Information and Management, 40,* 177–189.

Huntington, P. (2001). Introduction I – General background: History of the feminist reception of Heidegger and a guide to Heidegger's thought. In N. Holland & P. Huntington (Eds.), *Feminist interpretations of Martin Heidegger* (pp. 1–42). University Park, PA: Pennsylvania State University Press.

Hutchins, E. (1995). *Cognition in the wild*. Cambridge: MIT Press.

Ihde, D. (2002). *Bodies in technology*. Minneapolis: University of Minnesota Press.

Illich, I. (1977). *Medical nemesis: The expropriation of health*. New York: Bantam Books.

Inwood, M. (1997). *Heidegger: A very short introduction*. Oxford: Oxford University Press.

Jolly, B. (2006). Problem-based learning. *Medical Education, 40*, 494–495.

Juel, K., Mosbech, J., & Hansen, E. S. (1999). Mortality and causes of death among Danish medical doctors 1973–92. *International Journal of Epidemiology, 28*, 456–460.

Karasavvidis, I. (2002). Distributed cognition and educational practice. *Journal of Interactive Learning Research, 13*, 11–29.

Kieser, J., Dall'Alba, G., & Livingstone, V. (in press). Impact of curriculum on understanding of professional practice: A longitudinal study in students commencing dental education. *Advances in Health Sciences Education*.

Knorr Cetina, K. (2001). Objectual practice. In T. Schatzki, K. Knorr Cetina, & E. von Savigny (Eds.), *The practice turn in contemporary theory* (pp. 175–188). London: Routledge.

Knott, C., & Scragg, T. (Eds.). (2007). *Reflective practice in social work*. Exeter: Learning Matters.

Kuhn, T. (1962). *The structure of scientific revolutions*. Chicago: University of Chicago Press.

Kurtz, T. (2007). Sociological theory and sociological practice. *Acta Sociologica, 50*, 283–294.

Kyburz-Graber, R. (Ed.). (2006). *Reflective practice in teacher education: Learning from case studies of environmental education*. Bern & Oxford: Peter Lang.

Lamiani, G., Meyer, E. C., Rider, E. A., Browning, D. M., Vegni, E., Mauri, E., et al. (2008). Assumptions and blind spots in patient-centredness: Action research between American and Italian health care professionals. *Medical Education, 42*, 712–720.

Laurillard, D. (2002). Rethinking teaching for the knowledge society. *Educause Review, 37*, 16–25.

Lave, J. (1993). The practice of learning. In S. Chaiklin & J. Lave (Eds.), *Understanding practice: Perspectives on activity and context* (pp. 3–32). Cambridge: Cambridge University Press.

Lave, J., & Wenger, E. (1991). *Situated learning: Legitimate peripheral participation*. Cambridge: Cambridge University Press.

Leadbeater, C. (1999). *Living on thin air: The new economy*. New York: Viking.

Little, P., Everitt, H., Williamson, I., Warner, G., Moore, M., Gould, C., et al. (2001). Preferences of patients for patient centred approach to consultation in primary care: Observational study. *British Medical Journal, 322*(7284), 468–474.

Luke, H. (2003). *Medical education and sociology of medical habitus: It's not about the stethoscope!* Dordrecht; Boston: Kluwer Academic.

Magner, L. (1992). *A history of medicine*. New York: Marcel Dekker.

Major, C.H., & Palmer, B. (2001). Assessing the effectiveness of problem-based learning in higher education: Lessons from the literature. *Academic Exchange Quarterly, 5*, 4–9.

Mans, M. (2004). The changing body in Southern Africa – A perspective from ethnomusicology. In L. Bresler (Ed.), *Knowing bodies, moving minds: Towards embodied teaching and learning* (pp. 77–96). Dordrecht: Kluwer Academic.

Markula, P. (2004). Embodied movement knowledge in fitness and exercise education. In L. Bresler (Ed.), *Knowing bodies, moving minds: Towards embodied teaching and learning* (pp. 61–76). Dordrecht: Kluwer Academic.

Marshall, J. G. (1993). The expanding use of technology. In L. Curry, J. F. Wergin, & Associates (Eds.), *Educating professionals: Responding to new expectations for competence and accountability* (pp. 53–77). San Francisco: Jossey-Bass.

McCormick, J. (1992). The contribution of general practice. In R. S. Downie & B. Charlton (Eds.), *The making of a doctor* (pp. 153–164). Oxford: Oxford University Press.

McCuaig, L. (2007). Sitting on the fishbowl rim with Foucalt: A reflexive account of HPE teachers' caring. *Sport, Education and Society, 12*, 277–294.

McGuire, C. H. (1993). Sociocultural changes affecting professions and professionals. In L. Curry, J. F. Wergin & Associates (Eds.), *Educating professionals: Responding to new expectations for competence and accountability* (pp. 3–16). San Francisco: Jossey-Bass.

McIntyre, D. (1994). Preface. In M. Eraut (Ed.), *Developing professional knowledge and competence* (pp. viii–ix). London: Falmer Press.

McKeown, T., & Lowe, C.R. (1966). *An introduction to social medicine*. Oxford: Blackwell.

McWilliam, E. (2005). Unlearning pedagogy. *Journal of Learning Design, 1*, 1–11.

Merleau-Ponty, M. (1962/1945). *Phenomenology of perception* (C. Smith, Trans.). London: Routledge & Kegan Paul.

Mishler, E. (1984). *The discourse of medicine: Dialectics of medical interviews*. Norwood, NJ: Ablex Publishing.

Mishler, E. G. (1981a). The social construction of illness. In E. G. Mishler, L. R. AmaraSingham, S. T. Hauser, S. D. Osherson, N. Waxler, & R. Liem (Eds.), *Social contexts of health, illness, and patient care* (pp. 141–168). Cambridge: Cambridge University Press.

Mishler, E. G. (1981b). Viewpoint: Critical perspectives on the biomedical model. In E. G. Mishler, L. R. AmaraSingham, S. T. Hauser, S. D. Osherson, N. Waxler, & R. Liem (Eds.), *Social contexts of health, illness, and patient care* (pp. 1–23). Cambridge: Cambridge University Press.

Mishler, E. G., AmaraSingham, L. R., Hauser, S. T., Osherson, S. D., Waxler, N., & Liem, R. (Eds.) (1981). *Social contexts of health, illness, and patient care*. Cambridge: Cambridge University Press.

Mogensen, E. (1994). *Lara i praktiken: En studie av sjukskoterskeutbildningens kliniska avsnitt (Learning in practice: A study of nursing education's clinical segment)*. Stockholm: Stockholm University.

Moi, T. (2001). What is a woman? In *What is a woman and other essays* (pp. 3–120). Oxford: Oxford University Press.

Mol, A. (2002). *The body multiple: Ontology in medical practice*. Durham: Duke University Press.

Molander, B. (1993). *Kunskap i handling (Knowledge in action)*. Goteborg, Sweden: Daidalos.

Montgomery Hunter, K. (1991). *Doctors' stories: The narrative structure of medical knowledge*. Princeton, NJ: Princeton University Press.

Moon, J. A. (1999). *Learning journals: A handbook for academics, students and professional development*. London: Kogan Page.

Moon, J. A. (2008). *Critical thinking: An exploration of theory and practice*. London; New York: Routledge.

Newton, B. W., Barber, L., Clardy, J., Cleveland, E., & O'Sullivan, P. (2008). Is there hardening of the heart during medical school? *Academic Medicine, 83*, 244–249.

Nicholls, E., & Walsh, M. (2007). University of Wolverhampton case study: Embedding practical work-based modules into a traditionally, theoretical programme. *Education + Training, 49*, 201–209.

Noddings, N. (1992). *The challenge to care in schools: An alternative approach to education*. New York: Teachers College Press.

Norman, G. R., & Schmidt, H. G. (1992). The psychological basis of problem-based learning: A review of evidence. *Academic Medicine, 67*, 557–565.

Nutley, S., Isabel Walter, I., & Davies, H. T. O. (2003). From knowing to doing: A framework for understanding the evidence-into-practice agenda. *Evaluation, 9*, 125–148.

Osherson, S. D., & AmaraSingham, L. R. (1981). The machine metaphor in medicine. In E. G. Mishler, L. R. AmaraSingham, S. T. Hauser, S. D. Osherson, N. Waxler, & R. Liem (Eds.), *Social contexts of health, illness, and patient care* (pp. 218–249). Cambridge: Cambridge University Press.

Parsons, T. (1968). Professions. In D. Sills (Ed.), *International encyclopedia of the social sciences, XII* (pp. 536–547). New York: Macmillan and Free Press.

Perkins, D. N. (1993). Person-plus: A distributed view of thinking and learning. In G. Salomon (Ed.), *Distributed cognitions: Psychological and educational considerations* (pp. 88–110). Cambridge: Cambridge University Press.

Peters, M. (2004). Education and the philosophy of the body: Bodies of knowledge and knowledges of the body. In L. Bresler (Ed.), *Knowing bodies, moving minds: Towards embodied teaching and learning* (pp. 13–27). Dordrecht: Kluwer Academic.

Popkewitz, T. S. (1994). Professionalization in teaching and teacher education: Some notes on its history, ideology, and potential. *Teaching and Teacher Education, 10*, 1–14.

Porter, R. (1997). *The greatest benefit to mankind: A medical history of humanity from antiquity to the present*. London: HarperCollins.

Porter, R. (2003). *Blood and guts: A short history of medicine*. New York; London: W.W. Norton.

Prince, K. J. A. H., van Eijs, P. W. L. J., Boshuizen, H. P. A., van der Vleuten, C. P. M., & Scherpbier, A. J. J. A. (2005). General competencies of problem-based learning (PBL) and non-PBL graduates. *Medical Education, 39*, 394–401.

Ratcliffe, M. (2002). Heidegger, analytic metaphysics, and the being of beings. *Inquiry, 45*, 35–58.

Resnick, L., Levine, J., & Behrend, S. (1991). *Socially shared cognitions*. Hillsdale, NJ: Erlbaum.

Rhodes, G., & Shiel, G. (2007). Meeting the needs of the workplace and the learner through work-based learning. *Journal of Workplace Learning, 19*, 173–187.

Rolf, B., Ekstedt, E., & Barnett, R. (1993). *Kvalitet och kunskapsprocess i högre utbildning (Quality and knowledge process in higher education)*. Nora, Sweden: Nya Doxa.

Rosberg, S. (2000). *Kropp, varande och mening i ett sjukgymnastiskt perspektiv (Body, being and meaning from a physiotherapy perspective)*. Goteborg, Sweden: Department of Social Work, University of Göteborg.

Rose, N. (1994). Medicine, history and the present. In C. Jones & R. Porter (Eds.), *Reassessing Foucault: Power, medicine and the body* (pp. 48–72). London: Routledge.

Sacks, O. (1985). *The man who mistook his wife for a hat and other clinical tales*. New York: Summit Books.

Säljö, R. (1991). Learning and mediation: Fitting reality into a table. *Learning and Instruction, 1*, 261–272.

Säljö, R., & Wyndham, J. (1993). Solving everyday problems in the formal setting: An empirical study of the school as context of thought. In S. Chaiklin & J. Lave (Eds.), *Understanding practice: Perspectives on activity and context* (pp. 327–342). Cambridge: Cambridge University Press.

Salomon, G. (Ed.). (1993a). *Distributed cognitions: Psychological and educational considerations*. Cambridge: Cambridge University Press.

Salomon, G. (1993b). No distribution without individuals' cognition: A dynamic interactional view. In G. Salomon (Ed.), *Distributed cognitions: Psychological and educational considerations* (pp. xi–xxi). Cambridge: Cambridge University Press.

Sandberg, J. (1994). *Human competence at work: An interpretative approach*. Goteborg: Bas.

Sandberg, J. (2000). Understanding human competence at work: An interpretative approach. *The Academy of Management Journal, 43*, 9–25.

Sandberg, J., & Dall'Alba, G. (2006). Re-framing competence development at work. In R. Gerber, G. Castleton, & H. Pillay (Eds.), *Improving workplace learning: Emerging international perspectives* (pp. 107–121). New York: Nova.

Sandberg, J., & Dall'Alba, G. (in press). Returning to practice anew: A life-world perspective. *Organization Studies*.

Schatzki, T., Knorr Cetina, K., & von Savigny, E. (2001). *The practice turn in contemporary theory*. London: Routledge.

Schatzki, T. R. (2001). Introduction: Practice theory. In T. Schatzki, K. Knorr Cetina, & E. von Savigny (Eds.), *The practice turn in contemporary theory* (pp. 1–14). London: Routledge.

Schembri, S. (2005). *Consumer understanding of professional service quality: A phenomenographic approach*. Unpublished PhD thesis, University of Queensland, Australia.

Schernhammer, E. (2005). Taking their own lives—The high rate of physician suicide. *New England Journal of Medicine, 352*(24), 2473–2476.

Schmidt, H. G., Vermeulen, L., & van der Molen, H. T. (2006). Longterm effects of problem-based learning: A comparison of competencies acquired by graduates of a problem-based and a conventional medical school. *Medical Education, 40*, 562–567.

Schön, D. A. (1983). *The reflective practitioner: How professionals think in action*. New York: Basic Books.

Schön, D. A. (1987). *Educating the reflective practitioner: Toward a new design for teaching and learning in the professions*. San Francisco: Jossey-Bass.

Schön, D. A. (1995). The new scholarship requires a new epistemology. *Change, 27*, 27–34.

Seely Brown, J., Collins, A., & Duguid, P. (1989). Situated cognition and the culture of learning. *Educational Researcher, 18*(1), 32–42.

Self, D. J., & Olivarez, M. (1996). Retention of moral reasoning skills over the four years of medical education. *Teaching and Learning in Medicine, 8*, 195–199.

Semin, G. R., & Gergen, G. J. (1990). Everyday understanding in science and daily life. In G. R. Semin & G. J. Gergen (Eds.), *Everyday understanding: Social and scientific implications* (pp. 1–18). London: Sage.

Sennett, R. (2003). *Respect: The formation of character in an age of inequality*. London: Penguin Books.

Sidhu, R. K. (2006). *Universities and globalization: To market, to market*. Mahwah, NJ: Lawrence Erlbaum.

Slaughter, S., & Leslie, L. (1997). *Academic capitalism*. Baltimore: John Hopkins.

Snyder, B. R. (1970). *The hidden curriculum*. New York: Knopf.

Sobiechowska, P., & Maisch, M. (2007). Work-based learning and continuing professional development. *Education + Training, 49*, 182–192.

Sontag, S. (1983). *Illness as metaphor*. London: Penguin.

Spiegelberg, H. (1982). *The phenomenological movement* (3rd ed.). Haag: Martinus Nijhoff.

Stålsby Lundborg, C., Wahlstrom, R., & Dall'Alba, G. (1999). Ways of experiencing asthma management – Variations among general practitioners in Sweden. *Scandinavian Journal of Primary Health Care, 17*, 226–231.

Stein, H. D. (2003). *Challenge and change in social work education: Toward a world view*. Alexandria, VA: Council on Social Work Education.

Svenaeus, F. (1999). *The hermeneutics of medicine and the phenomenology of health: Steps towards a philosophy of medical practice*. Linköping: University of Linköping.

Szasz, T. S., & Hollender, M. H. (1956). A contribution to the philosophy of medicine: The basic models of the doctor-patient relationship. *Archives of Internal Medicine, 97*, 585–592.

Thomson, I. (2000). From the question concerning technology to the quest for a democratic technology: Heidegger, Marcuse, Feenberg. *Inquiry, 43*, 203–216.

Thomson, I. (2001). Heidegger on ontological Education, or: How we become what we are. *Inquiry, 44*, 243–268.

Thomson, I. (2004). Heidegger's perfectionist philosophy of education in *Being and Time. Continental Philosophy Review, 37*, 439–467.

Tirri, K., Husu, J., & Kansanen, P. (1999). The epistemological stance between the knower and the known. *Teaching and Teacher Education, 15*, 911–922.

Tiwari, A., Lai, P., So, M., & Yuen, K. (2006). A comparison of the effects of problem-based learning and lecturing on the development of students' critical thinking. *Medical Education, 40*, 547–554.

Toombs, S. K. (1993). *The meaning of illness: A phenomenological account of the different perspectives of physician and patient*. Dordrecht: Kluwer Academic.

Torre, D. M., Wang, N. Y., Meoni, L. A., Young, J. H., Klag, M. J., & Ford, D. E. (2005). Suicide compared to other causes of mortality in physicians. *Suicide & Life-Threatening Behavior, 35*, 146–153.

Toulmin, S. (1976). On the nature of the physician's understanding. *Journal of Medicine and Philosophy, 1*, 32–50.

Usher, R., Bryant, I., & Johnston, R. (1997). *Adult education and the postmodern challenge: Learning beyond the limits*. London: Routledge.

van Manen, M. (1977). Linking ways of knowing with ways of being practical. *Curriculum Inquiry, 6*, 205–228.

van Manen, M. (1991). *The tact of teaching: The meaning of pedagogical thoughtfulness*. Ann Arbor: The State University of New York Press.

van Manen, M. (1999). Knowledge, reflection and complexity in teacher practice. In M. Lange & J. Olson (Eds.), *Changing schools, changing practices: Perspectives on educational reform and teacher professionalism* (pp. 65–76). Luvain, Belgium: Garant.

Vernon, D. T., & Blake, R. L. (1993). Does problem-based learning work? A meta-analysis of evaluative research. *Academic Medicine, 68*, 550–563.

Virta, A. (2002). Becoming a history teacher: Observations on the beliefs and growth of student teachers. *Teaching and Teacher Education, 18*, 687–698.

Vu, T. T., & Dall'Alba, G. (2008). Exploring an authentic approach to assessment for enhancing student learning. Paper presented as part of a symposium entitled 'Re-imagining higher education pedagogies' at the conference of the Australian Association for Research on Education, Brisbane.

Vygotsky, L. (1978). *Mind in society: The development of higher psychological processes.* Cambridge, MA: Harvard University Press.

Vygotsky, L. (1987/1934). *The collected works of L.S. Vygotsky* (N. Minick, Trans.). New York: Plenum Press.

Walker, M. (2001). *Reconstructing professionalism in university teaching: Teachers and learners in action.* Buckingham: SRHE; Open University Press.

Walker, M. (2006). *Higher education pedagogies: A capabilities approach.* Maidenhead; New York: SRHE; Open University Press.

Webster-Wright, A. (in press). Reframing professional development through understanding authentic professional learning. *Review of Educational Research.*

Webster-Wright, A. (2006). *Understanding continuing professional learning.* Unpublished PhD thesis, University of Queensland, Brisbane, Australia.

Wenger, E. (1998). *Communities of practice: Learning, meaning and identity.* Cambridge: Cambridge University Press.

Williams, S. J., & Bendelow, G. (1998). *The lived body: Sociological themes, embodied issues.* London: Routledge.

Wilson, V., & Pirrie, A. (1999). Developing professional competence: Lessons from the emergency room. *Studies in Higher Education, 24*, 211–224.

Winograd, T., & Flores, F. (1986). *Understanding computers and cognition: A new foundation for design.* Norwood, NJ: Ablex.

Winterson, J. (2001). *The powerbook.* London: Vintage.

Wootton, D. (2006). *Bad medicine: Doctors doing harm since Hippocrates.* Oxford; New York: Oxford University Press.

Young, I. M. (1990). Throwing like a girl: A phenomenology of body comportment, motility, and spatiality. In *Throwing like a girl and other essays in feminist philosophy and social theory* (pp. 141–159). Bloomington: Indiana University Press.

Young, I. M. (2003). Lived body vs gender: Reflections on social structure and subjectivity. In M. Proudfoot (Ed.), *The philosophy of body* (pp. 94–111). Oxford: Blackwell.

Index

G. Dall'Alba, *Learning to be Professionals*, Innovation and Change in Professional
Education 4, DOI 10.1007/978-90-481-2608-8_BM2,
© Springer Science+Business Media B.V. 2009